Golden Dreams

Golden Dreams

GWEN BRISTOW

Lippincott & Crowell, Publishers

New York

FIRST EDITION

Designed by C. Linda Dingler

U.S. Library of Congress Cataloging in Publication Data

Bristow, Gwen, birth date
  Golden dreams.

   1. California—Gold discoveries. 2. California—
History—1846–1850. 3. Overland journeys to the
Pacific. 4. Voyages to the Pacific Coast. I. Title.
F865.B85   979.4'04   79–27579
ISBN 0–690–01678–6

---

80 81 82 83 84 10 9 8 7 6 5 4 3 2 1

For

Colette Burns (Kolsbun)

with thanks

Gold Mine Found.—In the newly made raceway of the Saw Mill recently erected by Captain Sutter on the American Fork, gold has been found in considerable quantities. One person brought thirty dollars' worth to New Helvetia, gathered there in a short time.

—San Francisco *Californian*, Wednesday, March 15, 1848, page 2, column 3. The first news of the discovery at Sutter's Mill published anywhere in the world.

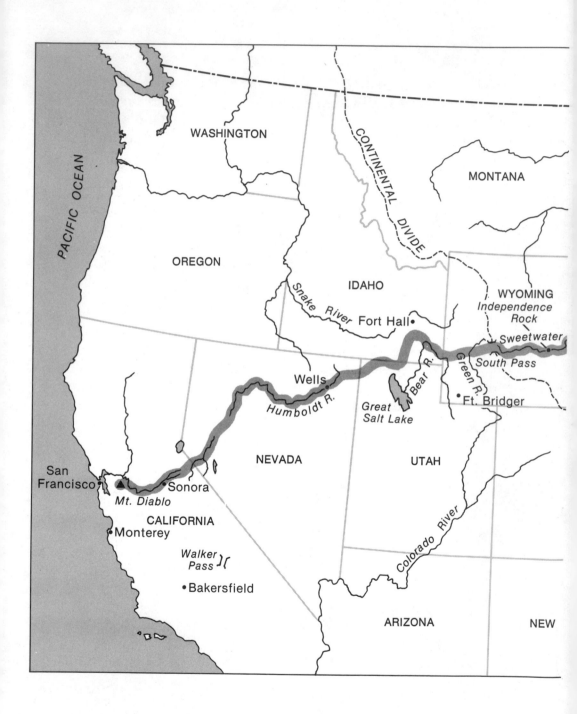

PACIFIC OCEAN

WASHINGTON

MONTANA

OREGON

CONTINENTAL DIVIDE

IDAHO

Snake River Fort Hall

WYOMING
Independence
Rock

Sweetwater

South Pass

Wells

Bear R.

Green R.

Humboldt R.

Great
Salt Lake

Ft. Bridger

NEVADA

UTAH

San
Francisco

Sonora

Mt. Diablo

CALIFORNIA

Monterey

Colorado River

Walker
Pass

Bakersfield

ARIZONA

NEW

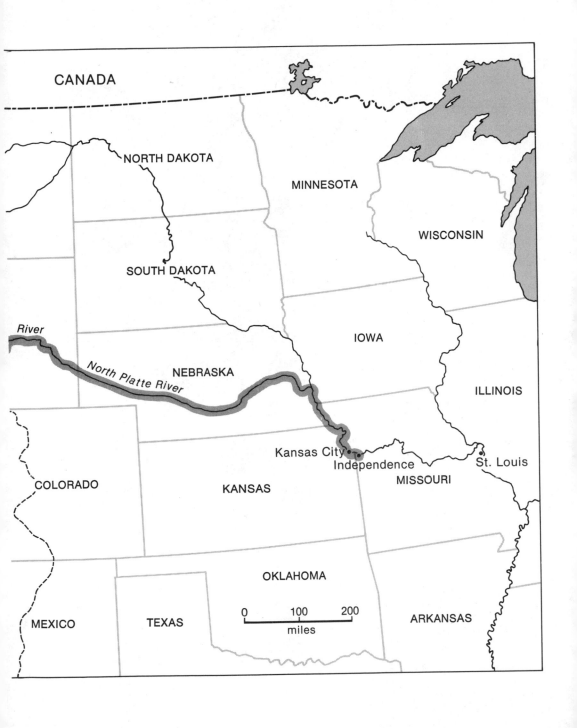

CANADA

NORTH DAKOTA

MINNESOTA

WISCONSIN

SOUTH DAKOTA

River

North Platte River

NEBRASKA

IOWA

ILLINOIS

COLORADO

Kansas City

Independence

St. Louis

KANSAS

MISSOURI

OKLAHOMA

MEXICO

TEXAS

ARKANSAS

0   100   200
miles

Golden Dreams

1

One morning in the spring of 1848, a puzzled fellow came into the office of Captain Joseph L. Folsom, quartermaster of the United States Army in San Francisco, and showed the captain a handful of yellow flakes. He wanted to know if these were bits of gold.

In those days, the army paid all its expenses with gold and silver coins. As quartermaster, Captain Folsom handled gold every day. Surely he would know the difference between real gold and something that merely looked like it.

The captain examined the fragments on his desk. He shook his head.

He said he had heard the rumors about men finding gold in the rivers. But this stuff was not gold. These were flakes of yellow mica.

His report got around. Soldiers and sailors repeated it in their letters home. Newspapers published it, both in this country and abroad. But of course, the stuff *was* gold. And when this was proved, a lot of people laughed at Captain Folsom. Some people are laughing at him to this day.

Folsom made a mistake and thereby made himself famous. But he was certainly not the first to do this. In A.D. 300 there was a wise man named Lactantius, tutor to the son of the Emperor Constantine and one of the most learned scholars in Europe. He wrote firmly:

"How can anyone be so foolish as to believe that there are antipodes where people walk with their feet up and their heads hanging down? Where the trees grow with their branches down, and the rain falls upward?"

Lactantius was wrong too; and both he and Folsom were proved wrong by people far less learned than themselves. The mistake of

Lactantius was righted for all time by Columbus, and Folsom (though he did not know it) had already been proved wrong by a bright though bookless young woman named Jenny Wimmer.

Jenny Wimmer was born Elizabeth Jane Cloud in Lumpkin County, Georgia. This was a hilly region, and through the hills were scattered little deposits of gold. In the intervals between their farming chores, Jenny's neighbors would scoop dirt from the creeks and wash it in their frying pans to separate the grains of gold from the grains of sand. From her childhood, Jenny had watched them. She knew how easy it was for a man to mistake any sort of yellow flash for the gold he wanted to find.

But there wasn't much doing around Lumpkin County. When Jenny married one of the local boys, Obadiah Bays, they decided to move on to the Missouri frontier. There, they hoped, things would be better.

They left home in the year 1840. To Lexington, Missouri, was a journey of about a thousand miles. A long way, but they got there.

Three years after her marriage, Jenny was the mother of two children. That fall, the settlement was struck by an epidemic of what they called "wasting fever," and her husband died. Also taken was the wife of a neighbor, Peter Wimmer. In the next year, Jenny and Peter were married.

Here in Missouri, Jenny and Peter heard a lot of talk about new lands in the West. Settlers bound for the newly opened country of Oregon made up their wagon trains here. And now people were talking about another country called California. They said if you wanted to go to California, you could get there safely if you went with the Oregon wagons as far as Fort Hall (in the present state of Idaho) and then turned south.

And so, in the spring of 1846, a party of fourteen families, the Wimmers among them, set out for California. By this time Jenny and Peter had seven children—his, hers, and theirs.

In California, the great landowner Johann Augustus Sutter was seeking a site for a sawmill to be built near his famous wilderness enclosure, Sutter's Fort. Peter Wimmer was employed at Sutter's Fort when the scouts reported that they had found a place for the mill— a forest stream high on a mountain, thirty-six miles from the fort. Sutter offered jobs to both Peter and Jenny. Peter was to be one of the builders, Jenny would cook for the work force. In August, 1847, Peter and Jenny and their two youngest children left the fort.

At the sawmill site, the workmen built log cabins to live in. The boss of the group, Jim Marshall, had a cabin all to himself, as befitted his superior status.

By the start of the year 1848, the sawmill was well under way. The men had built a dam, a millrace, and a good part of the mill itself. Behind the mill they had dug a ditch called a tailrace, where the water from the mill would run off. One evening in January, they turned water into the tailrace to deepen it overnight. The next day, Jim Marshall went out to see how the ditch was getting on. As he looked it over, he caught sight of a small shiny object lying in the ditch under the water. He stooped and picked it up.

Looking around, he found more bits like the first. Carrying them in his hat, he went indoors and showed them to the others. The men said this looked like gold. But was it?

One of the men, who had served in the army, had a five-dollar gold piece in his pocket, left from his army pay. He compared this with the pieces Jim had found. The coin was lighter in color, but the difference might be due to its alloy. How could they be sure?

There was one person in the camp, and only one, who had seen gold in pieces new from the earth. This was Jenny Wimmer. Not only had Jenny seen virgin gold, but she knew how women tested it in their backwoods kitchens. Could Jenny answer the big question? She could and she did.

Jenny took Jim's bits of metal and soaked them in vinegar. They came out unhurt. Now, she told the men, she would try a test more severe. Jenny was boiling a kettle of soap, strong lye soap that would take the dirt and sweat out of men's work clothes. She dropped some bits of the metal into her lye vat and let it boil all day and simmer all night. Nothing but gold, said Jenny, could stand a trial like this.

The next morning at breakfast time, while the men watched eagerly, Jenny poured the soap into her "cooling bowl"—the hollowed stump of a tree. And there, at the bottom of the kettle, lay the little nuggets, unchanged.

"It's gold, boys," said Jenny, and nothing in the world has been quite the same since then.

2

The stuff Jim had picked up *was* gold. The men whooped and rushed out to see if they could find any more gold lying around.

They continued to work on the sawmill, for they were practical fellows who knew that a steady job was more dependable than gold-hunting, but in their free time they picked up yellow grains and brought them to Jenny. Again and again, the grains proved real.

As for Jim, he grew more and more excited. He had found his first nugget January 24, 1848, and like the other men, he had been finding more. Now he could check his impatience no longer. On the night of January 27, Jim could not sleep. The next morning, he sprang on his horse and rode through a downpour of rain the thirty-six miles to Sutter's Fort, to tell Sutter about the gold before anybody else could do so and maybe take credit for finding it. Jim had found the first gold, and he wanted Sutter to know he had. For in this part of the world, Sutter was king.

Johann Augustus Sutter was a glittering pretender obsessed by dreams of greatness. Born in Germany, as a child he had been taken to Switzerland by his parents. He usually spoke of himself as a Swiss, and he spoke of himself often. He told of adventures in many lands, of thunderous heroism and splinter-thin escapes. He loved to talk. As one of his friends used to say, he talked so well that you believed him, even when you knew he was lying.

The truth was that Sutter had crept out of Switzerland because his creditors had filed bankruptcy charges against him, and in those days men went to jail for debt. He had run away in 1834, when he was thirty-one years old. Behind him at home were his wife, Anna, and their four children. He left nothing for their support. As Anna was a clergyman's daughter, maybe Sutter thought the Lord would provide. Or ought to.

Later that same year, Sutter reached New York aboard a French vessel. From New York he went with some German traders to St. Louis. At that time, the country across the Mississippi was a land of legend. St. Louis, close to the joining of the Mississippi and Missouri rivers, was the meeting place of East and West. Traders, trappers, frontiersmen of all sorts told about the marvels that beckoned men to the country beyond. They said that in the Mexican province of California, the governor was giving great tracts of land to men who would turn it into ranches. Most of this land went to natives of the country, but sometimes men from outside had succeeded in getting land grants. Now they were living like feudal lords on their estates.

Sutter decided to go to California.

In the spring of 1838, when he was thirty-five years old, he joined a party of fur trappers and started out. He had to go by strange and devious ways. First he traveled the Oregon Trail to Fort Vancouver, a trading post of the Hudson's Bay Company on the Columbia River, in the present state of Washington. When the company sent a vessel to Honolulu for supplies, Sutter went along.

In Honolulu he made many acquaintances. Sutter never had any trouble meeting people. One of these, a businessman, chartered a brig for trade and gave Sutter employment on board. The brig went first to the Russian fur station at Sitka, Alaska, then down the coast to Monterey, capital of California. Sutter went ashore.

As his friends had warned him, the rulers of California did not often give land to foreigners. But Sutter had engaging ways. In 1839 he received a grant of eleven Spanish leagues—nearly fifty thousand American acres—in the valley of the Sacramento River. Here, in a realm untouched by ax or plow, Sutter prepared to realize his dream.

Now, nine years later, he was lord of a vast and spreading empire. In the midst of it stood his fort, built in a corner where two rivers met, thus giving him protection from prowlers as well as plenty of water for his crops. His wheat fields stretched for miles, his grazing lands for miles farther still. His field hands were mostly Indians, brought in and guarded by their own tribal chiefs. The chiefs were paid for their trouble by being dressed in resplendent finery, called by handsome titles, and given all the food and squaws they wanted. Inside the walls of the fort were storehouses and workshops, a two-story building for Sutter's headquarters, and his own harem of the most desirable squaws.

5

This junction of the rivers was the end of the journey for people who, like the Wimmers, had traveled the Oregon Trail as far as Fort Hall and turned south to California. (Sutter had named one of the rivers El Rio de los Americanos; the other was the Sacramento.) By the time these travelers reached the fort they were tattered, gaunt, and exhausted. Sutter made them welcome. He gave them food and water and offered them work—as blacksmiths, carpenters, threshers, clerks, wagon drivers, tanners of hides, crewmen on his riverboat. Around the fort their settlement was growing. Perhaps with a twinge of homesickness, Sutter had given this settlement the old Latin name of Switzerland and called it New Helvetia. Today we know it as the city of Sacramento, the present capital of California.

As a result of the war of 1846–48 between the United States and Mexico, California was now occupied by the American army. More people were coming from the States. Sutter was building the sawmill to turn the forest trees into lumber, which he could sell to the new settlers for their homes.

And here came Jim, sweating with excitement as he untied a knot in a rag and poured out a pile of golden grains.

Sutter knew more about science than Jenny Wimmer. He had an encyclopedia. He also had a supply of drugs and chemicals, some for medicine, others for use in his workshops. After consulting the encyclopedia, he tried the grains with nitric acid. Baser metals would have given up and dissolved, but these perky little scraps paid no more attention to the acid than they had to Jenny's kettle of soap. The book gave several other tests. Sutter tried them all, and his own forehead began to show beads of sweat like Jim's. This *was* gold.

This was gold, and Sutter had need of it. He had fled from his debts in Switzerland only to pile up more debts in California. He was far behind on his payroll. The Russians had a second fur station at Fort Ross, near San Francisco Bay, and they had been sending a schooner down at intervals for wheat and other foodstuffs. Deciding to move all their interests to Alaska, they had offered Fort Ross for sale; Sutter had bought the property without thinking much about how he was going to pay for it. The Russians still sent the schooner down for supplies, only now, instead of buying these, they got them from Sutter as interest on his debt. He had paid very little on the principal, and the Russians were getting insistent. He had bought tools and materials from the Yankee traders in San Francisco, and they too wanted to be paid. Like most Yankees, they had scant patience with buyers who made charm a substitute for cash. In plain words,

Sutter was desperate. These grains might mean a gold mine.

But if they did mean a gold mine, whose gold mine was it?

Open land was so abundant in California that the boundaries of the grants were vague. But it made little difference whether or not the site of Jim's discovery was part of Sutter's grant. A vein of gold— or any other mineral—might run for miles beyond the point of discovery. Sutter decided to go and see for himself, right away.

The day after Jim brought the sample, Sutter went with him back to the sawmill. The laborers were still working on the mill, but they were using their free time to look for gold. And they were finding it.

Sutter thought fast.

Years ago, the Mexican government had made a law about mines. Upon giving formal notice to the authorities that a new mine had been found, or an old mine abandoned, a man could claim the mineral rights. When his claim was recognized, he could work the mine himself or allow other people to do so—on his own terms, of course. While California was now governed by the United States Army, no new laws had yet been passed to replace the old ones. The present governor was Colonel Richard B. Mason. If Sutter put in his claim now, Colonel Mason might grant it.

Meanwhile, Sutter wanted no break in his empire building. If word leaked out that the men at the sawmill were picking up handfuls of gold, the men at work on his other projects would drop their tools and rush to get their share of this sudden wealth. His vast domain would grow up in weeds. He would no longer be a mighty ruler because there would be nothing much left for him to rule over.

The sawmill workers were gleefully showing him the gold they had found in the river sands or scraped out of cracks in the rocks. They told him they planned to spend all their Sundays looking for more.

Sutter listened genially. Of course, of course. He didn't blame the boys for gathering up all the gold they could. They had a right to it. After all, wasn't it their work that had opened the ditch and turned up gold in the first place? But he did want to caution them.

"Let's not have this news getting around. You don't want every man between here and San Francisco coming in to take gold that by right belongs to you. We'd better not talk too much. Any of us."

The men nodded. The warning made sense. If they weren't careful, the place could get crowded.

"Keep quiet for six weeks," Sutter suggested. "That will give you time to finish the mill and collect your pay at the fort. Then, if you're

7

sure there's enough gold around here to make it worthwhile, you can come back and dig full time and bring your friends with you."

The men agreed. They promised to keep the gold find a secret for six weeks.

Sutter drew a breath of relief. Six weeks would give him time to make his claim. The men here at the mill weren't talking, and beyond the mill site nobody would know about the gold.

But like Lactantius and Folsom before him, Sutter was mistaken.

Jenny Wimmer had a little boy.

3

Sutter went into the woods and rounded up the Indian chiefs of the neighborhood. He made a "treaty."

For centuries, the ancestors of these Indians had been seeing yellow grains in the sand of the creekbeds but had set no value upon them. Now, in return for goods they did value—mirrors, knives, bright-colored clothes—the chiefs agreed to give Sutter exclusive rights for three years to gather up these grains. Also, in exchange for more pretty things, the Indians said they would have their tribesmen bring in more yellow bits for Sutter's benefit.

Sutter knew the Yankee settlers would pay no attention to such a "treaty" unless it was backed by real authority. His solid claim would have to come from the American governor of California, Colonel Mason. He went back to the fort and wrote a letter to be carried to the colonel's headquarters in the capital, Monterey, ninety miles down the coast from San Francisco.

This mission he entrusted to a clerk named Charles Bennett. Bennett had come from the States, first to Oregon and then south to Sutter's Fort. He is described by an acquaintance, John Henry Brown, as "an upright, honest citizen, much respected." Along with the letter, Sutter gave Bennett six ounces of gold in a buckskin bag such as men used for carrying tobacco. Sutter also gave him instructions.

When Bennett handed the letter to Colonel Mason, he was to say that his employer, Mr. Sutter, wanted to develop some unused land near his fort. To be free to do so, he was asking for certain exclusive rights. These were grazing rights in the country around the sawmill; rights to the water power, for this and other mills; and mineral rights in that section.

9

Suppose the colonel asked what sort of mineral he had discovered? Bennett was to answer that traces of lead and silver had been found in the soil. (This was true.) Only if Colonel Mason said this was not enough reason was Bennett to show him the gold in the buckskin bag. Sutter hoped his claim would be granted before Mason knew what the claim really was.

Bennett pocketed the buckskin bag and set out for Monterey. Sutter told himself all was going well. It was now early February, 1848.

Around the fort, work went on as usual. Sutter's launch went down the river, carrying wheat and other produce to William Leidesdorff, agent for the Russian interests in California. The fact that Charles Bennett was aboard caused no comment; Sutter often sent his clerks on business errands.

A few days later, Sutter sent his head wagon driver up to the sawmill with the regular shipment of food supplies, to be delivered to Jenny at her kitchen door. The driver's name was Jacob Wittmer. Like Sutter, Jacob was a Swiss; like Sutter, he had genial ways; and like Sutter, he loved to talk.

The mountain air was sharp, and Jacob was looking forward to the warmth of the kitchen fire. Leaving the wagons in a sheltered spot while his Indian helpers unhitched the oxen, he walked toward Jenny's cabin.

In front of the cabin Jenny's little boy, Martin Wimmer, was playing. Because of Jacob's frequent visits, he and Martin knew each other well. Martin ran to meet him, and Jacob, affable as always, paused and asked how things were getting on. Strutting importantly, Martin told him the men around here were picking up bagfuls of gold.

Jacob laughed with reproach. With a shake of his head, he warned Martin of what happened to little boys who told big lies.

Martin ran to the cabin and called Jenny to the door.

"Tell him it's true, Mother! I'm not telling lies, am I, Mother?"

Jenny glared at their visitor. Of course it was true. The men *were* picking up gold. If Jacob didn't believe it, he could come into the cabin right now and she would show him proof. Here was a sample of the gold her husband had brought in. Tying up the gold dust in a rag, she told Jacob he could take it and welcome. Now maybe he'd know her son was a truthful boy.

Speechless for once, Jacob took the gold. Jenny went back to her work. And now that his honor was vindicated, Martin babbled on, telling Jacob all about recent events.

When the workmen came in, they had no need to say either yes or no to Martin's story. Here stood Jacob with gold dust in his hand. But if they told him to keep quiet about the gold, they wasted their words. Jacob was not capable of keeping quiet about anything. And after all, he had made no promise to Sutter.

Jacob stayed several days, unloading the wagons and storing the foodstuffs. His work finished, he led the empty wagons back down the hill. When he reached the settlement of New Helvetia, he stopped to buy a drink at Smith and Brannan's store.

C. E. Smith and Samuel Brannan were leaders of a Mormon colony. After long religious harassment in their home state of New York, these Mormons and some friends of other faiths—238 men, women, and children in all—had chartered a ship and come to San Francisco in 1846. Brannan lived in town, where he was now a man of many enterprises; Smith had come to Sutter's Fort to mind his part of their business. The store was a busy trading post, where ranchers delivered their hides and produce and took back goods brought by the merchant vessels.

When Jacob joined the other men at the counter and ordered a drink, Smith asked to see his money. Jacob was a likable fellow. But fondness for liquor was his major fault, and he had been known to say he could pay and then, when he had his drink inside him, to admit that he couldn't. Reminded of this, Jacob took the knotted rag out of his pocket and showed the grains he had received from Jenny Wimmer. He said these were gold. He had just come down from the sawmill, and the workers there were picking up bagfuls of gold.

His hearers nudged each other and murmured, "There he goes again." Nobody ever believed anything Jacob said.

For though Martin was not a liar, Jacob was. Jacob was famous for his yarns. He meant no trouble and seldom caused any; he simply had a many-colored fancy and could not help using it.

Jacob did not get his drink. But while his friends thought he was romancing, Jacob knew that this time he was not. Re-tying the knot in the rag, he put it back into his pocket and drove on to the fort.

Here he kept on talking about the gold find at the sawmill. Shaking with excitement, he told his fellow workers what Martin had told him— how Jenny had boiled the nugget in her soap kettle; how the men had tried other tests she knew about, such as beating a scrap of gold with a hammer and watching it grow broader and thinner with every stroke.

Sutter may have wanted to stop him, but Sutter must have known this was not in his power; nobody on earth could make Jacob stop talking. At first the workmen at the fort, like the men at Smith's store, heard him with tolerant amusement, but this mood did not last long. The blacksmith, Levi Fifield, took a speck from Jacob's rag, laid it on his anvil, and pounded it with a hammer. While he pounded, a popeyed group of watchers saw the golden dot spread into a wafer, half an inch across, thinner than the sheerest silk, with never a crack.

Fifield and the others gasped with amazement. At last, one of Jacob's fantastic tales had proved to be not fantasy but sober truth.

Fifield was another Mormon. Back in the States, people who disliked the Mormons had called them un-American. To prove their patriotism, the elders had organized a battalion of Mormon soldiers and offered them to the army for service in the Mexican War. After marching to the Pacific Coast under the command of Colonel Philip St. George Cooke of the regular army, the Mormon Battalion had served in Los Angeles and San Diego until its members were mustered out. Their plan was to join the Mormon settlement on the Salt Lake, in the present state of Utah. But as it was too late in the year to cross the mountains, they had sought work for the winter. Many of them had found jobs at Sutter's Fort. Fifield the blacksmith was one of these.

Fifield and two other veterans of the Mormon Battalion, Wilford Hudson and Sidney Willis, quit their jobs that day. They scampered off to Smith and Brannan's store to buy provisions and then as fast as they could, they set out for the golden hill.

But when they reached the sawmill, February 27, Jim Marshall was grumpy about their presence. Jim thought the gold hereabouts belonged to him, and when Hudson, using his knife, scraped up a little nugget weighing nearly half an ounce, Jim was not happy. One of the men said he even drew his gun and told the newcomers to clear out.

Fifield and his partners were good-humored about it. Very well, they would look for a spot of their own.

They decided to go down the hill toward the fort, but to go in two groups, so as to double their chances of finding gold. Willis and Hudson offered to follow the river, while Fifield chose to go by the wagon trail. Fifield would be accompanied by another man they had known in the old battalion, Henry Bigler. (This young man kept a diary, and it is because of Henry Bigler's diary that we know the date when Marshall found gold and other details recorded by nobody else.)

The four men agreed to meet at a flour mill being built by other battalion men in Sutter's employ. Leaving Jim to his sulks, they started out—the first men in history to go prospecting along the golden vein that later was to be known as the California Mother Lode.

Their good nature paid them well. Willis and Hudson were walking down the hill, following the south fork of the American River (the stream Sutter had called El Rio de los Americanos). Between the saw-mill and the flour mill, they came to a place where the river made a sharp turn. In the course of centuries, here in the turn, the river had piled a heap of sand shaped like a frying pan with a long handle. As it piled up the sand, the river had also piled up the golden flakes that Nature had mixed with the sand. It was one of the richest deposits ever found in the land of gold.

Willis and Hudson did not yet know the value of their find; all they knew was that they had come across a gravel bed with specks of gold in it. But, more generous than Jim, they told not only their partners; when they went back to the fort for more supplies, they also told their friends there.

Many of these friends were dubious. But week by week, Smith's store began to do extra business in shovels and pans and salt beef, as one man and then another left his job and went to see for himself. Gradually the heap of sand became a busy mining camp. Since the river often overflowed the strip that looked like the handle of the frying pan, many people thought this camp was set on an island; and as most of the men panning gold here were Mormons, this spot became famous under the name Mormon Island.

So far, in February, 1848, only a few people had heard the tale of gold, and none of these had any idea of how stupendous a tale it was. But the great exodus had begun. With his chubby little hand, Martin Wimmer had turned a page of history.

And while all this was going on, Charles Bennett had conferred with Colonel Mason in Monterey and had come back to San Francisco.

San Francisco was a town of almost nine hundred people. Among them, as if a mischievous Fate had brought him there to take his particular part in the Gold Rush, was a man named Isaac Humphreys.

And what was so remarkable about Isaac Humphreys? Nothing. Except that by sheer coincidence Isaac, like Jenny, had grown up among the gold diggers of Lumpkin County, Georgia.

There seems to be no evidence that Isaac and Jenny ever knew each other. But they both knew about virgin gold, and they both just happened to be around when they were needed.

4

Charles Bennett had gone to Colonel Mason's headquarters and presented Sutter's request. Colonel Mason had said no.

He made his reason clear. He said that just now California was at a halfway point, no longer under the laws of Mexico but not yet under the laws of the United States. The fighting had ended, but officially the war would not be over until a treaty of peace had been signed and ratified by both countries. When this happened, Congress would be expected to set up a civil government in California. In the meantime, said Colonel Mason, he and his troops were here merely to keep order.

Mason said he would write a reply for Bennett to take back to Sutter. In his letter, and in his talk with Bennett, he said it made no difference what the newly discovered mineral might be. He had no authority to make land grants or give mineral rights in any section to any one man. The public land was open to everyone alike.

Bennett did not jump out of his chair. He kept himself calm, calm enough to make sure he understood. He asked: Did this mean that any man who wanted to dig for minerals in the unoccupied lands of California was free to do so?

Yes, that's what it meant.

Now Bennett knew. The gold in the ground did not belong to Sutter. Nor to Jim Marshall. It belonged to anybody who would take it out. His mission was over and he could dig gold for himself.

But a man who went up into those wild hills would need boots, blankets, pick, shovel, gun, and food to last for weeks. Such an outfit would cost money, and Bennett did not have enough. He needed a partner to provide what later miners were going to call a grubstake.

14

He transferred Sutter's six ounces of gold dust from the buckskin bag to a metal snuffbox with a tight cover. Visiting the taverns, he showed the gold to the men he met there. They shook their heads. They did not believe it was gold. Even if it was, how could they know there was enough in the ground to be worth so much cost and trouble?

Bennett moved on to San Francisco, where the launch that had brought him down was loading the supplies Sutter had ordered for the fort. At the same time, a courier rode to San Francisco with a letter signed by Colonel Mason, dated February 12, 1848, saying the old Mexican mining law was no longer in effect. The courier carried copies of the letter in English and Spanish. He gave them to the newspapers—called the *Californian* and the *Star*—to be published.

Both papers complied. This was only one of a series of orders issued from time to time by the military government, and it stirred no excitement. Neither did Charles Bennett stir any excitement with those yellow grains in his snuffbox, which he was now showing around the City Hotel.

The City Hotel was destined to become famous. Two stories high, made of brown adobe bricks, the hotel was built around three sides of a courtyard at the southwest corner of Clay and Kearny streets, facing the old plaza. Most of the army officers lived there, and leading businessmen had their offices in the rooms along the porch. On this porch, or at the bar and dining table, men gathered to chat and hear the news. They heard Bennett's story with wise smiles of doubt.

As seen down the long road of history, their rejection looks like a wooden-headed reluctance to accept something new. But they had their reasons.

First, they had already heard a story like this and it had proved not worth listening to. Six years earlier, a man named Francisco Lopez, who worked on a ranch near Los Angeles, had pulled up some wild onions to eat with his lunch and had seen golden specks in the earth clinging to the roots. He showed the specks to his friends, the story went around, and men thronged to the ranch to pull up more wild onions. A few weeks later, they were trudging back home.

The specks on the onion roots were gold. But there was not enough gold on the ranch, or anywhere near it, to pay for the time and labor of searching. Men who had heard of this fiasco were not impressed by Bennett.

But another reason, more important, was that these men had no need of gold. When Sutter saw the first grains brought to him by Jim Marshall, he was excited almost to ecstasy because he was deep in debt. But these men in San Francisco were doing very well as they were. Their town was growing and thriving, as few towns had ever grown and thrived anywhere in the world.

During the summer before Jim found gold, the people of San Francisco had taken a town census. In the spring of the next year— while Charles Bennett was looking for a partner—they counted themselves again. They found that in nine months the population had more than doubled.

They were a highly literate group. With fewer than nine hundred people, they supported two newspapers. One of the first sales ever held in town was an auction of books. They had taken the census because they were building a schoolhouse and they wanted to know how many boys and girls of school age there were in town. The teacher was to be Thomas Douglas, a graduate of Yale.

The school opened April 3, 1848. By this time the children already had a Sunday school. The Sunday school met every Sunday morning in the office of the chief magistrate (still called by the old Mexican title of alcalde) and was supervised by Sarah Buetner (Mrs. Charles) Gillespie. Mr. and Mrs. Gillespie were New Yorkers who had lived for seven years in China, where Mr. Gillespie had been engaged in the Pacific trade. In his home port, Macao, near Canton, he had kept a warehouse filled with Oriental goods to be put aboard the great merchant ships that carried these Eastern treasures to the Western world.

Now that San Francisco was becoming a center of Pacific commerce, the Gillespies appear to have decided that they would like to live again among their own people. They arrived in San Francisco February 3, 1848, aboard the brig *Eagle.* The early San Francisco newspapers have enticing lists of merchandise: silks, tea, gunpowder, firecrackers, spices, lacquered bowls, velvet slippers, "mosquito curtains of grass-cloth, for bedsteads," and a thousand other exotic wares that Mr. and Mrs. Gillespie had brought with them. They had also brought three Chinese employees—two men and a woman—the first Chinese to make their home in San Francisco.

In this spring of 1848, the chief businessmen of the town were Pacific traders, like Charles Gillespie, or merchants who sold supplies to the vessels engaged in this trade. But there were many others. The first census listed thirty-five occupations in which the people were employed. Any man who wanted a job could get one, and any woman too, for the lodging houses hired women to cook and to hem sheets and blankets. Often, during this spring, the newspapers had more space taken up by advertisements than by news.

The people of such a town were slow to believe in a shower of gold because they did not need to believe in it. Still, here and there Bennett did find a man who listened seriously to what he said. One of these was John Henry Brown.

John Henry Brown was a seasoned pioneer. Born in England, as a boy he had served as apprentice to his uncle on a packet ship. Evidently his uncle was not an indulgent master, for Brown ran away, found a berth on a vessel that took him to Havana, worked his way somehow to Philadelphia, and then headed west. After some bloodcurdling years as a fur trader among the Indians from Ohio to Oregon, he had now, at the age of thirty-seven, settled down as an innkeeper in California.

He had rented the City Hotel from its owner, William Leidesdorff. Their relationship was stormy, so with a new partner, Robert A. Parker, Brown was building another hotel, to be called the Parker House. But it was in the City Hotel that he met Bennett and looked at the grains in the snuffbox. While he knew little about the looks of newly mined gold, Brown was a shrewd judge of men, and he believed what Bennett told him.

But while he believed in Bennett's gold, Brown could not go looking for it. The Parker House, still under construction, was taking all his time and strength. Lumber for the hotel was cut in the woods on the other side of the bay, and most of the woodcutters were sailors who had deserted their ships and were working there because the woods made a safe hiding place. In San Francisco, as in all ports in those days, there were professional sailor-catchers paid to find runaways and drag them back to their ships. But if any man came to this camp looking for a sailor, the whole brotherhood would gang up and kill him. The catchers had learned to keep away.

At intervals, Brown took provisions to the woodcutters by boat and brought back the lumber they had cut since his last visit. To keep the men contented, whenever he took food, he also had to take a barrel of liquor. Of course they all got drunk, and not until the barrel was empty would they go back to work. Putting up the hotel in town was less nerve-racking because most of the carpenters were Mormons, a sober and dependable lot; but they demanded high pay and got it, as workmen were needed everywhere.

By high wages, perseverance, and barrels of booze, Brown and

Parker were getting their building up, but they could do no more. They had to let somebody else go after gold.

Brown thought first of George McDougal, a broker whose main business was buying town lots and holding them for a rise in price. But, as Brown wrote later, "McDougal thought it was a put-up job to get money out of him" and so declined. Brown thought again. This time he remembered a man around town named Isaac Humphreys, who had said he used to dig gold in Georgia. Brown sought out Isaac Humphreys and brought him to the City Hotel. He introduced Bennett and told him to open the snuffbox.

This interview had momentous consequences.

Near the corner of Montgomery and Sacramento streets was a cabinetmaker's shop. Here the workmen made furniture, carts, wheelbarrows, and anything else a customer asked for. One day during the last week of February, 1848, a man came into the shop; he said his name was Isaac Humphreys and he was looking for a carpenter named Spencer, whose work he had seen before. Did they know him?

Yes, they knew him, a good carpenter. Spencer was a boarder in the home of a man who worked in the shop, William Foster. Humphreys went to see them.

William Foster also was an expert woodworker. He had married a beautiful girl named Sally Murphy, one of three beautiful sisters whose names occur over and over in the memoirs of early Californians as women noteworthy both for their good looks and their good sense. Spencer and Foster welcomed their new customer and asked what he wanted. While they listened with puzzled frowns, Humphreys began to describe a contrivance the like of which they had never heard.

Humphreys said he would stand by and direct them. They said they would make the thing, whatever it was.

In a few days the "thing" was finished. To the builders it was a mighty strange object, but it was going to make hundreds of men rich before the year was over. For Isaac Humphreys, fresh from the hills of Georgia, not only knew how to recognize gold but also how to get gold out of the earth that held it.

The "thing" was a gold rocker. It was based on the fact that gold is heavy. Put a lump of gold-bearing dirt into a container of water, stir up the dirt to loosen any wee nuggets that may be embedded there, and the gold will sink to the bottom. That's all.

The rockers used in that first year of gold mining were copies— or copies of copies—of Isaac's model. The miners made a box three or four feet long, about twenty inches wide, and eighteen inches deep,

18

mounted on curved rockers like a baby's cradle. One end of the box was closed and the other end left open. The mount under the closed end was a little higher than that under the open end, so water would trickle down and out by the opening. Across the bottom of the box they nailed wooden crosspieces, two or three inches apart. Into the higher end of the box they fitted a smaller box, about sixteen inches wide and four inches deep. This smaller box had a sheet-iron bottom pierced with holes about half an inch across.

The miners set up the rocker between a hill and a creek. If two men were working as partners, one of them would dig earth out of the hillside and bring it to the rocker in a bucket or wheelbarrow while the other man brought water from the creek. They put a shovelful of earth into the upper box. One man poured in a slow stream of water; his partner rocked the cradle gently—as gently as a mother rocking her baby to sleep.

This rocking turned the earth into mud. The mud dripped through the holes to the wooden bottom, where the crosspieces were, and drifted down toward the open end. As it crept along, the bits of gold in the mud sank and caught on the crosspieces, while the mud flowed on and out.

Such was the basic idea. However, many rockers were nothing but hollowed logs, with the upper box a roughly sawed board instead of sheet iron. Some were made by men who had never seen a rocker and had to be guided by hearsay. But during that first lavish summer, those rockers took out prodigious quantities of gold. Men who became expert devised changes that made their work faster. Before long, the early rocker had turned into the "long tom," nine or ten feet from end to end, and more complex in design. But the principle stayed the same.

Bringing their rocker with them, Bennett and Humphreys went to Sutter's Fort. When he had made his report to Sutter, Bennett led Humphreys up to the sawmill. Several of the builders had quit to go gold-hunting, but those who were still at work had nearly finished the job. The mill began operations March 11, 1848, and for some weeks it really did saw lumber. But by this time, Bennett and Humphreys, like the Mormons from the fort, had gone looking for a golden spot of their own. In those days, this was not hard to find.

That first rocker brought them good fortune. John Henry Brown wrote that when Bennett took a ship back to his home in Oregon, he had about fourteen hundred ounces of gold to take with him. At 1848 value, fourteen hundred ounces of gold would be worth about

$22,000 (about $800,000 at the start of 1980). Brown may have garnished the facts, but when we read well-based accounts of what other men picked up in that plentiful summer, we can be sure he did not exaggerate much.

But this is ahead of the story. When Bennett and Humphreys took their rocker up to the hills, the tale of gold was still wandering around like a ghost looking for somebody to believe in it. However, when Bennett had been showing his gold around the City Hotel, he had started talk. As the weeks passed, other men came down from the hills with more samples of gold. Still others brought reports of other minerals found in California. A quicksilver mine, near the present town of Santa Clara, had been worked since Mexican days. At length the editor of the *Californian*, Benjamin R. Buckelew of Long Island, decided to mention these reports. He did not think they were worth much space, but he did include them among other small items of news.

After saying the quicksilver mine was doing well, he reported that copper and coal had been seen north of San Francisco Bay. Other items took up most of the page, but down at the end of the column, almost like an afterthought, he added a few lines about gold. Here is what he said:

Gold Mine Found.—In the newly made raceway of the Saw Mill recently erected by Captain Sutter on the American Fork, gold has been found in considerable quantities. One person brought thirty dollars' worth to New Helvetia, gathered there in a short time. California no doubt is rich in mineral wealth, great chances here for scientific capitalists. Gold had been found in almost every part of the country.

This appeared in the *Californian* of Wednesday, March 15, 1848, at the bottom of column 3, page 2. It was the first mention in print of Jim Marshall's discovery anywhere in the world.

Seven copies of this newspaper are known to exist, six of them in the United States and one in Canada. If these were for sale, one copy would probably be worth close to a million dollars.

People who bought the paper the day it was published paid twelve and a half cents.

5

During March and April, a few men left San Francisco and went up
to the hills. But only a few, and most of these did not say they were
leaving to look for gold. Lest they come back empty-handed and be
laughed at, they said they were going to hunt venison, or trade in
cattle hides, or attend to some business with men who just happened
to live near Sutter's Fort.

But such a momentous fact could not long smolder under the
surface of life. Somewhere it had to explode.

The explosion occurred Thursday, May 11, 1848. The people of
San Francisco were going about their affairs as usual when they heard
a commotion outdoors. Men in their workshops, children saying their
lessons in the schoolhouse, women buying dinner at the market
dropped their tools, books, and market baskets and rushed out to see
what was going on. They saw such a happening as none of them had
ever seen before.

The Mormon leader Sam Brannan was running down the street.
He was holding aloft a glass bottle that had once held quinine and
was now full of shimmering flakes. As he ran and waved the bottle,
he was yelling as loud as he could yell, "Gold! Gold! Gold from the
American River!"

A husky fellow, twenty-nine years old, Sam Brannan could make
a lot of noise. He ran and shouted, and other men ran after him and
shouted for him to stop and show them the gold, and still other men
ran after these and shouted to ask what the excitement was about.
With every step he took, the train behind him grew longer and the
noise grew louder. At last, when his legs and lungs had to rest, Sam
paused. The crowd clustered around him. He showed them his bottle

21

of gold. They stared and listened avidly as Sam caught his breath and told them where it came from and how to get there.

Later generations have wondered: Why did Sam Brannan act like this? Talk of gold had been buzzing around for weeks. Why did he make such a racket about it, all of a sudden?

Some people have said it was because he did not always abide by the Mormon rule against strong waters, and this was one of those days. According to others, Brannan and his partner Smith had stuffed their store at New Helvetia with beans and salt meat, picks and shovels and pans, boots and shirts and other goods men would need to buy on their way to the hills. They say he chose this dramatic way to stir up business.

Whatever his reason, the effect was like the effect of a bomb. That day, the Gold Rush began from San Francisco. Carpenters who had run out of the half-built Parker House did not even go back to pick up their tools. The saws and hammers lay where they had fallen and were still lying there when the men came back from the hills with their bags of gold. The market man, George Eggleston, hung out a sign that said, "Gone to the diggings, help yourself," and set out for the goldfields. Before evening, every man who owned any sort of boat was beset by other men asking what he would charge to take them across to the east side of San Francisco Bay. There were not enough boats in town. Within a week, the beach was crowded with men and women and children—some of them babies in their mothers' arms—waiting their turn to cross.

Families who had wagons drove around the bay to Carquinez Strait, a strip of water two miles wide, which they had to cross before they could drive on to the land of gold. Here, on the south bank of the strait, they took a ferry to the north side. The ferry was a big flatboat owned by a Kentucky giant nearly seven feet tall, named Robert Semple. With some other land speculators, Semple had planned a settlement called Benicia on the north side. Wanting to sell town lots, he had been using his boat to take over prospective buyers. Now he found himself getting rich in a way he had not planned.

A San Francisco trader, Charles L. Ross (whose place of business was grandly named The New York Store), had crossed the strait two or three days before Sam Brannan made his run. That day, he had been the only passenger on the ferryboat. On his return, two weeks later, he found the boat nearly empty as he crossed southward toward San Francisco, but on the south side, he met two hundred wagons and five hundred persons, waiting to cross northward toward the hills.

Semple had nobody to help him run the ferryboat. The men he had employed had quit to dig gold. He ran the ferry day and night, pausing only when he had to sleep. On each crossing toward the gold-fields he carried two wagons, with their horses or oxen, and the people traveling with the wagons. If there was room for more, he would also take single men who had no baggage but what they bore on their backs. No matter how he raised his fares, still they came.

In the midst of all this push and clatter, when excitement was flitting through the population like some glorious epidemic, one day a man gave the malady a name. Almost as if by chance, he used a phrase that was destined to be heard wherever people spoke the English language, and in translation everywhere else. He called the infection gold fever.

Benjamin Buckelew, for some months editor of the *Californian*, wanted to give more of his time to the profitable business of land speculation. He had recently engaged a printer from Newport, Rhode Island, named Henry Sheldon, to take his place. When Brannan made his run and the town burst into action, Henry Sheldon, with remarkable calm, wrote a news article about what was going on. This appeared in the paper May 17, 1848. He said:

We have been informed by a gentleman recently from the gold region that digging continues brisk. Many persons have already left the coast for that region, and considerable excitement exists in our midst, which bids fair to become quite a gold fever.

How casually he used the term! It seems to have slipped off his pen without his having any idea that he was making an immortal linkage of words.

But Edward Kemble, editor of the *Star*, recognized what a great description it was. Three days later, in the *Star* of May 20, Kemble blazoned it forth:

A terrible visitant we have had of late, a fever which has well nigh depopulated the town. It has preyed upon defenseless old age, subdued the elasticity of careless youth, and attacked indiscriminately sex and class. This is the Gold Fever.

His remark about "defenseless old age" is more flowery than exact. The town census of the year before had shown that 93 percent of the people in San Francisco were less than forty years old. But Kemble was only nineteen when he wrote this, and he may have thought old age began at thirty. At any rate, he was right in all he said about the gold fever itself.

23

He used the phrase so vividly that he is usually given credit for having invented it. In fact, as time passed, Kemble himself came to believe he had. He said so in his *History of California Newspapers*—not boastfully but in an offhand sentence, as if it were something that most of his readers already knew.

His history was first published in 1858, as a supplement to the Christmas issue of the Sacramento *Union*. In it, Kemble describes every newspaper and magazine published in California from 1846 to the end of 1858. This was no small achievement, for there were 324 of these publications, and many of them did not last a year.

In his book, Kemble is modest. At the beginning, he refers to himself by name. He says the former editor of the *Star*, a quarrelsome fellow named Jones, had quit, and "his place was filled by one of the printers in the office, a mere lad. The printer's name was Kemble." But through most of the book, he refers to himself only as "the editor of the *Star*." He is modest also in another way. He frankly laughs at the clumsiness of "the editor's" early writings. But he makes an equally frank comment: "Under his management the *Star* prospered very well."

And so it did, until the subscribers and advertisers saw Sam Brannan's bottle of gold dust and began rushing off to the hills. "The editor" went to see for himself. Finding only a "few grains of gold," he decided the reports were "all sham." He said so in his paper; and, continues Kemble in 1858, "He gave the popular infection the name of the 'gold fever.' "

Actually, nobody is sure who invented the phrase "gold fever." It dates from long before Sam Brannan's noisy run down the street in San Francisco. The words had appeared a year earlier in a religious paper published in Honolulu called *The Seamen's Friend and Temperance Advocate*. This time the writer used "gold fever" to describe the excitement among the crews of two whaling ships just back from the Arctic Sea, who thought they had found gold "on an island in Marguerita Bay, California." There is no Marguerita (or Margarita) Bay on modern maps, but wherever these seamen were, they loaded several tons of what they thought was gold ore. But, *The Seamen's Friend* reported, "It was not gold ore. Recently a quantity was landed on one of our wharfs and is to be employed for the useful purpose of house building. After the gold fever was over, these ships were very successful in taking oil in the bay."

This article was reprinted in the San Francisco *Californian* May 22, 1847. Sheldon may have read it, and maybe Kemble did too. Or maybe they heard the words "gold fever" somewhere else.

The fever raged on. By June 1, 1848, nearly every store and office in San Francisco was vacant. Many of the storekeepers had not even locked their doors but, like the market man, had put up signs saying, "Help yourself."

Again, people have wondered: Why this thundering response to Sam Brannan's run? Why did all the people who had been scoffing at the talk of gold change their minds as suddenly as if they had been bewitched?

The answer seems to be that Sam Brannan proclaimed the fact just when they were *ready* to accept it. For two months—ever since Charles Bennett had begun looking for a partner in the City Hotel— the idea of gold had been seeping into their minds. They could not believe it, but they had wished they could. And now Sam Brannan had shown them proof. They caught the gold fever and it made them delirious.

And no wonder, when we look at the facts behind the fever. At the "Dry Diggins" (site of the present town of Placerville), men who worked steadily were averaging three ounces to five pounds of gold a day. Indians were giving a handful of gold for a fancy handkerchief or a bright-colored shirt. One Indian directed a party of miners to a spot where they took out an average of eighteen ounces a day each, for ten successive days. (At the 1848 price of gold, this would mean $288 a day; the value at the start of 1980, more than $10,000.

The gold fever was not mere delirium.

They called a deposit of gold a *placer*. This was a Spanish word that meant a pleasure, a delight. Now the Americans agreed that it was a mighty apt word for a spot where gold lay around, waiting for them to pick it up. They usually pronounced it to rhyme with "passer."

The first town outside California to hear the golden tale was Honolulu.

Hawaii was still an independent country with its own king, but Honolulu had a vigorous colony of Americans and Europeans who lived and worked there. During the week after Sam Brannan's run, two schooners from Hawaii, the *Louise* (Captain Menzies) and the *Mary* (Captain Belcham), came into port at San Francisco. The rush out of town had started, and both captains had trouble with sailors who tried to jump ship and rush off. A few of them did run away, but the captains managed to keep enough men aboard to put their vessels to sea again.

There has been some confusion about the sailing dates, but according to the *Star* of June 3, 1848, the *Louise* sailed for Honolulu May 28, and the *Mary* sailed the next day. The distance from San Francisco to Honolulu is 2,091 miles. Both vessels made the voyage in the usual time—three weeks. Both brought gold and newspapers from San Francisco. The resulting outbreak of gold fever in Honolulu did not drain the town, for one reason: there were not enough ships' berths available for all the people who wanted to leave.

The San Franciscans had doubted; the people of Honolulu had no reason to doubt. They had proof. The *Louise* and the *Mary* had brought not rumors but real gold and real newspapers. Officers and crewmen had spoken to men who held nuggets in their hands; they had seen gold exchanged for goods at the stores.

They set Honolulu agog. Yankees, Britons, Frenchmen, native Hawaiians, all were begging the ships' captains to take them to San Francisco. But though Honolulu was the major port of call for Pacific vessels, most of these vessels were traders with few berths for passengers, or none at all. Some of the gold seekers would have to wait for weeks or months before they could sail. But they had caught the fever. Their minds were made up. They would go to California somehow, and hundreds of them did.

While all this was going on, word of California gold was creeping eastward. But so far, nobody on the Atlantic side of the continent knew anything about it. The news was traveling, but it traveled slowly.
Slowly.

6

Today we can sit in New York and watch men playing a ball game in San Francisco. We can pick up a phone in Los Angeles and talk to friends in London. Instant communication is such an ordinary part of our lives that we feel a sense of confusion as we try to adjust our minds to the days when news took months to go from one of these cities to another.

We are used to thinking of the Forty-niners as pioneers in the goldfields. The fact is, the Forty-niners got there a year late.

The Forty-niners did not even start their journeys until the real pioneers—such as the men who used those first gold rockers—had already gathered up fortunes. Why didn't they start sooner? There were several reasons. One reason was that the news took so long to reach them.

When Jim Marshall found gold at the sawmill, he was two thousand miles from any post office or telegraph station. Less than four years had passed since Samuel Morse had sent the world's first telegram over a wire from Washington to Baltimore. By the time Jim found gold, telegraph wires linked the cities of the Atlantic coast from Portland to Savannah and reached as far west as New Orleans and Milwaukee. But no farther. As for mail, there was not one post office between the town of Independence, Missouri, and Honolulu.

If a man in California wanted to send a message back east, he had two ways to do it. Yankee trading vessels on their way home from Oriental ports usually stopped at San Francisco for supplies. When such a ship sailed, the Californian might give a letter to the captain and ask him to mail it when he reached his home port. But nobody knew when to expect a homebound ship; they might be months apart.

27

When a captain did take a letter, he had to sail around Cape Horn at the tip of South America, then up the east coasts of both Americas until he reached New York or New Bedford or whatever his home port might be. This was a voyage of seventeen thousand miles. Few vessels made it in less than six months. Many took longer.

Or the Californian might use the summer mail couriers, who went by land. These were men daring enough to ride horseback across two thousand miles of mountains and deserts and prairies, and hardy enough to reach Missouri alive. The mailmen left as soon as the snow had melted in the mountain passes. Their journey took two or three months, depending on weather, horses, and luck.

In the spring of 1848, while the gold rush from San Francisco was still only a trickle, an army mail and a private mail left California. These two parties brought the first news of gold to reach the people who lived east of the Great Divide.

The government mailmen, led by the great western scout Kit Carson (who had the rank of lieutenant in the army), were allowed to carry letters only. No newspapers; too bulky. The private mailmen carried some letters, but they had been hired mainly to take newspapers.

These papers were copies of a special edition of the *Star*, meant for readers in the East. This edition had California news, advice for settlers, and articles on local subjects. The Westerners sent two thousand copies to their friends back home.

Both mail parties rode to Missouri. Here they put letters and papers into the post office.

In Kit Carson's mailbag was a newsletter. It was written by a soldier in the First Regiment of the New York Volunteers; it was addressed to James Gordon Bennett, editor of the New York *Herald*; it was dated from San Francisco April 1, 1848, six weeks before Sam Brannan's run. The letter appeared in the *Herald* August 19. This was the first news of California gold to be published on the East Coast.

The editor thought the letter so interesting that he put it on the front page. But he identified the writer only as one of the New York Volunteers. Nobody has ever found out the soldier's name.

The soldier was a keen and impartial observer. He told about the crops, the cattle ranches, the town and harbor of San Francisco. He described the customs of the Californios (the Spanish word meaning people born in California). But though his letter filled nearly two columns, there were only a few lines about gold. He was so casual that the editor did not think gold important enough to be noted in the headline.

Gold was also mentioned in the special issue of the *Star*. This was in an article called "The Prospects of California" by Dr. Victor Fourgeaud.

Dr. Fourgeaud was a man of scholarly mind and romantic soul. A native of Charleston, South Carolina, he was of French ancestry and was sent to school in Paris when he was ten years old. After graduating from the University of France, he came home and took his degree in medicine at the South Carolina Medical College, following this with three more years of study in Paris. Back in his native country, he was struck by the western urge.

First he went to St. Louis, which seemed mighty far west in those days. Here he practiced medicine for several years. But the tales he heard from fur traders and mountain men drew him on. In 1847, when he was thirty-two years old, Dr. Fourgeaud made the long journey overland. When he saw California, he fell in love.

Writing for eastern readers, he had none of the cool detachment of the New York soldier. He wrote from his heart. Like most lovers, he was so fervent that even when he told plain facts about his darling, he was hard to believe.

According to him, California was a paradise without flaw. Nearly every fruit, vegetable, and flower known to mankind grew there in abundance. Sheep and cattle multiplied beyond counting. As for minerals, California had them in startling variety. Among a long list of others, he said a gold mine had been found, so rich that men were picking up gold "at random and without any trouble."

This was true and might have started the Gold Rush if anybody had taken it seriously. But before they got this far, Fourgeaud's readers had gone through so many columns of glittering prose that it is no wonder if they were too dazzled to see any of it as simple fact.

Other private letters were passed around. Some were printed in the hometown papers. But many of them made no mention of gold, others said the supposed gold had proved to be mica, and all had been written too early to tell the real story. By the time the letters crossed the Mississippi River, the gold fever had changed everything in California for all time. But the people who read the letters did not know it.

As the summer moved on to fall, more rumors drifted in. Some were published here and there. People talked about them but were not excited about them. In the East, the reaction to the reports of gold went through the same stages as in the West: disbelief, doubt, slow acceptance, and then a sudden storming rush to the goldfields. Only in the East it took longer.

Another reason for this was that for a long time the people in the East had only *words* about California gold. In the West, they soon had the gold itself as proof of the words. There at hand were nuggets that they could see, hold, test for realness.

But the strongest reason for the slow start of the Forty-niners was the large number of Americans who detested the whole idea of California.

Many of the most effective leaders of public opinion did not want the western country at all. They never had wanted it. They were still saying, in print and in Congress, that California was an idiot-inspired burden on the taxpayers and never would be anything else.

For years, the United States had been split on the subject of western expansion. This had been the main issue—almost the only issue—in the Presidential election of 1844. The candidates were James K. Polk and Henry Clay. Polk wanted the United States to grow westward, and said so. Clay thought the country was big enough as it was, and said so.

Polk and his supporters favored a plan of western expansion that would begin with Texas.

Formerly part of Mexico, Texas had won independence in 1836 and was now a republic with Sam Houston as president. Most of the Texans were Americans who had settled there during the past twenty-five years, and they wanted Texas to become a state of the Union. Throughout the campaign, Polk and his friends had urged statehood for Texas, but they had let it be known that their plan included much more than Texas. They wanted the United States to reach still farther west, as far as the Pacific Coast.

Henry Clay and his supporters thought this a preposterous fantasy. They insisted that the United States could not possibly occupy and defend so vast an area, and it would be ruinous to try.

Polk was elected. But while he received 170 electoral votes and Clay only 105, Polk's victory was not as sweeping as it sounds. The people were sharply divided; 48 percent of them voted against Polk and his dream of western growth. Plainly, nearly half of Polk's countrymen wanted the country to stop where it was.

But Polk felt that he had a mandate to go ahead. During the campaign he had said exactly what he would do if he became President.

Now he did it. Right or wrong, he followed his campaign promises more closely than any other President in our history.

He had Congress on his side. Less than a month after Polk took office, Congress offered to make the Republic of Texas a state of the Union. The Texans promptly agreed. Now Polk and his friends looked still farther west.

The admission of Texas caused the Mexican War. When the envoys met to draw up a treaty of peace, the Mexicans consented to cede to the United States an area that included not only California but also the present states of Nevada and Utah, most of Arizona, and part of Wyoming, Colorado and New Mexico. For this territory, Mexico would receive a payment of $15 million. In those days, $15 million meant twenty-nine tons of gold.

Now went up storms of wrath.

The people who had not wanted western growth in the first place had been opposed to Texas and the war. They were even more enraged at being asked to pay twenty-nine tons of gold for California or any other place of western territory.

They said California was a miserable desert where nothing would grow. It was too far off to be of any value to a nation based on the Atlantic shoreline. The anti-slavery people noted that a large part of the new country lay in the same latitude as the slave states. They feared that the plan would mean the spread of slavery. The pro-slavery faction saw that much of the country was in the latitude of the free states. This would add to the free territory. And of course there were those people, present in every place and every age, who object to anything new just because it *is* new, and whatever is new upsets them.

A leading spokesman for the anti-California side was Horace Greeley. Besides being editor of the New York *Tribune,* Greeley was a man active in many phases of public life. He had violent likes and dislikes, mostly dislikes. Among other grievances, he was opposed to theaters, alcohol, divorce, votes for women, and new lands in the West. While the treaty was pending, Greeley expressed his opinion in plain words. He began, "Absurd as it is on our part to give fifteen millions of dollars for an accession of territory which we have no use for . . ."

And later, when the Senate approved the treaty, he was outraged to find that the United States had agreed on still further payments to Mexico. This made the cost of the western country not $15 million (twenty-nine tons of gold), but $20 million (thirty-nine tons). Greeley's newspaper bluntly gave his opinion. "We have fought two years for nothing, and pay $20 million dollars to get leave to stop."

31

Millions of Americans agreed with him. Chief of these was Daniel Webster.

The greatest orator in the Senate, Webster had used all his talents to warn his colleagues against the folly of acquiring California and the rest of this western land. Even after he had lost his fight, Webster would not budge. Six months after the treaty was signed, Webster made a speech in the Senate. He said, "I regarded the war as a calamity; and I fear that it is likely to prove, by the annexations which it has brought to us, a great calamity, in being more permanent than the war itself."

The followers of Greeley and Webster concurred. California had been forced upon them, and they resented the maneuver. They were not mentally prepared to believe the reports of gold.

To be sure, the people who wanted California were also doubtful. But their headshaking was like that of the San Franciscans—the story was just too good to be true. Such men as Greeley and Webster were different. Theirs was no mere doubt, but an aggressive disbelief.

But as it happened, on the very day that Daniel Webster was making his speech (Friday, August 11, 1848), the people of San Francisco were shouting all over town.

A courier had arrived the previous day with a letter from Colonel Mason telling them that Mexico had joined the United States in ratifying the treaty. California was now a United States possession.

The celebration had begun that evening, and it lasted all the next day. The whole town took a holiday. At sunrise, the ships in the harbor hoisted flags and fired salutes. On shore, every man who could lay his hands on a gun fired in reply. Boys and girls set off firecrackers brought from China on Charles Gillespie's brig, the *Eagle*. A lordly cavalcade paraded through the streets, led by Lieutenant Edward Gilbert of the New York Volunteers. The Kentucky giant, Robert Semple, made a speech in which he thanked Providence that he was standing on American soil again. All the stores were closed, so that any man wanting to buy an outfit for the mines had to wait until the following day. All the saloons were open, so he could be happy while waiting. Throughout the day, the guns and firecrackers popped and crackled. When night fell, lights shone from every house and tent and makeshift dwelling. Barrels of tar blazed in the plaza and on the street corners. Amazingly, nobody got killed and the town did not burn up.

The merrymakers did not know what Daniel Webster was saying that day in Washington. They did know—at least, the well-informed among them knew—that a naval officer named Edward Beale was on his way to Washington, and an army officer named Lucien Loeser was about to set out. Both men carried gold, to be proved at the Mint, and newspapers that would shake not only Washington but the world. Beale and Loeser were going to start the Forty-niners on their way to California. They were even going to make Greeley and Webster change their minds.

7

Edward Beale and Lucien Loeser were carrying letters written by three of the most important men in California. One writer was Thomas Oliver Larkin, who had been United States consul for California in the Mexican days. The other two letter writers were Commodore Thomas Ap Catesby Jones of the navy and Colonel Mason of the army.

These men had their offices in Monterey. Although this was only ninety miles from San Francisco, news limped so slowly in those days that by the time they heard their first word of gold fever, San Francisco was already emptying to the mines. However, they were astute men, and it did not take them long to realize that this was no small affair like the specks on the onion roots. They decided, all three at about the same time, to write, each man to his own department of the government.

Larkin wrote first.

Thomas Larkin was well known and well esteemed. A native of Massachusetts, he had been living in Monterey for sixteen years when Jim Marshall found gold. He had married Rachel Hobson Holmes, young widow of a sea captain. Rachel also was a native of Massachusetts, and they had first met when they were fellow passengers on the long voyage from Boston around Cape Horn. In later years, Rachel and her husband were to boast proudly that their children were the first native-born Californians, both of whose parents had been born in the United States.

Starting as a small trader, Larkin had become a man of wealth and influence. His home was an eleven-room house, superb for its place and time. (This house is still standing. Nearby is the home of Larkin's half-brother, John B. R. Cooper, who married Encarnación

34

Vallejo, daughter of one of the great California dons.) Most Americans in early California became Mexican citizens, but Larkin would not. He and Rachel lived there on a visitors' permit, which they had to renew every year. When his country made him consul, he filled the office well.

Larkin owned a ranch on the Sacramento River. One day in May, 1848, he set out for the ranch on a routine visit. When he reached San José, about fifty miles above Monterey, he found the trail bustling with men carrying picks and shovels. They told him they were on their way to dig gold.

No report of gold had come to Monterey since last February, when Charles Bennett had tried in vain to get somebody interested. Larkin was sure these men's yarns were overblown, but he sent a brief report to Colonel Mason. Then he went on to San Francisco, still planning to visit his ranch.

But in San Francisco, men were coming in every day bringing gold dust. Boats packed with people were crossing the bay toward the gold country, fast as the wind would move them. Larkin's interest was aroused. He squeezed himself on one of the boats and went to the hills. In spite of all he had seen and heard, he was wonderstruck.

When he came home to Monterey, he found the once-busy town almost silent. During his absence, more tales of gold had come in. Monterey had emptied like San Francisco.

Larkin wrote a letter addressed to the Secretary of State, James Buchanan (the same Buchanan who later became President). A few days later he wrote again. He told of the fortunes pouring out of the hills. He told of soldiers and sailors deserting to dig gold; of vessels rocking at anchor in the harbors, unable to get out because their crews had run away.

In port at Monterey was the USS *Ohio,* flagship of Commodore Jones. Larkin spoke to the commodore. Although Larkin had written to Mr. Buchanan, he told the commodore that news of such importance should be sent to Washington by an official military courier.

The commodore agreed to write a letter also. His letter would go to the Secretary of the Navy, John Young Mason. To carry the letters to Washington, the commodore chose a naval lieutenant, Edward Fitzgerald Beale. Lieutenant Beale was young, brave, and proud to be chosen.

At the same time, Colonel Mason was making up his own report for the War Department. Like Larkin, the colonel wanted to do more than merely repeat what other people had told him. He wanted to see for himself before he wrote.

Colonel Mason set out for the mines June 17, 1848. With him were his valet, a black man named Aaron; four enlisted men selected because of their fine records; and a promising young lieutenant named William Tecumseh Sherman. When they reached San Francisco, the colonel accepted the company of three other men. Two of these were civilians. The third was Captain Folsom, who by this time was convinced that the yellow flakes he had seen were not mica. The party rode to Sutter's Fort, Mormon Island, the sawmill, and several mining camps.

Assisted by Lieutenant Sherman, the colonel took notes. Working together, the two men made maps of the gold country. They recorded the names of the men they talked with, the amounts of gold displayed to them, the spots where the miners had found it, the time they had taken to gather it. They wrote careful descriptions of the gold rockers and other aids the miners were using. They also noted that a man at the mines could pick up, in a day, more than the army paid an enlisted man in a month. Soldiers were deserting the army for the goldfields, and who could be surprised?

Taking their records, the two officers rode back to Monterey. The four carefully chosen enlisted men who had gone with them to the mines rode back to Monterey with them. But a few days later, a soldier who had not deserted, but had been on a twenty-two-day furlough, arrived at Monterey. He brought gold worth the pay and rations given to a soldier during five years in the army. The four men with flawless records could resist no longer. They deserted.

Commodore Jones had written his report to a man named Mason; now, by coincidence, Colonel Mason wrote his to a man named Jones. (The two Masons were distant cousins. Born in Virginia, they were descendants of a family distinguished in public life since colonial times.) Addressing Adjutant General Roger Jones under the date of August 17, Colonel Mason sent a letter destined to become a classic. He enclosed his maps. He sent a specimen of the gravel from the creekbeds, with the grains of gold among the grains of sand. He told Captain Folsom to take government money and buy a good-sized sample of gold. This gold—nearly twenty pounds troy weight—he put into a little box that had once held tea. The newspapers were appearing only now and then, but on August 14, Henry Sheldon had managed to bring out an issue of the *Californian* in which he gave late news from the gold country. Colonel Mason bought copies of the paper to be sent along.

His evidence was ready. Now, like Commodore Jones, he had to appoint a man to deliver it. Colonel Mason chose Lieutenant Lucien Loeser of the army. Like Lieutenant Beale of the navy, Loeser was young, brave, and proud to be chosen.

For the colonel and the commodore, the choice of couriers had been no ordinary decision. These couriers could not be ordinary men.

There was no regular route from the Pacific Coast to the Atlantic. A courier would have to take care of himself. He had to be a man quick to sense danger and deal with it, and just as quick to sense a good chance and make the most of it. He must be constantly aware that he would meet a thousand turns of luck over which he had no control. Above all, he must be practical enough to know that a mission accomplished is better than a dead hero, and act accordingly. His job was to get there.

Beale and Loeser were both capable men. They were both well qualified for the charge before them. But beyond this likeness, they were different.

Beale was a man of courage, the quiet sort. He was devoted to his duty and he did it well. But he was not a showy fellow. He had no wish for public acclaim. In his personal life, he wanted to be let alone.

Loeser was a man of courage, the zestful sort. He was talkative, exuberant, outgoing. He had no wish to be let alone; he saw to it that he was not let alone. Wherever he went, something started to happen.

Beale and Loeser both did exactly what they had been told to do. They brought their great news to the country east of the Mississippi River; they delivered their letters promptly and safely. But because they were themselves so unlike, they had different sorts of influence on what happened next. If Beale had been like the rollicking Loeser, if Loeser had been like the unflustered Beale, the Gold Rush would not have been the same.

Beale started first.

Beale knew that a man crossing from coast to coast, no matter which way he went, would have to go through some horrendous country. But he felt honored to have been given this mission, and he meant to prove that he deserved it.

He wanted to take a specimen of gold with him, but unlike Colonel

37

Mason, Commodore Jones did not think he should spend government money for this. Beale decided to buy the gold himself. When he met the members of the President's Cabinet, he wanted to show them more than sheets of paper. He wanted to show them gold—real gold that could be tested at the Mint.

But he had another reason, perhaps even stronger than the first. Beale was a young man in love. He was hoping to marry a girl named Mary Edwards, descendant of a Quaker family who had come to this country with William Penn. He wanted to offer Mary a tribute no man had ever offered a girl before, an engagement ring made of California gold.

He could not afford to buy much. In those days, a naval lieutenant was paid $1,500 to $1,800 a year, depending on his duties. At the prices of the time, this was adequate, but even then it left little for luxuries. However, when Beale set out on his journey, he was carrying two samples of gold dust: one for the Mint, the other for Mary's ring.

In the first week of July (while Colonel Mason and his party were celebrating Independence Day at Sutter's Fort), Commodore Jones and Lieutenant Beale left Monterey on the commodore's flagship. They sailed to La Paz, near the tip of the long peninsula called Baja (Lower) California. Here, Commodore Jones wrote his dispatch. He gave this to Beale and said good-bye.

Beale was now carrying a packet of regular naval reports, the commodore's letter to the Secretary of the Navy, Larkin's letters to Buchanan, government money for his expenses, and his own little cache of gold. His job was to take these safely from La Paz to Washington.

On August 1 he began his cross-country journey. First he bought passage on a trading vessel that went from La Paz across the Gulf of California to Mazatlán on the west coast of the Mexican mainland. Here he boarded a coastwise vessel that took him southward to the port of San Blas. Now the real challenge began.

He planned to travel across Mexico, from San Blas on the west coast to Veracruz on the east. Veracruz was a busy harbor. Beale knew if he could get there, he would have no trouble finding a vessel bound for some United States port. But the distance from San Blas to Veracruz was about a thousand miles, and for nearly every mile of the way he would be taking chances on his life.

In the interior of Mexico, towns were separated by long stretches of mountains and forests. Beale would be crossing in the rainy season. The rivers would be at flood height and the trails deep in mud. His journey would have been dangerous enough if Nature had been his only enemy; but lurking along the trails were gangs of killer bandits, waiting to attack any traveler who looked as if he might have something worth stealing.

Beale had made perilous journeys before. He knew the safest traveler was the one least noticed. As his uniform would be an invitation to the jungle thugs, he made himself look as much like an average Mexican as he could.

After several years among the Spanish-speaking Californios, he was fluent in their language, and he had a deep tan from the California sun. Now at San Blas, he put on the usual costume of the country— red flannel shirt, sombrero, leather breeches, and high boots. He hired a native professional guide recommended by the governor of San Blas. Beale equipped himself and his guide with the best of weapons; thus armed, they rode toward the town of Tepec. The roads were deep with mud, and the desperadoes were swarming. The two men were attacked, but with their guns and knives, they fought their way through to the town of Guadalajara and then to Mexico City.

On the whole journey, Beale's main idea was to keep moving, and moving as fast as he could. He and his guide rode night and day. They caught snatches of sleep at the stations along the trail where travelers stopped to have their saddles transferred to fresh horses for the next lap of the journey. Five days from San Blas they reached Mexico City. Beale's red shirt was almost solid with mud, but he was well and triumphant. He reported to the United States minister, Nathan Clifford of Maine.

After a night's sleep, Beale wanted to push on. But Mr. Clifford made him stay for a second night, saying he had to write some reports of his own for Washington. (Probably he ordered the pause also because he did not want this over-dutiful young man to elude the bandits, only to drop of exhaustion before he could reach Veracruz.)

Beale set out as soon as he was allowed to do so, riding horseback. The distance from Mexico City to Veracruz is 264 miles, but the road was well traveled and safe, so he needed his guide no longer. At Veracruz he found the American sloop-of-war *Germantown*, preparing to sail for Mobile, Alabama. Though Beale chafed because he had to wait several days before sailing, the delay did give him time to get some rest and better clothes.

He went to Mobile aboard the *Germantown*. At Mobile he could have taken a coastwise steamer for Washington. But steamers from ports on the Gulf of Mexico did not take the shortest route. They had to go around the tip of Florida, so they usually went a few miles more, to Havana, for mail and passengers. As Beale wanted to accomplish his mission as fast as he could, he chose instead to go by stagecoach from Mobile directly to the Atlantic seaboard. Here he boarded a steamer for Washington.

He reached Washington aboard the steamer *Augusta* on Saturday, September 16, 1848. He had done his duty bravely and well. The letters entrusted to him were intact, and his journey of forty-seven days from La Paz had been the fastest crossing ever made from the Pacific coast to Washington.

His arrival was reported Monday, September 18, in the Washington *Union*. That same day, Beale called on the various officials to whom his letters were addressed and delivered the letters, including those from Larkin and Commodore Jones, confirming the reports of great gold finds in California. This news was published by the *Union* Tuesday, September 19, and by the Baltimore *Sun* the next day. Both papers reported it rather cautiously. It was as if the editors thought it deserved attention, but they did not want to risk being sensational about it.

The little sample of gold Beale had bought for the government was sent to the Mint in Philadelphia for testing. The Mint sent the gold back to Washington with the report that it was 22 carats fine. The sample was put on display at the Patent Office. It was no more than a pinch, but it did prove that California gold was real. Larkin's letters appeared in the papers; the streets began to buzz with talk.

Beale had nothing to do now but wait for further orders and return dispatches. He began asking his superiors how soon he could go out of town.

At this time, Beale might have become a public hero, but he had no wish for any such attention. He had no interest in starting a gold rush. Apparently, no such idea ever crossed his mind. He was happy to have won the approval of the Navy Department and the admiration of his friends. But he was not thinking about his impact on history. He was thinking about Mary Edwards. As soon as he had permission, he left Washington. He did not give his address to the papers, but his friends knew he had gone to the Edwards home in Chester, Pennsylvania, to see Mary and ask if she would accept a ring made of California gold.

Here, too, he accomplished his mission. Mary accepted the ring.

As he was the best continent-crosser in the navy, Beale had to leave her to take dispatches from Washington to Monterey, but in the summer of the following year, he was back east. One day in June, 1849, leading the column headed "Married," the New York *Herald* reported:

At Chester, Delaware County, Pa., on the 27th inst., by the Rev. Mortimer Talbot of the United States Navy, Lieutenant Edward F. Beale of the United States Navy, to Mary Engle, daughter of the Hon. Samuel Edwards.

Just how Beale and Mary had expected to spend their honeymoon, we do not know. But whatever their plan, they did not carry it out. The day after they were married, grim reality blasted their dream. A courier appeared with an order from the navy. Lieutenant Beale was to leave for California, carrying dispatches for the naval officers there. He was to sail Saturday, June 30, on the steamer *Crescent City*, now in port at New York. He was not allowed to take Mary with him.

Beale had to obey. The *Crescent City* sailed at three o'clock in the afternoon of June 30. Her passenger list had more than two hundred names, all but one signifying men. The exception was "H. D. Kimball and lady." But the name "Lieutenant E. Beall" (spelled that way in the list) had no "and lady" attached. Beale, married three days before, had had to leave his wife behind.

In spite of its stodgy beginning, their marriage was a happy one. They had several children. One of them was named Truxtun Beale, in honor of Edward Beale's grandfather, Commodore Thomas Truxtun, a naval hero of the Revolution.

When Mary had accepted her engagement ring—autumn, 1848— it was generally known in the East that somebody had found gold somewhere in California. All sorts of reports had been drifting in. However, before Beale's arrival, the letters from California had all been written by men who had not themselves seen the goldfields. They were reporting only what they had been told. This was true also of the letter Beale had brought from Commodore Jones. But Larkin had visited the goldfields before he wrote his two letters, both of which Beale had brought to Washington. His letters were being published all over the country. They could not be disregarded.

People who favored western growth were elated. The editor of the Washington *Union*, a staunch California man, triumphantly addressed those who had not wanted the West. "There," he exclaimed in his paper, "is the country you sneeringly declared not worth having! Why, it is a solid mass of gold!"

But people in general were not so sure. They were interested. They talked about it. But most of them said, "Let's wait and see." There was gold on this side, too. Men were mining it right now in the hills from Vermont to Georgia, but the amount was not sensational. These wild-sounding reports from California might be true. Or they might not.

James Gordon Bennett expressed the prevailing mood: "Now for our part, we do not know what to think of this gold story. It looks marvelously like a speculation to induce a rapid emigration."

Horace Greeley was even less ardent. He published only one of Larkin's letters, and this one he put on an inside page. Instead of calling it news, he headlined it, "The Gold Mania in California."

But people in the East still thought "mania" a good word for it. They went on with their usual business. "All Washington" might be "in a ferment," as one California zealot said it was; but either this "ferment" did not last, or it took a long time to reach New York. On October 6, 1848, three weeks after Edward Beale had arrived with the Larkin letters, a steamboat left New York for San Francisco. To emphasize where she was going, her owners had named her the *California.* She was new; she was equipped with the finest engines and the most modern comforts. She had berths for 150 passengers. But she carried not one passenger bound for the land of gold.

The *California* had been built by a new business firm, the Pacific Mail Steamship Company. She was the first of three steamers that were to go around the tip of South America and up the Pacific coast to San Francisco, then ply regularly between San Francisco and Panama.

For some weeks before the *California* left New York, the company had been advertising that she would carry mail and passengers. When she sailed, she did have passengers aboard, but they were all bound for Rio de Janeiro in Brazil, where the steamer was to make her first stop, or for Valparaiso in Chile. If anybody wanted to buy a ticket for San Francisco, he could have done so, but nobody did. When the *California* went around the tip of South America, except for the Valparaiso passengers, she had not a soul on board but her captain and crew.

But though the captain and crew did not know it, they were steaming right into the Gold Rush. Before they reached San Francisco, they were going to have an adventure that would make history.

In New York, the sailing of the *California* was no great event. As in all port cities, the papers ran a daily column giving the names and destinations of vessels that had sailed the day before. The day after the *California* left, the *Tribune* printed the names of yesterday's departures. At the bottom of the list were two lines: "Sailed—steamship *California*, for Valparaiso and other ports in the Pacific."

Never did a more fantastic voyage have a less fantastic start.

8

Edward Beale had brought gold with him. He had not brought gold fever.

But the fever was not far behind. On November 23, 1848, while the *California* was in port at Rio, Lucien Loeser reached the United States. Loeser arrived on a vessel that docked at New Orleans. He exploded into town like a fireball, and before he had been there twenty-four hours he had started the Gold Rush.

Lucien Loeser was born in Pennsylvania. He graduated from West Point in 1842. He was now a first lieutenant in Company F, Third Artillery, which had been stationed at Monterey for nearly two years. Monterey was a town of about a thousand people. Garrison duty was dull. The young officers fumed at being kept there in near idleness while others, no older and no braver than themselves, were on active duty with the chance to win distinction. Loeser was elated when Colonel Mason chose him to take the gold to Washington.

Colonel Mason gave him a good start.

While Mason and his party had been on their tour of the mines, the bark *Lambayecana* (named for the Peruvian town of Lambayeque) had left San Francisco on her way to ports in Peru and Chile. She had stopped at Monterey for supplies and was there when Mason's party returned. Mason summoned Captain Sparrow of the *Lambayecana* and gave him an army mission.

Captain Sparrow was to sail back to San Francisco and pick up the gold Folsom had been told to buy. When he brought the gold to Monterey, Loeser would join him and go as far as the vessel's first stop, which was Paita, Peru. A British trading steamer made monthly

44

trips between Paita and Panama City on the Pacific side of the isthmus. Loeser would leave the ship at Paita and wait there for the next sailing of the steamer to Panama. From Panama City he would cross the isthmus. This would be dangerous but not impossible for a sturdy and well-armed young man. At the port of Chagres, on the Atlantic side of the isthmus, Loeser would take whatever vessel he could find to forward him on his way.

Captain Sparrow went back to San Francisco. Hearing of the journey planned for Loeser, two civilians asked permission to join him. One was a wealthy merchant, David Carter, who with his partner, William Heath Davis, had a store at Clay and Montgomery streets. The second was another businessman, Thomas A. Minard. Both men had thousands of dollars' worth of gold. They had taken it in trade, and now they wanted to exchange it for coin at the Mint in Philadelphia.

With these two passengers, Captain Sparrow sailed again for Monterey. Loeser came aboard, no doubt glad to have the added safety of numbers while crossing the isthmus. They sailed from Monterey on August 30, 1848.

Late in September they reached Paita. Here they bought tickets for the British steamer's October voyage northward to Panama. Now they had nothing to do but sit and wait.

But if there was one thing Lucian Loeser could not do gracefully, it was sit and wait. He was the bearer of great news and he wanted to tell it. As for Messrs. Carter and Minard, either they were as eager as Loeser to be heroes of the gold story or they had caught his enthusiasm on the voyage. They too wanted to spread the news of gold.

Loeser could not of course open Colonel Mason's letter, but he had newspapers which he was free to show to anybody who could read English. And he could talk. There is no record that Loeser was ever called a man of few words. Most convincing of all, he and Carter and Minard were all carrying *gold*. By the time the three Yankees boarded the British steamer, hundreds of Peruvians were eagerly asking where they could find a boat that would take them to California.

At Panama City, Loeser and his friends hired mules and made their perilous way across the isthmus to Chagres, on the other side. At Chagres they met a West Indian cargo vessel that had stopped to take on water before going on to Kingston, Jamaica. The vessel was not meant for passengers. The quarters were not comfortable. But Kingston was nearer the United States than Chagres, so the three

45

men gladly took such berths as they could get. At Kingston they found a schooner, the *Desdemona,* about to sail for New Orleans. They bought tickets and went aboard.

The *Desdemona* reached New Orleans the morning of November 23, 1848. Loeser and Carter and Minard hurried ashore.

They registered at the best hotel in town, the St. Charles. A good soldier, Loeser went first to the telegraph office. He sent a message to the War Department, saying he was bringing a dispatch from Colonel Mason. Next he inquired about boats and coaches to Washington. Then he asked the way to the newspaper offices. The time now was about noon.

All three men went to the newspapers. They took their copies of the papers from San Francisco; they took nuggets; and they took their own experience of life in the land of gold. They talked.

While the editors listened goggle-eyed, the men from California told them facts, and facts, and more facts. They told what they had seen themselves. They answered questions from their own observation. Their accounts, spoken face to face, were more vivid and more impressive than any letters from afar.

The first report appeared that same afternoon in the New Orleans *Mercury.* It had a breathless sound, as if the writer had scribbled as fast as his hand would move. But he told the story.

We today had the pleasure of a personal interview with Lieutenant Loeser, just arrived from California. He fully confirms the most glowing accounts heretofore received in the States of the richness and extent of the gold region. Gold is found from the tops of the highest mountains to the bottom of the rivers. He has seen the mines and knows what he says to be a fact.

The next morning, in the New Orleans *Picayune* and the *Commercial Times,* the arrival of the men from California was the biggest news of the day. In fact, the editors gave them so much space that this was almost the only news they published that morning.

These articles were longer and clearer than the *Mercury*'s hastily written account of the evening before. The editors had had more time to listen and more time to calm down. But they too wrote some dizzying lines: "California . . . the real El Dorado dreamed of by the old buccaneers . . . scene of inexhaustible wealth . . . one vast deposit of gold . . . the imagination is lost in wonder. . . ."

But these writers also gave facts and figures. Their statements were sensational, but they had the sound of truth.

Loeser and Carter and Minard had described the abundance of gold and the scarcity of goods to spend it for. They told of the astound-

46

ing prices men were paying for shirts and shoes and flour. They told how men had deserted army and navy to dig gold, how crews of whaling ships and trading vessels had vanished, and how captains were offering amazing sums for seamen to move their ships. They told what it was like to live in a place where everybody was so rich that nobody wanted to work. They said carpenters in San Francisco were earning a dollar and a half an hour; this was what men in New York were being paid for a ten-hour day. These men had seen it all, and they knew it was happening. They made it more real than anybody had done before.

They passed around their nuggets so the editors could weigh and handle them. They left copies of the San Francisco *Californian* on the editors' desks, and the papers used copious quotations.

People who read the papers that morning were thunderstruck. Loeser's stopover did for New Orleans what Sam Brannan's run had done for San Francisco. This was the day Gold Fever broke out in the country east of the Mississippi River.

Loeser and Carter and Minard went on their way. But they left behind them a city in tumult.

For a week past, a steamboat company had been advertising a steamer for Chagres, the port on the Atlantic side of the isthmus. This steamer, called the *Falcon,* had been for some time plying between New York and New Orleans, with stops at ports between. Now she was to start a new schedule, going on down to Chagres on each trip with mail for the troops and other Americans in California. The mail-bags were to be carried across the isthmus by mules. At Panama City they would be put aboard the *California,* the steamer that had left New York in October to sail around South America to San Francisco.

The *Falcon* was an excellent vessel, well furnished. She could carry ninety passengers with ease; more if they did not mind being crowded. When she left New York, her passenger list had consisted of ninety-five names. Most of these people had booked passage only as far as Charleston, Havana, or New Orleans. But twenty-nine of them were listed as "bound for Chagres and California."

These twenty-nine passengers were not planning to dig gold. Most of them were government officials and army officers, some with their wives. There were also four young clergymen, one with his wife, who were being sent out to establish churches; four ambitious young carpenters going to California to work at their trade; and several businessmen whose names appear later in the city directories of San Francisco. They all intended to cross the isthmus to Panama City, board the *California* there, and go on to their posts in Monterey or San Francisco.

47

The *Falcon* was expected to leave New York December 1 and reach New Orleans two weeks later. Here she would take on any travelers who might want to join those others bound for Chagres and California. "For freight or passage," said the advertisements in the New Orleans papers, "having splendid accommodations, apply to Paradise, Saffarans, and Co., agents, 67 Gravier Street." But up to now, few if any tickets to Chagres had been sold in New Orleans.

Loeser's first interview had appeared on a Thursday evening. The others were published Friday morning. By Friday noon, the office on Gravier Street was cluttered with men shouting questions.

A ticket to Chagres—what would it cost? Could a man reserve a berth on the *Falcon* now and pay later? How much baggage could he take? Would there be an extra charge for the baggage?

These men who suddenly wanted to go to California had noticed the California prices. Barrels of salt beef, crates packed with picks and shovels, might make a man rich the day he got there.

The clamor was so great that the next morning, Saturday, Messrs. Paradise and Saffarans had a new notice in the papers. This time they said nothing about "splendid accommodations." They knew now that if the *Falcon* had been the shabbiest vessel at sea, every berth she had could have been sold twice over. They said tersely, "No berth secured until paid for. Passengers to Chagres will be charged freight on everything except wearing apparel."

The company sold every foot of space where a man might roll up and sleep. Still the customers poured in. Less than a week after Loeser's stop, two more companies in New Orleans announced vessels bound for Chagres. They were less expensive than the steamer, but slower. The men who had caught gold fever were in a hurry. They wanted to get across the isthmus in time to board the *California* when she reached Panama.

These gold seekers in New Orleans had three weeks to prepare for their journey aboard the *Falcon*. This was not a simple matter. The distance to San Francisco by way of the isthmus was nearly six thousand miles. Travel was slow and hard. If they did not find California the land of their dreams, for all they knew, it might be months or years before they could find a way back.

The men who had bought tickets in New York were envoys of state, church, or established business. They had the support of their institutions behind them. They had been allowed time to take care of their other concerns before sailing. They had a fair idea of the duties that lay ahead of them. But a man who took the *Falcon* at

New Orleans had to cut himself abruptly from his past and present and go into a future that he could not foresee. And the journey was expensive. Ne'er-do-wells could not pay for it, and few men of property cared to undertake such a risk.

But New Orleans had a large class of people who were risk takers by profession. They were gamblers, barkeepers, adventurers of all sorts and both sexes. They came in by sea and river, and they stayed just as long as it pleased them. They had no ties that they could not easily break. They were always ready to go somewhere else and try a new enterprise. Some observers said New Orleans had more romantic rogues than any other city in the country. They may or may not have been right, but they never said it was a dull place to visit.

The gambling parlors were famous. The finest of these were in the two most patrician hotels, the St. Charles and the Verandah. Besides the gamblers who lived in town, there were many who played cards on the vessels that plied between New Orleans and other ports on the Gulf of Mexico. Many more worked on the Mississippi River steamboats, which carried the richest and raciest voyagers of the day. They all met in New Orleans.

And now, they had a fascinating chance to move on.

It would not be fair, or accurate, to say that all those who bought tickets on the *Falcon* at New Orleans belonged to this group. Some of them were young fellows looking for adventure. Others were men who wanted to work and thought a town of such wealth as San Francisco would be a good place to work in. But people who were there at the time agreed that at least two thirds of the New Orleans passengers were gamblers and their lady friends. And the fact that so many casinos in the San Francisco of '49 were named for the New Orleans resorts—St. Charles, Verandah, Crescent City, and others—suggests that these people were right.

During the Gold Rush, hundreds of gamblers, both men and women, took this way to California. So many of them sailed from New Orleans and crossed the isthmus that before long this became generally known as "the gamblers' route."

The *Falcon* entered the Mississippi River December 12, 1848, and docked at Lafayette, a river port twenty-three miles above New Orleans. The captain, W. T. Thompson, would not have been surprised to find half a dozen persons waiting to join those who were already bound for Chagres. But he was not prepared for the horde that burst upon him, holding tickets they had bought at the office of Paradise, Saffarans, and Company on Gravier Street.

49

But when the morrow came, they still could not start. The most important passengers of all had not yet arrived. These were Brevet Major General Persifor Frazer Smith, his wife (the former Frances Jeannette Bureau of New Orleans), and his staff. General Smith had been ordered to California, but he had been delayed in Washington on official business. For a week, the gold seekers paced the wharf. At last General and Mrs. Smith arrived. He brought a valet (some people said several valets), and she brought a maid, a pretty girl in a frilly cap and apron, for they expected to live as suited their rank.

The next day was Monday, December 18. At five o'clock that evening, the *Falcon* left her berth at Pier 1, Lafayette, and sailed for Chagres.

It was a splendid occasion.

General Smith was escorted to the steamer by officers of the state militia and leading state and city dignitaries. Hundreds of people crowded the wharf. Some of them had come to watch the goings-on, others to say envious good-byes. The gold seekers were debonair. They laughed and talked of California as they would have talked of a place that lay no more than a day's journey ahead. When the time came for visitors to go ashore, travelers and stay-at-homes said their farewells like friends who expected to meet again in a week. As the *Falcon* got under way, a salute of artillery cracked the air.

Now they were off to the land of gold. They were a strangely varied company.

The *Falcon*'s passenger list has 178 names. Some of these are easily recognized. The clergymen, the army personnel, and the government envoys are all there. Among the others are names of several men who later became prominent citizens of California. Eight men were accompanied by their wives; two had also brought children.

But the rest?

The possible guesses are tantalizing. "Lawrence Denison" may have been the man who opened the San Francisco gambling resort called Denison's Exchange. "W. Johnson" sounds like Willie Johnson, proprietor of the Verandah, another great casino of Gold Rush days. "Peter Smith" may be the notorious Dr. Peter Smith who, in the 1850s, involved the city of San Francisco in long and costly lawsuits over his claim to public funds.

It is one of the ironies of history that the wild Gold Rush took place at a time when nice people, served fowl at dinner, asked for "white meat" or "drumsticks" because "breast" and "leg" were unspeakable words. Many of the *Falcon*'s passengers listed puzzling names. They gave only a single initial, linked to a surname borne by millions of other people. It is likely that among these one-initial passengers were several madams from the New Orleans bordellos and their girls.

Loeser and his friends had mentioned that men far outnumbered women in the golden land. These madams had grasped their chance to set up shop in a town that offered them such brilliant prospects. But they did not want to be noticed before the ship sailed. They might be recognized, and the clergymen or the army wives might insist that they get off. So they asked their gentlemen friends to buy their tickets, giving those nearly anonymous names. Once aboard, they kept out of sight until the steamer had passed the mouth of the river and was well out to sea. Then they appeared, ready for business.

One of the four clergymen aboard the *Falcon* was the Reverend Samuel Hopkins Willey, twenty-seven years old. Young Mr. Willey had just graduated from the Union Theological Seminary in New York. He had been ordained only the day before the *Falcon* began her voyage from New York to Chagres. Writing his memoirs thirty years afterward, he dropped a hint.

"On the way to Chagres," he wrote delicately, "we had a little experience of rough life that was new to us."

Anyway, whatever the reason, when people identify themselves only as E. Smith, J. Brown, and C. Robinson (all names on the *Falcon*'s passenger list), they hardly seem eager to draw attention to themselves.

9

When the *Falcon* sailed from New York, the New Yorkers had heard of California gold, but the gold fever had not yet struck them. A few fast-acting businessmen had sent out vessels with goods they hoped to sell in San Francisco. But up to now, the New Yorkers had not shown themselves eager to go there.

Now, however, the gold fever was rushing upon them.

Lucien Loeser had left Monterey with Colonel Mason's letter August 30, 1848. Colonel Mason was a cautious man. For safety's sake, he had ordered Loeser to make a roundabout journey by sea. Three weeks after Loeser left, a party of men more venturesome than the colonel set out on an overland trek to the States. Mason gave them a second copy of his letter to the War Department. The travelers also carried letters from several other men to their friends at home.

Nobody today seems to be sure who these carriers were. They may have been successful miners. On November 24, a newspaper called the *Gazette*, in the frontier town of St. Joseph, Missouri, said a party had gone through town recently, bringing "large quantities" of gold dust. A local jeweler had tested a sample and said it was "the real grit."

These men, or another such party, could have brought the second copy of Mason's letter. At any rate, somebody left California in September, bringing letters that reached the East Coast late in November. One of these was Mason's duplicate of his letter to Adjutant General Roger Jones.

On the last page of the duplicate, Mason had added a postscript to say that Loeser was on his way. Then he continued, "Lieutenant Loeser bears, in addition to the specimens mentioned in the foregoing letter, a tea caddy containing two hundred and thirty ounces, fifteen pennyweight, and nine grains of gold."

This copy of the letter reached Washington before Loeser did. President Polk ordered that it be sent to the government printing office. He wanted copies made so he could present them, along with his annual message to Congress, due December 5.

The letter was no secret. It was news. Men who had read it told their friends. Word spread to the newspapers, in New York and elsewhere. People began to talk, with excitement. Colonel Mason was no dreamer of dreams. He was a tough-minded soldier. What he said could be believed. Especially when he was sending a man with a box of gold to prove it.

Copies of the letter were to be handed out along with copies of the President's message the following Tuesday, December 5. People waited, with impatience.

Then, on Saturday, December 2, a mail express rider from New Orleans reached New York. He brought New Orleans papers in his saddlebags. On Sunday, the New York *Herald* reprinted the *Mercury's* breathless interview with Lucien Loeser. The next day, the *Herald* reprinted a second interview from New Orleans. This was Monday, December 4. The President's message was to be read to Congress Tuesday.

That Tuesday, when the members of Congress met, they felt great interest in what they were about to hear. So did the newsmen from New York and other cities.

The day had a brilliant beginning. The sun shone, the air was balmy. One observer called it "a June day in December." Members of the two houses of Congress gathered in their respective chambers. Outside waited a group of horseback riders. Each of them had a packet holding copies of the message, copies of the letter from Colonel Mason, and other reports. Their tasks were to take these packets to the newspapers, telegraph offices, and important persons in and out of town.

Just before noon, the President's secretary, Knox Walker, would present packets like these to both Houses of Congress. When he had done this, a signal would be given from the Capitol to soldiers stationed beside a cannon. The soldiers would fire. The riders would start their horses. The wires would tell the nation that Congress was now hearing the message. It was a great day.

Mr. Walker first went to the House of Representatives. He placed a packet before the speaker, Robert Winthrop of Massachusetts. This packet contained copies of the President's message, furnished by the government printing office, one for each member of the House. Mr. Winthrop formally accepted the packet. Mr. Walker then went to the Senate chamber and presented a similar packet to the president pro tem, David Atchison of Missouri.

The signal was given. The cannon boomed. The horsemen sprang to their saddles. In their two meeting rooms, the secretary of the Senate and the clerk of the House began to read aloud.

It was a great day. But as far as Congress was concerned, the President's message was a fizzle. The New York *Herald*'s irreverent Senate reporter summed up the events by writing, "The message took three hours to read and some senators actually sat through all of it."

As he implied, most of the senators had walked out, yawning, long before the reading was over. So had most members of the House.

Colonel Mason's letter had been the most talked-about topic of the day. It had not been made public, but the talk was not only that Mason confirmed the gold story but also that he had checked and made sure of so many details, so carefully, that no man could ever again doubt it. Certainly this belonged in a report on the State of the Union.

But President Polk somehow had not realized how eager the men in Congress were to hear what Mason had written about gold. Polk had overlooked the old, old rule for letter writing, which was the same as the most modern rule taught to news broadcasters today: When you have more than one subject to report, start with the most important. And worst of all, he forgot—or maybe he had never heard—the warning of Voltaire: The way to be a bore is to tell everything.

The members of Congress had assembled in their respective meeting rooms with almost breathless interest to hear what Mason had written. Instead, Polk told them about the new lands acquired in the Mexican War. He praised the gallantry of the men who had fought the war. He stressed the importance of Texas. He described the value of San Francisco as a port for Pacific trade. He went on and on and on, telling the members of Congress facts that were surely worth knowing, but facts that every man of them already knew. The President's message sounded like the minutes of the last meeting.

In both houses of Congress, the men began to get restless. Outdoors glistened that June day in December. Indoors the readers droned on.

In the Senate there were little coughs and fidgety rustles. In the House the reaction was more candid.

At a paragraph stop, the clerk paused to take breath. Congressman

Frank A. Tallmadge of New York stood up. He asked that the page boys be told to give each member his own copy of the message from the packet brought by Mr. Walker. The speaker agreed. When this was done and the clerk was about to go on reading, Mr. Tallmadge stood up again. He moved that the clerk be told to stop reading. Every member now had his own copy, said Mr. Tallmadge, and could read it for himself. (And in the meantime they could get out of there.)

The speaker ruled that the reading could be discontinued, but only by unanimous consent. Another member, Samuel Vinton of Ohio, rose to object. He said that this action would be disrespectful. The clerk cleared his throat and went on.

As published in the newspapers the following day, the President's message occupied twelve columns. The first reference to the California gold discovery appeared in column ten.

As the *Herald* reported, the reading took three hours. In both House and Senate, the readers grew hoarse and the members grew weary. No doubt they were disrespectful, but by twos and threes they drifted out. By the time the readers came to the paragraphs about gold, both meeting rooms were half empty and the men who had stayed respectfully in their places were half asleep.

It was close to three o'clock in the afternoon when the reading at last came to an end. In each house, one of the tired holdouts moved to adjourn. They adjourned.

When they went outside, they found their disrespectful colleagues having a talkfest about gold. These men had skipped through the dull subjects until they reached the lines that referred to Colonel Mason's letter. After thousands of other words about other matters, Polk had said of California, "The accounts of the abundance of gold in that territory are of such an extraordinary character as would scarcely command belief were they not corroborated by the authentic reports of officers in the public service who have visited the mineral district." He described Colonel Mason's tour of the mines and added, "His report to the War Department is herewith laid before Congress."

When, on December 6, the papers printed the message in full, it is doubtful that many people read it all. But they did find the lines telling them that everything they had heard about California was true.

This was the day Gold Fever broke out in New York. Before night, hundreds of men were clamoring to know how they could get to the land of gold.

Horace Greeley still would not give way. He likened the President to "the bar-room disputant" whose talk is so loud and fierce that nobody else can be heard and then says his argument is "unanswerable, because no one has had a chance to answer it."

Greeley was not ready to admit that the western lands were worth much. He wrote, "The gold of California (the finding of which was pure accident, and has nothing to do with results of the war) may strengthen and benefit, or it may deprave and destroy us."

But if anybody agreed with him now, there was little sign of it. And the next day, December 7, Lucien Loeser reached Washington, bringing the tea caddy holding twenty pounds of gold.

With his usual verve, Loeser made haste and told his story as fast as he could. That same day, the gold was put on exhibit in the library of the War Department.

All the gold Beale had brought with him could have been put into Mary Edward's thimble. But Loeser had brought gold enough to impress the most doubtful, and hundreds of people crowded in to look at it. They saw a dramatic display.

The gold was in glass vials. Some held tiny scales, others the larger lumps, still others the black sand sparkling with golden specks just as it had come from the riverbeds. It was there, it was real, and they said it was the greatest show that had ever come to town.

The next day a messenger took the gold to the Mint for testing. The Treasurer of the Mint, Colonel James R. Snowden, reported that it proved 894½.1000—almost perfectly pure gold.

His report flashed over the wires. The papers published Colonel Mason's letter. They published interviews with Loeser and quotations from the San Francisco papers Loeser had brought. Ships leaving for foreign ports took the news with them. A year earlier, few of the world's people had ever heard of California; now the whole world began to hear of it. The exuberant young lieutenant had made his mark on history.

History did not again give Lucien Loeser a chance so dramatic. But he had a long and honorable career. During the Civil War he served as lieutenant colonel of a cavalry regiment in the Union Army. After the war, he retired to civilian life. He died in 1897, at the age of seventy-nine.

Now in December, 1848, on the Atlantic Coast of the United States, suddenly it seemed that people were talking about nothing but gold. Hundreds, thousands of them wanted to go to California.

But how to get there? In December they could not start overland. Wagons had to be drawn by mules and oxen. Mules and oxen could not cross the prairies until the snow melted and the spring grass began to grow. These fuming gold seekers wanted to start *now*.

This meant they had to go by sea. A man could take a vessel that would sail around Cape Horn on the tip of South America. Or he could go to Chagres, cross the isthmus, and meet the Pacific Mail steamship *California* when she reached Panama. The voyage around meant seventeen thousand miles in distance and four to six months in time. But the *California* had left New York last October. She was already more than halfway to Panama City. If a man left New York now and crossed the isthmus, he could get to Panama City in time to board the *California* there.

The New York office of the Pacific Mail Company was at 54 South Street. Gold-hungry men crowded the doors, trying to elbow each other out of the way. The clerks told them the *California* was expected to reach Panama in January. The second steamer of the line, the *Oregon,* had left New York a few days ago. She would get to Panama in February or March. The third steamer, the *Panama,* had met with an accident and would not start for several weeks.

Some men bought tickets on the *Panama* and sat down to wait. Men who were in too much of a hurry for this bought tickets on any ship that promised to take them to Chagres in time to cross the isthmus and meet the *California*.

The first vessel to leave New York carrying gold seekers to Chagres was a sailing vessel called the *John Benson*. This ship sailed December 11, 1848, five days after the New York papers published the President's message. She carried seventy passengers. Twenty-four of them were on their way to Chagres, bound for the land of gold.

In less than a week, fifteen more vessels in New York harbor were taking on passengers for California. Some of these vessels would go only as far as the isthmus, some all the way around the Horn. In nearly every port on the Atlantic seaboard, other young men, giddy with impatience, were boarding the vessels for the golden coast.

Men who had no money to buy tickets begged for jobs as cooks or stewards on the ships. Men who had land but not cash mortgaged the land to pay their fares. Others looked for "partners" who would pay for the tickets, on promise of half the gold the traveler brought back. Groups of men organized "California companies," planning to travel together and share expenses and then share their takings of gold.

While men who owned ships sat up nights rerouting them to Chagres or Cape Horn, men who kept stores were just as busy. Any gadget that could have "gold" or "California" attached to its name was now "designed for California emigrants." During those early weeks of the rush from the eastern seaboard, the bedazzled young men were sure to buy it.

They bought "gold pans" for stirring the sand, and "gold sifters" for shaking the earth from the nuggets. (If they had been seeing straight, they might have noticed that these were remarkably like the pans and sifters in their mothers' kitchens.) They bought "gold bags"—leather pouches that men had hitherto used for carrying tobacco. They bought "steam engines suitable for California"—to do what, they were not sure. For health in the strange land they bought medicines with strange names: "Indian Vegetable Pills," "Cold Candy for California," "California Canchalagua." This last was said to have special value because it was made from a plant that grew on the Pacific Coast.

Some astute men figured that there were easier ways to get gold than digging for it. Since all Californians were said to be rich, these men took goods to sell when they got there. They packed rubber tents to keep off the rain, and rubber sheets for men to sleep on when the rain got in and soaked the ground. Hearing that San Francisco was a rough town where men got shot in barroom brawls, several enterprising fellows took out tombstones ready for use. These had Scripture verses already cut. The buyer needed only to add the name of the deceased and the proper dates.

They heard that, in California, clothes were in short supply because everything wore out fast at the mines. Now in New York, these would-be tradesmen asked clothing dealers to empty their shelves of garments that had been lying around unsold. The clothes were out of date, but away out there, who would know it? They bought the clothes at low prices, planning to sell them at great profit for gold. One man set out from Boston with five thousand women's bonnets. There were not five thousand women within a hundred miles of Sutter's Fort, but apparently nobody had told him so.

While all this was going on, the steamship *California* was calmly puffing her way southward. Her first stop after leaving New York had been Rio de Janeiro.

The steamer was having a good voyage. She had reached Rio in twenty-six days. This was the shortest time any vessel had ever made between New York and Rio, and the longest nonstop voyage ever made by any steamship in the world. Captain Cleveland Forbes and his crew had good reason to be proud of their work.

But such bright times were not to last. Before he reached Rio, Captain Forbes had begun to feel unwell. The exact nature of his illness seems not to be known; possibly the doctors of the time were not sure. The captain himself did not think it serious and believed a rest on shore was all he needed. At Rio he took as much rest as he could, while his vessel loaded coal and supplies for the long voyage around the tip of South America. On November 25, 1848, the *California* left Rio. Two days before this, Lucien Loeser and his friends had reached New Orleans and started the fire. But Captain Forbes did not know it.

Instead of doubling Cape Horn as the sailing vessels did, Captain Forbes planned to thread the Strait of Magellan, a narrow passage about 350 miles long, between the south end of Chile and the islands of Tierra del Fuego. It was a dangerous run, but Captain Forbes was the best of seamen. The steamer entered the strait December 7, the day Loeser reached Washington with the tea caddy full of gold. Five days later, Captain Forbes guided his ship into the Pacific Ocean.

But his health was growing worse. As the ship steamed up the coast of Chile, he realized that he could not go on carrying the burden of authority alone. When he reached Valparaiso, he would have to look for help.

Valparaiso was a center of trade, and there were many vessels in port. One of these was a sailing ship whose captain, John Marshall, had already been up and down the Pacific coast several times. The two captains agreed upon an exchange; an officer of the *California* would take command of Marshall's ship, while Marshall would become assistant captain of the steamer.

Here at Valparaiso, Captain Forbes and his crew met for the first time the gold excitement spreading from California. When they had left New York, the New Yorkers had thought so little of the gold talk that not one of them had bought a ticket to San Francisco. At Rio, the talk had hardly started.

But there was a lively trade between the ports of Chile and those of Peru. Ever since Loeser had stopped at Paita in Peru, vessels from Paita had been bringing down news of gold. When the people of Valparaiso learned that there was a steamer in port, on her way to the golden land, men rushed to ask for tickets.

Captain Forbes was sick, but not too sick to think clearly. He said no. His vessel, and other vessels of the Pacific Mail Company, had been licensed by the United States government for American mail and American travelers. If the gold discovery was as important as they were saying here, he thought by this time it must have roused interest in the United States as well. Maybe some other Americans had joined those clergymen and army officers he had been told to expect at Panama. He said his first duty was to them, and he refused to take the foreigners aboard.

With all her passenger berths empty, the steamer went up the coast to Peru. At the port of Callao she stopped for supplies.

Here she met a surge of gold fever that made the fluster at Valparaiso seem lukewarm. The ship was almost stormed by Peruvians wanting to go to California.

At the city of Lima, near Callao, the Pacific Mail Company had an office. Captain Forbes called there, to make his report and ask where he could get medical advice.

The directors of the office were men who had invested their own money in the company. They felt a natural desire to get a return on their investment as soon as they could. They insisted that Captain Forbes take on passengers here. Suppose he did find that a few others had joined those Americans he was to meet at Panama? The *California* had berths for 150 passengers. With a little doubling up she could easily carry more. And there stood these Peruvians with money in their hands. Why not let them board the ship? If he took, say, 100 Peruvians, there would still be plenty of room.

So when the *California* sailed from Callao she had on board about 100 men from Peru. Seventeen of them were in the more expensive cabin berths. The rest had space in the steerage.

The ship made another stop at Paita, but here the captain was firm. No more foreigners. His own countrymen must be taken care of. On January 12, 1849, the *California* left Paita and set out for the isthmus, to pick up the forty or fifty persons Captain Forbes now expected to meet him there.

10

But the isthmus was getting crowded.

Americans were pouring into Chagres. They were all planning to cross the isthmus and sail from Panama City to San Francisco.

The first steamboat to reach Chagres was the *Falcon*, the first sailing ship the *John Benson*. After them came a long line of others. The steamer *Crescent City* left New York for Chagres December 23, 1848. The steamer *Isthmus* left Christmas Day, the steamer *Orus* early in January. Slower than the steamers, but more plentiful, were the sailing ships. On a single day, the New York *Tribune* announced five of them about to leave for Chagres. They all carried passengers packed in like cigarettes.

And it was not only the passengers who came for gold. When the schooner *Sovereign* from Baltimore reached Chagres, every soul on board, including the captain and crew, came ashore and started for Panama City. They left their ship empty.

The *Falcon* and the *John Benson* had reached Chagres in December. Passengers from these two vessels were the first gold dreamers to cross the isthmus. Their adventures were typical of what befell the rest.

They found Chagres a village of about a hundred huts. The huts were made of bamboo canes, roofed with palm leaves and set on stilts in the swampy ground near the mouth of the Chagres River. It rained every day. The heat was stifling. On December 29, a New Yorker named James Grant wrote to a friend at home, "It is hotter here at present than I ever felt it in New York on the Fourth of July."

The people of Chagres were a hodgepodge. Their ancestors were Indians, Spanish invaders, black slaves the Spaniards had brought with

61

them, and sailors of many breeds. To the horror of the lady travelers, they wore scarcely any clothes. Many of them wore palm-leaf hats, to keep the sun off their heads, and nothing else. They had never heard of California gold, and they stared in wonder at this strange throng that had burst upon them.

An agent of the Pacific Mail, Arnold Harris, had come from New York on the *Falcon*. He had been sent to help the army and government personnel hire boats to take them up the Chagres River. But the gold seekers who had boarded with such gusto had to take care of themselves.

And they found no royal road across the isthmus. They found no road at all.

The distance from Chagres to Panama City was only about fifty miles. But most of the isthmus was covered with tropical jungle and ridden with cholera, malaria, and other deadly fevers for which the Americans had no names. If they hired river boats, these would take them about two thirds of the way. Or they might cross all the way on muleback. There was a difference of opinion about which way was worse.

Three hundred years before, when the Spaniards were plundering Peru and Mexico, they had laid stones and logs in the swampy ground to make a causeway over which mules could carry their booty from the Pacific to the Atlantic side. But now this was nothing but a vague track, so overgrown as to be in places totally lost. Mules were scarce. Men who could not get them walked across. A walker carried what baggage he could on his back and hired natives to carry the rest. These natives might seem lazy, but they were not stupid. When they saw how much they were needed, they put their prices up and up.

People who tried to cross through the jungle often got sick. More often they got lost. Like most North Americans they had thought that to cross the isthmus from the Atlantic Ocean to the Pacific, a man would move from east to west. Few of them knew that the isthmus was shaped like an *S* lying on its side, and the track from Chagres to Panama led from west to east. The sun always seemed to be on the wrong side.

Some of them thought it might be easier to go by boat.

The only "boats" they could hire were bongos. A bongo was made of the trunk of one of the enormous isthmus trees, ten feet wide, or even wider, and fifteen to twenty feet long. The builders hollowed out the log and put up palm-leaf awnings for shade. A bongo was poled upstream by four or five boatmen, usually stark naked except for their sun hats. They poled until they felt like stopping for a rest, and started again when they felt like it. No threats or urging or offers of more pay could make them work harder. Their speed averaged one mile per hour.

The hapless passenger could take some baggage with him in the bongo, but if he had brought more, he had to trust the rest to native carriers, who walked across. The bongo passenger took along his own food, mainly salt meat and ship's bread, which he had bought in Chagres. Some of the lucky ones had also been able to buy umbrellas. They huddled in the bongos, scared and sweltering.

A bongo went up the river to a village called Gorgona, or a few miles farther to a village called Cruces. Depending on the boatmen's rate of movement, the ride took from three days to a week. Some travelers slept in the bongos. This was risky, because if a sleeper was restless, a bongo had a way of turning over and dumping him and his fellow sleepers into the river. More cautious people made a fire on the riverbank to discourage mosquitoes, and got what sleep they could on blankets spread around it.

When the passengers from the *Falcon* and the *John Benson* heard about this journey, a few of them said they were going home and got back on the ships. But only a few. Most of them went ahead. With granite gallantry, these first Forty-niners went right on doing what they had set out to do. They hired mules or boatmen and started on their way.

One man who was frightened was Captain Edward G. Elliott, a member of the staff of General Persifor Smith. Captain Elliott had recently married. His bride had come to Chagres with him, expecting to go on to California. But when Captain Elliott learned of the hardships ahead, he feared for her safety. He begged her to go back on the *Falcon,* and she consented.

The *Falcon* left Chagres New Year's Day, 1849. Mrs. Elliott never saw her husband again. Five days later, at the village of Cruces, Captain Elliott died of cholera.

Another American died of cholera at Cruces that same day. He was William Burch, one of the group of four young carpenters who had boarded the *Falcon* at New York. Gold fever had not then struck the Northeast, but they had read about the high wages paid in San Francisco and were sure diligent workmen could do well there. (While Burch did not live to finish the journey, his three friends reached California safely, and they did well.)

At Cruces, some of the travelers managed to hire mules. The rest had to walk. Again, they disagreed on which was worse. Not far beyond Cruces, the swampy ground gave way to mountains made almost of solid rock. The cliffs were so abrupt that every step was a new danger. Once at the top, they had to go down the other side, which was even harder than climbing. In the olden days, the Spaniards had cut slashes across the steepest mountainsides, to give footing for the mules that carried their treasures. The Americans called them "mule staircases" and used them thankfully.

Five more men from these first vessels died on the way across the isthmus. Probably many others wished they had never started. But they kept on. Group after weary group, they reached the port of Panama.

Three hundred years before, this had been a rich and splendid city, but now it had sunk into lethargy and decay. It was nothing but a stopping place for vessels in the Pacific trade, which made brief calls for water and supplies on their way somewhere else. There were a few families of Spanish descent; the rest were a mixture like the people of Chagres. More civilized than the people of Chagres, they wore clothes and lived in houses made of adobe bricks set among picturesque ruins overgrown with bright-blooming vines. They were an easygoing lot, but they were dismayed by this sudden influx of strangers.

The United States had a consul here, William Nelson. Also, the Pacific Mail line had set up an office. Mr. Nelson and the company agents had known to expect the army and government personnel and had found places for them to live until the steamer *California* should appear. The gold seekers had to do the best they could.

There was no hotel. There was a little market where they could buy rice and yams, tomatoes and pumpkins, sometimes beef. Men who were good at hunting could bring in game from the woods. Most of the Americans had to cook and sleep outdoors. The weather was clear— at least this was an improvement over Chagres.

When at last these Forty-niners reached San Francisco, they wrote fearsome letters to their friends at home, urging them, if they meant to come to California, to take any way but the way across the isthmus. Said one man, "No urgency short of life and death should bring a man on this route; for a female, it is utterly out of the question."

In his state of horror, this writer appears not to have noticed that a good many "females" had crossed the isthmus with him. Among them were Frances Jeannette (Mrs. Persifor) Smith and her ever-so-elegant maid; Mrs. Elizabeth Hamilton Wheeler, wife of the Reverend

Osgood C. Wheeler, one of the four young clergymen who were being sent to establish churches in San Francisco; and Mrs. E.R.S. Canby, wife of the officer who was to relieve Lieutenant Sherman. There were also the girls who are said to have used some of those one-initial names on the *Falcon*'s passenger list. Many more women were to cross the isthmus in the next two or three years. They never found the crossing easy, but it did improve as the government set up regular mail routes with army guards.

Several days after the first passengers from the *Falcon* and the *John Benson* reached Panama, passengers from the *Crescent City* began to arrive. Then came passengers from the *Isthmus*, and the *Orus*, and more, and more, and more. They all wanted tickets on the *California*.

The vessels that had brought these people to Chagres were not part of the Pacific Mail line. A few of those who had started from New York had farsightedly bought through tickets at the Pacific Mail office before they left. The rest had to get their tickets here at the office in Panama.

Within a week after the first arrivals reached Panama, the agents at the office had sold tickets to more people than there were berths on the *California*. At first they said the buyers could double up, but at length they simply refused to sell any more. Still the people poured in. Nobody counted them, but by mid-January there were at least five hundred gold dreamers in Panama City, and more were on the way. They had brought money with them, and they wanted to spend it for tickets to San Francisco.

Now the New Orleans gamblers began to do a flashing business.

With the other passengers from the *Falcon*, these gentlemen had been the first to cross the isthmus. The shrewdest of them had gone promptly to the steamboat office and bought tickets—not only for themselves, but extras for people who might need them later. When no more tickets could be had at the office, the gambling brotherhood set up shop.

They organized raffles, with steamboat tickets as prizes. They held auctions. Breathless young argonauts, sure they would get rich if only they could reach the goldfields, bid the prices up to five or six or ten times their first cost. The gambling men said this was a better game than any they had played on the riverboats.

But sellers or buyers, they were all nervous, impatient, scared. While they waited for the *California*, they were getting sick from bad food and cholera. They heard more and more reports of deaths among them. With every day, their fright came closer to panic.

In Panama's time of glory, the Spaniards had built a stone wall to protect the city from marauders by land and sea. This wall had fallen into ruin, but several of the great guns that had threatened pirates were still there. Every day, restless Americans climbed up and sat straddling these guns, looking out for the steamer. They did not have to wait long, though while they waited, the time seemed endless. On the morning of January 17, 1849, the men on the beach heard a shout from the men on the guns. They had sighted the *California*.

As she moved closer, they watched in quivering suspense. But even those who held tickets were not sure they could all crowd aboard. They could only wait. At last, a rowboat brought Acting Captain Marshall and other officers to shore. A horde of Americans stormed the rowboat.

Captain Marshall was nearly stunned. Who were all these people? What did they want?

It was not long before he knew. These were people holding tickets on the steamer. They wanted to be taken to the land of gold.

Then the dreadful fact emerged. At most, the *California* had berths for 150 passengers. She already had 100 on board.

The fury of the Americans was just what Captain Forbes had foreseen. He was still very ill, and Captain Marshall was in command, but neither of them could change the fact. Those Peruvians were there.

The Americans thronged the steamship office. They said the line had been licensed by the United States government to carry American mail and American passengers. Those foreigners had to get off the boat.

But the foreigners refused to budge. The only way to get them off would have been to throw them overboard.

The red-faced agents of the line said their company had the right to sell a ticket to anybody who wanted to buy it. But all the same, they themselves had sold the tickets to their clamoring countrymen. What could they do now?

An American sailing vessel, the *Philadelphia*, was unloading a cargo of coal at Panama. The Pacific Mail chartered this ship to take as many as possible of the angry people stranded here. This did nothing to calm their tempers. The sailing ship would take twice as long as the steamer to reach San Francisco. They had paid for tickets on the *California* and they loudly said so.

They put up such a howl that Captain Marshall turned the Peruvians out of their berths and told them they would have to sleep on deck. This meant that there were as many berths for Americans as if the foreigners had not been there. But still, there were not nearly as many berths as there were people who held tickets for them.

After several days of chaos, the Pacific Mail announced the order in which the ticket holders would be taken care of:

First, the army officers and government envoys.

Second, those who held through tickets they had bought in New York.

Then, the people who had bought tickets at the office of the Pacific Mail in Panama. These could be allowed on board in the order in which their tickets were registered there. This gave first chance to the passengers from the *Falcon* and the *John Benson*. Those who had come by later vessels were as furious as ever.

The scramble to get on the *California* was so frantic that the ticket holders were glad to take any space they could get. The steamer had a crew of thirty-six men. They were set to work putting up bunks in the hold, where the baggage was normally carried. Because of the press of people, the agents said the ship would not carry their baggage.

But the price of a ticket included the transportation of a trunk! Too bad. The agents said the steamer would not carry it. (They did not point out, but the enraged travelers did, that every extra human body meant an extra fare paid, while a trunk did not.)

A little baggage was stuffed in. But many a passenger who had paid full fare for himself and his trunk had to get aboard with no luggage except a handbag, which he had to keep beside him all the way. Sometimes his trunk reached San Francisco by a later vessel. Sometimes it did not.

On January 30, they were allowed to board the ship. There was such confusion that nobody had time to count them. Estimates varied from 300 to 500. They were all frustrated, resentful, short-tempered. But they did feel a certain triumph. In spite of all the stuffing and squeezing, a lot of people were still left behind to take the sailing ship or wait for the second steamer of the line.

On the last day of January, 1849, early in the morning, the steamer chugged out of the harbor of Panama and headed north toward the golden shore. It was a long journey. The distance from Panama to San Francisco is 3,245 nautical miles. (This is 113 miles more than the distance from New York to Liverpool.) It was also one of the most disagreeable journeys any travelers ever made. But they got there. They slept in the airless hold. They slept on coils of rope on deck. They slept on the dining table, in hammocks swung from the rigging, anywhere they could find room for one more. And in spite of the

67

dense crowding and the shortages of food and water, as they moved out of the tropics their health improved. Several persons who had been ill when they left Panama began to recover. One of these was Captain Forbes. By the time they sighted the California coast, Captain Forbes was nearly well. In San Francisco he took command of his ship again.

The *California* was to stop at Monterey to let off the army personnel. She would then take the other passengers on to San Francisco. Colonel Mason was expecting the steamer early in January.

Life in Monterey just then was not agreeable, either for the army men or for the people who lived there. The young officers at the garrison were bored and restless with the routine of their days. As for the civilian residents, while many of them had gone to the goldfields, many others had not, and the stay-at-homes were having their own problems. Chief among these was the problem of getting enough to eat.

Prices of food were skyrocketing. But even if they could pay the prices, often the people found that there was little to buy. So many ranch workers had gone to look for gold that the fields were turning into weed patches, and few cattle were brought to market. Ranchers lucky enough to have workers were finding it more profitable to change their produce for gold dust at the mines than to bring it to town.

But the soldiers of the American garrison were well fed. The army quartermaster bought food with gold and silver coins collected as duties on goods that foreign vessels brought to California ports, and these coins were better than gold dust. A silver dollar was always worth a dollar, while the value of gold dust at the mining camps was never certain. The ranchers sold food for coins whenever they could, and the army had the coins in plenty. There can be little doubt that the reason many enlisted men stayed on duty was not patriotism, but the gruesome reports of scurvy and starvation that were already coming down from the hills. As long as they stayed at their posts they were sure of three good meals a day.

In ordinary times, this assurance would have been true only for enlisted men. Then as now, the commissioned officers were expected to live on their pay. But in 1849, if the officers in Monterey had had to buy food at the prevailing prices, they would have gone hungry. Colonel Mason therefore let them draw their pay in foodstuffs.

Tired of pantries half empty, many of the native families were glad to have these food-rich Yanquis as their house guests. The men paid for board and lodging by bringing their rations to their hostesses

every payday. They had comfortable living quarters, and the Californios who entertained them had lavish meals.

One of the leading citizens of Monterey, Don Manuel Jimeno Casa-
rin, took as boarders with his family four young army men: Lieutenant
Sherman, Lieutenant Henry W. Halleck, Dr. Robert Murray, and Lieutenant Edward O. C. Ord. They were fortunate. Don Manuel was a
highly respected gentleman, and his wife, Doña María de las Angustias
(Mary of the Heartaches) de la Guerra, was one of the most beautiful
and most cultured women in California. Doña Angustias, as she was
usually called, was thirty-five years old. Every American who included
her in his memoirs described her as a woman of charm, intellect, and
noble character. Doña Angustias had several children, and her admirers
said the eldest of them, a teen-aged girl named Manuela, bade fair
to be as bewitching as her mother.

But though they might be comfortable, the Yanqui soldiers were
bored and impatient. Every day seemed just like the day before. They
eagerly waited for the steamer to bring them news and fresh company.

The enlisted men had built a fort on a hill overlooking the sea.
Colonel Mason had ordered them to keep a constant lookout. At their
first glimpse of the steamer they were to fire the guns of the fort, so
the garrison and the whole town would know she was coming in.

Every morning the young officers hoped that this would be the
day they would hear the guns. But day after day poked along with
no booming from the fort.

The month of January passed. The first week of February passed,
and still they saw no puff of smoke along the horizon. The men tried
to enliven the time with every sort of amusement they could think
of. As Washington's birthday drew near, they hailed this chance to
celebrate with a party.

They planned it joyfully, a ball with patriotic decorations and the
best refreshments in town. Their guests were the leading citizens,
and all the pretty señoritas they would bring with them.

They gave the ball in the new building put up by order of the
American alcalde, Walter Colton, as a schoolhouse and place for public
gatherings. This was a two-story structure made of stone. The school-
rooms were on the first floor, and on the second floor was a hall thirty
by sixty feet. (This building, now known as Colton Hall, is still standing.)

The ball was a great success. The señoritas and the gallant young
men from West Point danced until the chaperones said the girls must
go home. After they had left, the señores and the Yanqui officers went
on making merry in honor of George Washington. Writing his memoirs

many years later, Sherman recalled, "The ball was really a handsome affair, and we kept it up nearly all night."

But there is always a morning after. When Doña Angustias and Manuela came to breakfast as usual, they were reluctantly joined by three of their four house guests, Lieutenants Sherman and Halleck and Dr. Murray. Don Manuel did not come to breakfast, nor did Lieutenant Ord. Maybe they could not get up. As for the three who did appear, Sherman wrote, "We were dull and stupid enough."

Then, all of a sudden, they heard a noise like a crack of thunder. It sounded again and again—today, of all days, they were hearing the roar of those guns at the fort. This meant the steamer. It was something happening. Dull and stupid they had felt the minute before, but now they almost leaped from the table and started toward the beach. The fresh morning air was a bracer, and as they neared the beach they were running. The steamer was still a good way off, and almost hidden by a cloud of fog, but already a crowd was gathering on shore. The first rowboat that went out carried, among others, Sherman and Halleck, Thomas Larkin, and William E. P. Hartnell, an Englishman who had lived in Monterey for some years.

Passengers on the steamer crowded the deck to meet them. Among these passengers was the Reverend Samuel Willey. Though a devout churchman, Mr. Willey did not always keep his mind fixed on Higher Things. When he wrote his memoirs thirty years later, he recalled that the dress of Messrs. Larkin and Hartnell showed how long they had been out of touch with the fashions. Their manners, he said, were as urbane as the manners of men on Broadway. But their clothes were at least two years behind the times.

The *California* stayed in port four days and then went on. Already Mrs. Persifor Smith's pretty maid had eloped to the goldfields with a man she had known only two days. She was not heard from again.

It was the last day of February when the steamer reached San Francisco. Here, as in Monterey, the people had been scanning the horizon for weeks. When the steamer came in sight, every man, woman, and child in town rushed out to give her welcome. They shouted and cheered and tooted horns; they waved flags and scarves and kerchiefs and torn-up newspapers. The commodore's flagship and five other ships of war fired salutes as the steamer came through the Golden Gate and into the bay. The passengers straggled ashore, tired and battered but aglow with victory. They were *here*.

The *California* opened a new chapter of history. She was the first steamship ever to make the voyage from an Atlantic port of North

America, around the southern continent, to a port on the Pacific side. She was the first steamship from anywhere to enter San Francisco Bay. She brought the first men and women who came from the United States to California because of the gold find. Gamblers and laborers and businessmen, clergymen and courtesans and mothers holding their children's hands, they were the first American Forty-niners.

11

Lucien Loeser had reached New Orleans November 23, 1848. This meant that the gold fever had struck the country just as winter was beginning.

The prairies were a wasteland of snow. Months would pass before gold seekers from the States could cross the country in covered wagons. They had to wait for spring before starting, or they had to take other routes. Thousands of them, too impatient to wait, chose other routes.

The first Forty-niners to reach California from the States had come over the isthmus. The second wave came as passengers on sailing ships that went around the tip of South America. They began to arrive in spring. The third category of Forty-niners was made up of people who came across the plains. The first of them reached Sutter's Fort in July, 1849. Later gold seekers continued to use all three ways.

In the days of the Gold Rush, when the strangers met in California, they would ask each other, "Did you come Around, Across, or Over?"

And no matter which of the three routes a traveler had chosen, by the time he got to California he was sure he had taken the worst route of all.

But in December, 1848, no one could choose to go Across. They had to go Around or Over.

The way over the isthmus was new and strange. So were the routes some people tried across Nicaragua and Mexico. But the route around South America was well known because of the many ships in the Pacific trade. People who lived in the Atlantic seaboard towns might never have heard of San Francisco until this year, but they had heard of Cape Horn. They had seen the ships setting out for the western ocean and coming back with silk and tea from China, spices and sandalwood from the South Sea Islands, whale oil from the Arctic Sea. More important to the people dreaming of gold, if they went to California by sea they could start right away.

The President's message was published in the New York papers December 6, 1848. Within a week, shipowners began to announce vessels they were making ready to sail for California by way of Cape Horn. Before the month's end, Cape Horners were announced in nearly every port along the Atlantic coast. During 1849, hundreds of vessels left the United States for San Francisco. They carried thousands of men and hundreds of women dreaming of gold. The condition of the ships ranged from good to horrible. Most of them were horrible.

Even on the best Cape Horners of '49, the voyagers found the journey hard going.

For one thing, they made it at the wrong time of year. From New York to San Francisco around Cape Horn, the average sailing time was 160 days. Captains of trading vessels nearly always left their home ports in the autumn so they would reach Cape Horn in December or January, the Antarctic summer. Fighting the wind at Cape Horn was always a rugged task for a ship going from east to west because the prevailing winds blew from west to east. The ship had to push against the wind all the way.

This was hard enough in summer, when the sea was fairly calm and the seamen had sixteen hours of light in the day to show them what they were doing. But setting out early in the year meant that the gold seekers would double the Horn in the winter of the Southern Hemisphere. They would have only eight hours of daylight in the twenty-four. The calendar would say May or June, but they would be going through torrents of snow. The sea would be a howling monster that knocked them down if they tried to stand up. And they would be *cold*. Cape Horn is at latitude 50 degrees south, which is about equivalent to the northern latitude of Ketchikan, Alaska.

They were seasick. Few of the Cape Horn Forty-niners escaped days or weeks of misery.

Even the best ships were crowded. Men were so eager to get to California that they were glad to double up. They had no privacy. In the most placid weather, they were always stumbling over each other. They often wished their shipmates dead, and they said so.

And they all had to bear the long, long monotony. What could they *do* all day? They would read until they hated the sight of a printed page. They would talk until they were sick of one another's voices. They studied the stars, they kept diaries, they played every game they could think of; still the days seemed to stretch longer and longer.

A strict-minded editor in Philadelphia was shocked when he heard that men were bringing dice and playing cards aboard vessels bound for the gold country. "There are ample means of pastime and agreeable recreation always at hand," he wrote sternly, "without resorting to cards or dice."

One cannot help wondering what "means of pastime" he would have mentioned if he had been asked. Nearly everyone who made the voyage around the Horn agreed that almost worse than seasickness was the boredom of the empty days.

This is how it was on the good ships with good captains. But when so many men wanted passage all at once, there were simply not enough good ships or good captains. And when the captain was not fit for his office, the passengers were helpless.

In our own time, when men travel to the moon, they can keep in touch with their home planet. In the days of the Gold Rush, when a ship put to sea, she sailed into a lonely silence. On long journeys she might go for weeks without sight of land, or even of another vessel. The ship was an isolated world. The captain was in command. His power was absolute.

In ordinary years, American vessels were in general well equipped and well commanded. But 1849 was not ordinary. Thousands of gold-crazy young fellows were crowding the offices along the docks from New Bedford to New Orleans. They had money in their hands. They were begging for a chance to spend their money on tickets to California. The temptation was great. There were men who did not even try to withstand it.

They patched up ancient whaling ships and worn-out hulks of all sorts. The gold dreamers eagerly paid for tickets. They were ready to get aboard anything that would float.

Men of cooler heads gave them warning. Early in January, the New York *Herald* said bluntly of the vessels about to sail, "One half at least are nearly if not entirely unseaworthy, and unsafe for a short voyage, much less for around Cape Horn."

The men of cool heads warned with deeds as well as words. The directors of an insurance company in Worcester, Massachusetts, started a trend when they voted to refuse life insurance to any person going to California. They announced their decision: "It needs but an inspection of the accommodations of some of the passenger vessels now fitting out, to convince the directors of any company that such risks are not likely to be profitable." A stately way of saying, "We don't expect you to live through it."

But if this deterred any of the gold dreamers, they showed little sign of it. The captains of the Cape Horners were still deluged with applications for passage.

Some of these captains were able and honest men. But too many of them were like a man named Joseph W. Richardson, captain of a dirty old tub called the *Brooklyn*.

The *Brooklyn* left New York January 12, 1849. She reached San Francisco August 12. Seven months. Two hundred and ten days. She was a bad ship and her captain was a greedy brute.

The American laws covering passenger ships were good. Besides limiting the number of persons that vessels of different sizes could carry, Congress had made rules for cleanliness and set minimum standards for food and water. But with hundreds of vessels going to sea at the same time, there were not enough officials to enforce the laws. To make his voyage pay better, the *Brooklyn*'s captain ignored every one.

He packed in passengers like litters of pigs. He gave them food pigs would not have wanted to eat. When they bought their tickets, he had told them he would stop at Rio de Janeiro for fresh food and water. But when he neared Rio he sailed past. Stopping at any port meant that he would have to pay tonnage duty—a fee collected at all ports from ships that anchored there and used the accommodations of the port—and he was in business to make money, not spend it. By the time the ship came near Valparaiso, nearly all the passengers were staggering with scurvy. They pleaded with him to stop so they could buy fresh food. He refused. The excuse he gave was that if he let them go ashore they would get drunk and waste their money.

But by this time the ship's water supply was almost gone, and the captain had to stop somewhere for more. He chose a rocky island 300 miles off the Chilean coast, where there was no port and hence no port duty. The sick men found little food here except such fish as they could catch. Before the ship reached San Francisco, several of these men were dead. They had died of scurvy and other diseases caused by bad food, verminous water, and dirt.

By law, the *Brooklyn* should have carried no more than 120 passengers. When she reached San Francisco she had 171 passengers still alive. Every one of them was sick with scurvy. Conditions on the ship had been so chaotic that nobody was sure just how many passengers had been aboard to begin with, or how many had died on the way. Four of the men still living were so weak they could not walk. They had to be carried ashore. A few days later, one of them died.

A month after the *Brooklyn* reached port, five men, by this time strong enough to stand up and talk, brought suit against Captain Richardson. The jury awarded them substantial damages. Having to pay out all this money probably broke the captain's heart, but it did not raise the dead or restore vigor to men whose health had been damaged beyond repair.

But no reports of greedy captains and horrible voyages could cool the ardor of the young men buying tickets to California. Passenger lists of ships bound for San Francisco still crowded the columns of newspapers along the whole East Coast. And by this time, gold dreamers were setting out from nearly every country on earth. The editor of the *Alta California* was almost gushy about it. "Never in the history of man," he exulted, "has a single event so affected the history of the world as the discovery of the gold mines of California!"

This newspaper, the *Alta California,* was a new venture, already becoming known as a dependable recorder of its place and time. The two earlier San Francisco papers, the *Star* and the *Californian,* had collapsed in the summer of 1848 when printers and subscribers alike had rushed off to the hills to pan gold. The young editor of the *Star,* Edward Kemble, had also gone to the hills, but when he came back to town in the fall of that year, he observed that hundreds of other miners were returning. Knowing he was a better editor than gold digger, Kemble decided to launch a newspaper of his own. He bought the presses and other equipment of the two extinct papers, and on November 18, 1848, he issued a paper called the *Star and Californian.*

While he was earning a living with this paper, he was pursuing a more ambitious purpose. He had formed a partnership with Edward Gilbert, the officer who had led the military parade through San Francisco when the people were celebrating news of the treaty of peace. When they became partners, Kemble was twenty years old and Gilbert thirty.

For several years before coming to California, Gilbert had been a newspaper writer in his home town of Albany, New York. He leavened Kemble's exuberance with his own practical knowledge. Between them, they made plans for a newspaper that would not be like the papers on the Atlantic side but would reflect the uniqueness of California and the attitudes, unfamiliar and often misunderstood, of the people who lived here.

Alta (Upper) California was the name of the part of California north of the Mexican boundary line, and Baja (Lower) California was the name of the peninsula south of the line. Gilbert suggested that they make *Alta California* the name of their newspaper. Beginning as a weekly, the paper first appeared Thursday, January 4, 1849. During the following year it became a daily, and for more than forty years the paper—usually called the *Alta* for convenience—continued to record the history of early California while that history was being made.

It was almost certainly Kemble who wrote the lines about the impact of the gold discovery on the whole world. He may have exaggerated, but California gold was certainly bringing forth a lot of curious behavior.

A New York dentist announced that he was now using only California gold to make fillings for his patients' teeth. In Boston, insurance companies refused to write policies for trading ships that even stopped for water at San Francisco because they were afraid the crews would run off to the mines. At Panama the throng waiting for ships had grown so large that these travelers now had a newspaper of their own. They chose a timely motto—"Press onward." The paper lasted for years as the colony continued to grow, and when an editor managed to press onward to San Francisco, a new man was always there to take his place.

A writer who signed himself Cantell A. Bigly was inspired to dash off a novel called *Aurifodina* (the Latin word for gold mine), about a man who found a spot in California where the people had so much gold that they set no value upon it. Their daily "paper" was not printed on paper but on sheets of gold. Poor folks wore cloth of gold because it was cheap, while the princes of the land strutted about in cotton because only they could afford it. Readers did not have to be *very* bright to observe that if they read the author's name aloud and slowly, it came out "Can-tell-a-big-lie." But so great was the interest in anything about California, real or humbug, that Horace Greeley put a review of this gabble on the front page of the *Tribune*.

For Horace Greeley had changed his mind. He was a man of violent opinions. But when he knew he had been wrong, he was not afraid to put a new opinion in place of the old. He knew now that when the American people had paid thirty-nine tons of gold for California, they had picked up one of the biggest bargains of all time. Greeley showed his change of heart when he endorsed a proposal made by a venturesome young widow named Eliza Farnham.

Though Horace Greeley approved it, and so did other distinguished men and women, Eliza's plan was too daring to win widespread favor. What she wanted to do, in those days of prudery and properness, was to take a party of single women to woman-starved California. Object: matrimony.

Her plan did not work. Not all at once. But Eliza Farnham was a woman who usually had her own way in the end. She got it by wit and courage, a cool persistence, and the ability to stand almost anything.

Eliza had had a dreary girlhood. Its barrenness was not caused by poverty; she had never gone hungry or suffered from lack of cloak or blanket. What she had lacked was love.

Born in upstate New York in 1815, Eliza Burhans became an orphan when she was six years old. The children of the family were scattered among relatives. Eliza was sent to an aunt and uncle, who made it clear that they would have been just as happy if she had been sent somewhere else. Her growing-up years were not cheerful.

But her misfortune gave her a deep strength. Since she knew nobody cared about her, she learned to depend on nobody. She developed independence of spirit and a self-reliance that lasted all her life.

When she was sixteen, Eliza managed to get away from her unhappy home and live with another uncle. At his home she found more affection than she had received before, and here she was given a chance to make friends with her brother and her two sisters. One of her sisters married and went to live in Peoria, Illinois, and one day Eliza received a letter. Her sister was lonesome. Would Eliza come and live with her?

Eliza was delighted. She had grown fond of her sister, and besides, the trip meant adventure. Peoria (named for a tribe of Illinois Indians) was a remote little village on the prairie, and in those days, most people in New York State knew less about the prairies than we know today about the moon. Escorted by her brother Henry, Eliza set out for Peoria. It was now the spring of 1836. She had had her twentieth birthday in November of the previous year.

They went by stagecoach and riverboat, first to St. Louis, then up the Illinois River to Peoria. It was a long, slow journey. The farther west they traveled, the more dislikable it became. The boats were dirty and the staterooms primitive, and most of the passengers were the roughest sort of frontiersmen. They stared wishfully at Eliza, with her neatly combed hair and the fresh new dresses she had made for her journey. Her brother seldom dared to leave her side.

But Eliza had learned patience in a hard school, and she had a vivid sense of humor. She did not exactly enjoy the dirt and discomfort, but she found the whole experience so challenging that she never regretted having had it. When she reached the prairie, bright with midsummer bloom, she loved being there.

In Peoria Eliza met and married a lawyer named Thomas Jefferson Farnham. She was twenty-one years old, he thirty-two. Tom had grown up in New England, but he did not stay there any longer than he had to. Yearning for adventure, he had set out early for what was then the western frontier, and he meant to go still farther. His temperament was not suited for quiet domestic life; probably one reason he and Eliza were attracted to each other was that they were both rebels against routine. Neither of them could bear the prospect of going through life meekly doing what other people expected of them. (And they did not.)

Tom recognized Eliza's poise and courage. No helpless creampuff, Eliza could take care of herself. It was a good thing she could, for before they had been married two years, Tom had caught the westerly urge again.

He and Eliza were now parents of a baby son, but neither this nor any other circumstance could make Tom stay in one place when he felt like moving on. This time he wanted to cross the continent all the way. He wanted to reach that far frontier he had dreamed of, the Oregon Territory.

It happened in the fall of the year 1838. Except for Indians, most of the people who lived in the Oregon Territory were employees of the Hudson's Bay Company. This was a British trading firm, with headquarters at Fort Vancouver, in the present state of Washington. There were also a few settlers, clearing land for farms, and missionaries sent out by their churches.

One of these missionaries, the Reverend Jason Lee, had started back to the States to raise funds for his work among the Indians. On his way east, he stopped in Peoria, where he gave a talk. Listening and asking questions were some zesty young men, among them Tom Farnham. Before Dr. Lee had gone on to New York, Tom had made up his mind. He would never be happy until he had seen the Oregon Territory.

It was too late in the fall to start out, but as soon as the spring thaws made the journey possible, Tom headed a party of nineteen young fellows who started westward over the Oregon Trail. They left in May, 1839.

The Oregon Trail—marked by explorers, fur trappers, and adventurers of all sorts—led from Independence, Missouri, to Fort Vancouver. The distance was 2,000 miles. It was a wild and dangerous journey and required a rugged persistence that most people did not possess. Only five of the nineteen young fellows held out to reach the Territory, but Tom was one of them. Not only did he get there, but he brought with him abundant notes of what he had observed on the way.

At Fort Vancouver, he made friends with the head of the post, a wise and affable Scot named John McLoughlin. When the next company ship set out for Honolulu with a cargo of furs, Tom was on board, notebook in hand.

On the way back, the ship stopped in Yerba Buena, a supply station on the California coast. This was a settlement of about fifty persons, most of them Americans who had wandered west, each for his own reasons. In his notebook, Tom recorded that Yerba Buena was a dingy little town. He did not say—he could not know—that this dingy little town would, in another ten years, be world-famous as the city of San Francisco. He did note, however, that San Francisco Bay was "the glory of the Western world."

Tom went next to Monterey, where he called on Thomas Larkin (not yet United States consul), and Mrs. Larkin. They introduced him to another Yankee, a rancher named John Marsh. The three of them told Tom about the vast resources of California. They also told him that a surprising number of their countrymen were living in California even then. These men—ranchers, traders, storekeepers—controlled much of the local business. Their influence was great, and their prospects almost unlimited. Tom began to feel a conviction that the other three clearly felt already. California was too fair a land to belong to any country but their own.

At first Tom was as sure as they were that Yankees were welcome in California. Then an incident occurred that gave him a sudden dislike for the place.

Most of the local Americans had won the respect and liking of the Californios. But not all. Some of them were seamen who had jumped ship, drifters who had strayed to California by chance, or no-goods who would not have been welcome anywhere. A general rendezvous for this footloose crowd was a distillery near Monterey owned by an ex-trapper named Isaac Graham.

Isaac's friends did a little work in return for liquid entertainment.

When they felt restless, they roamed off to Monterey, where they loafed in the taverns, drank *aguardiente* (which is literally translated "firewater"), and talked.

They talked too much and too noisily. They said the Californios needed a lot of Yankees to teach them some Yankee gumption, and one of these days the Yankees were going to come right in and take over. The Britishers among them shouted that California would more probably be taken by heroes from Queen Victoria's domain. It was sheer barroom bluster, but the governor got tired of it. One day he sent troops to Isaac's distillery. The troops arrested a lot of these braggarts and took them to Mexico to be tried as enemies of the country. They were not active enemies, certainly, but they had undoubtedly made nuisances of themselves. However, the whole affair suggested to Tom Farnham that Americans were not wanted in California, nor were they safe there.

By this time Tom had made enough notes on his travels to write a book, and he wanted to go home and write it. He joined a group of travelers who were planning to go to the United States by way of Mexico. With them, he crossed from San Blas on the Pacific coast to Veracruz on the Atlantic. From Veracruz he took a ship for New Orleans, then came by riverboat to Peoria.

It was now midsummer, 1840, more than a year since Tom had left. He reached Peoria on what would have been the third birthday of his son. But the baby was dead. Eliza took him to see the grave.

12

Tom and Eliza went back east, so that Tom could discuss his book with publishers in New York. But, still angry about the Isaac Graham affair, before he began his book, Tom wrote an article for a New York newspaper in which he gave vent to his wrath. He wrote that California might be a fine country, but the people there did not want any outsiders among them. If any of his readers were thinking of going to California, Tom advised them to change their plans.

He wrote the article impulsively and hastily. He did not know what might be happening now to Isaac Graham and the other barroom blusterers. What he wrote was to have important consequences, but Tom Farnham seems to have been one of those people who seldom if ever look ahead to the possible results of their deeds. (What happened to Graham and his cronies was that they were brought before a Mexican court and released. About half of them, including Graham, went back to live in California. When Tom heard about this, he had already changed his mind on the subject of California and was yearning to live there himself. But his newspaper article was still being printed, and reprinted, and read.)

For the present—the year 1840—Tom found a publisher interested in his book, and he set about writing it. He had so much to say about his journeyings that his book turned out to be two books—or, rather, one book in two fat volumes. While he was writing, Mr. Larkin of Monterey was made United States consul in California. This happened in April, 1842. Neither Larkin nor John Marsh had seen Tom's newspaper article, and they were both sending him letters extolling California as a land of sunshine and untapped wealth. They repeated their hope that more Americans would come to California to live. Tom had liked

California when he first saw it, and as he wrote about it he returned to his former opinion. California was a fair land, and it ought to belong to the United States. The more he wrote, the more he wanted to go back.

Writing the book kept Tom busy for four years. During this time, Eliza became the mother of two little boys, called Charlie and Eddie. She also began a career of her own as a friend and confidante of people in trouble.

"Philanthropist" is such an imposing word that it has a haze of self-righteousness about it. There is no evidence in what Eliza wrote, or in what others wrote about her, that she ever thought of herself as an angel of mercy. She really enjoyed giving her time and energy to making people happier or helping them bear hardships that she could not ease.

Eliza knew how it felt to be unloved and unwanted. When she had lost her first child, she had also known heartbreak, and with her husband far away, she had had to face it alone. All this had given her a sense of kinship with other unloved and unwanted and heartbroken people of the world. She wanted to give, to as many of them as she could, the understanding she had missed.

She began visiting the prisons. Not to preach or pass cookies to the prisoners, but to find out why these people were there, what had made them take this way of life instead of a better one. Eliza knew that many lawbreakers were so at odds with the world that they would never learn to live in it peacefully. But she did believe some of them could be helped. She believed they would respond to sympathy and to somebody who would listen to what they had to say.

Eliza was willing to work with them and to listen. She began by doing her work for nothing. But she soon found that she needed a job. Tom's second book was finished and he was as restless as before. He told her he wanted to go west again.

Tom could have had a lucrative law practice in New York. But he disliked New York and every other place where he had to be surrounded by four walls and live by standard rules. He said he would go back to the West Coast on a trading vessel or with a party of trappers on their way overland to Fort Vancouver. Yes, it would be a long journey, and the necessary supplies would cost a lot of money, but he could gather material for another book. And Eliza could take care of herself. And their two children. Couldn't she?

By this time Eliza knew she had better. Tom had a first-class mind, an honorable spirit, and winning ways. But he had no talent for coping with the dull and ofttimes burdensome details of everyday life.

So it came about that early in 1844, when she was twenty-eight years old, Eliza became matron of the women's division of Sing Sing prison in Ossining, New York. The next year, leaving Eliza and the two little boys in New York, Tom set out again for the West. It may be that Eliza was not unhappy to have him off her hands. And it may be that Tom went west again because he found Eliza, for all her fine qualities, irksome as a constant companion. Many excellent people are hard to live with. Tom and Eliza were both free spirits who could keep only self-imposed rules. This independence of character, so strong in them both, was almost certainly what had drawn them together in the first place. Now apparently it was this same trait that made it impossible for them to stay together.

In the women's prison at Sing Sing there were seventy-three prisoners. Most of them were there because of theft, prostitution, drunkenness, or all three. Only twenty-three of them could read and write. Thirty others had picked up enough knowledge of letters to read street signs, and short lines of print, but could not write. The rest were totally illiterate.

At night they were locked up, each alone in her cell. They spent their days at work, mostly sewing. They had little chance for exercise, except as they took their turns to sweep or scrub the floor. They were forbidden to speak to each other at any time, lest they conspire to riot or otherwise make trouble. Sometimes they did devise ways to talk. This generally brought on quarrels in which they would go into a howling fury and beat each other up. Punishment for such disorder usually meant solitary confinement on a diet of bread and water, for as long a time as the person in charge thought needful.

The custodians were not basically cruel. But it was a hard task to keep order among so many women, all hating the rules, hating their guards, and in danger at any moment of turning into a pack of screaming viragoes. The members of the prison board said they would be glad to have any help Eliza could give. It is not likely that they thought she could give much.

But Eliza was no mawkish do-gooder. She was a practical person. She knew these women were an unruly lot; otherwise they would not have been there. She knew some of them were too stupid or too hardened to be changed. But she suspected that many of their outbreaks were simply revolts against the deadly hopelessness of their

84

lives. She believed that some of them, at least, would improve if they could realize that she truly cared about them.

They could and they did. When Eliza came to the women's prison, offenses against major rules averaged forty-seven a month. By the time she had been on the job a year, the number had dropped to eleven. The women might not have developed better characters, but their tempers had calmed down. They were happier—or at any rate, less desperate—than they had been.

Eliza had great energy. She took good care of her charges in the prison, and she took equally good care of her children at home. The second task was even more exacting than the first, for while her older boy, Charlie, was a sturdy child, little Eddie had been frail from birth. Probably to raise the money she needed for him, in her spare minutes Eliza wrote a book, *Life in Prairie Land,* in which she told about her journey to Peoria and about day-by-day incidents in the settlements scattered over the plains. She was also asked to edit and write a preface to an American edition of a book on crime and prisons by an English penologist. Both books were published in 1846.

Meanwhile, Tom was practicing law in Yerba Buena, which most people were now calling San Francisco to agree with the bay. (The name was officially changed when an announcement to this effect was published in the *Star* on February 7, 1848, by order of the alcalde, W. A. Bartlett.) Tom liked this bustling little town, where there were no traditions and a man could do as he pleased. He was a good lawyer and, as usual, he speedily made friends.

Then Jim Marshall found gold. Edward Beale and Lucien Loeser brought the news to Washington. The westward rush began. In the midst of the gold fever, Eliza received a letter from San Francisco. The letter told her that Tom was dead.

He had died suddenly on September 13, 1848. At that time, San Francisco was wild with gold fever, and hardly anybody was thinking about anything else. But Tom had been so well liked that the San Francisco *Californian* had made room in its crowded columns to announce Tom's death and give a memoir of his life.

After describing Tom's career and his books, the writer added, "In his profession he ranked among the best. . . . His name will long be remembered by a large circle of friends."

The letter bringing word of Tom's death—apparently written by one of his legal confrères—also told Eliza about business details. The population of California was increasing as fast as people could get there. Foreseeing a rise in land values, Tom had bought a tract in the Santa

Cruz Valley, north of Monterey Bay. Fertile and well located for a ranch, the land now belonged to Eliza and the two boys. The writer knew that even in the quietest times, the long journey to California had been perilous for a woman without an escort. The confusion of the gold rush made it even more dangerous. Still, if Eliza could come to California and establish her claim to the property, she would be wise to do so.

Eliza may have already known about the property. In any case, her immediate outlook was clear. Her little boys, the older only seven, had nobody but her to depend on. Whatever the dangers, it was her duty to go to California and take possession of the land their father had left them. It was her duty, in fact, to join the Gold Rush.

Eliza had never turned down a chance to do something unexpected. When she decided to join the great migration, everything she said or did suggested that she liked the prospect. But it was typical of Eliza that now, as usual when she decided to do something, she asked herself, "Can't I help somebody while I'm doing it?"

She had an idea. Some people said it was excellent. Others said it was not only foolish and unworkable but also immodest, indecent, and shocking.

13

As prison matron, Eliza had spent four years at Sing Sing. During this time she had been made keenly aware of how many women turned to crime and prostitution not because they were sinful but because they were hungry. Few trades were open to women, and many women needed work. The result was that they had to take whatever pay they could get, and this was only a little more than nothing.

In New York and elsewhere, the women who made men's shirts— by hand, of course—were paid a dollar a dozen. The seamstress was given the work to take home. This meant that her earnings had to pay not only for food and clothes and rent; they also had to pay for lights on dark winter days, and fire to keep her fingers from getting so numb that she could not sew. Even at a time when beef sold for twenty cents a pound, no seamstress could make shirts fast enough to earn a decent living at a dollar a dozen. If she had a child, her life was doubly wretched. A woman who worked fourteen hours a day and was still hungry must have had a mighty noble character if she did not snatch goods or money left unguarded. Sooner or later she would get caught. And with a jail record behind her, what could she do?

On both sides of the Atlantic, voices were raised in protest. In the United States, outspoken writers such as Timothy Shay Arthur and C. T. Hinckley wrote angry articles about the plight of women who had to earn their own living. In England, Thomas Hood tried to rouse his countrymen by his bitter poems "The Song of the Shirt" and "The Bridge of Sighs," with such lines of torture as "Oh, God, that bread should be so dear,/ and flesh and blood so cheap!"

These and other efforts brought forth floods of tears and a few charity funds, but they did not make tight-fisted employers pay higher wages. If a seamstress went to jail or died of want, or turned from sewing to streetwalking, there were always more to take her place.

Now Eliza thought she saw a chance to help these women. She would soon be on her way to California. Why not take a party of seamstresses with her, to that land of high wages and lonely men who wanted wives?

Already, early in 1849, the Easterners were hearing about the need for women in the gold country. Typical of these laments was a letter written by a man in California to a friend in Boston, published in the New York *Herald*. The writer advised his friend that if he should ever come to the land of gold, he should bring a wife with him; "for a good wife," said he, "is the scarcest article in California." Quoting this, the New York editor noted that most of the men now leaving for California were young bachelors. He suggested, "The best shipment hereafter to the gold diggings would be a consignment of young ladies."

Sometime before this, a New York newspaper had published a news item about an indignation meeting of New York seamstresses, trying to call attention to their scanty pay. The *Alta California* had published a summary of this article, and commented:

> We would advise a colony of these same working girls to come to California as soon as possible. They can earn from $5 to $35 per day in the manufacture of clothing; and if they be anxious to do better than that, they will find hundreds of young, good-looking, and enterprising men, ready to embrace an opportunity which promises a good wife.

The first city east of the Mississippi River to receive this issue of the *Alta* was New Orleans. The account of the indignation meeting, followed by the *Alta*'s invitation, was promptly reprinted in the New Orleans *Picayune,* and the *Picayune* editor added, "Girls, do you hear that?"

The whole series, including the question at the end, was quoted by papers in other parts of the country. The editors of these papers seemed to be saying, in effect, For you women who can't make a decent living at home, here's a chance to do better. Go to California! Eliza Farnham seems to have been the first person to take a practical view of the subject.

A journey to California was a costly undertaking. Eliza had read the advertisements crowding the papers, showing how young men were desperately trying to raise money for this journey. Clear-headed as usual, she wondered: How did all those editors think the underpaid sewing women were going to pay their fare to California? Having asked herself the question, she devised a possible answer.

Eliza knew that many people were uncaring skinflints. But she knew also that many other people were generous and kind. Told of a chance to help these workwomen, they would respond. Eliza intended to travel about the country, making talks to church societies and similar groups and asking for contributions from her hearers.

She began by writing a circular that gave an account of her plan. She sent the circular to newspaper editors, civic leaders, and outstanding men and women in many walks of life. It was widely published and discussed.

To reassure even the most proper-minded of her readers, Eliza's circular described the plan in detail. She was not going to take inexperienced young girls, who might be victimized by wicked men. Nor any "fallen women" of any age. To join her company, a woman must be at least twenty-five years old, she must bring a warrant of good character from her clergyman or some other responsible person, and she must prove that she had enough skill at sewing or some other trade to support herself.

The working women responded at once, more than two hundred of them, in person or by letters. A few of these respondents said they had been making a fair living and had saved enough money to pay their own fare. The vast majority, however, could hardly pay for their next day's meals. These were the women for whom Eliza intended to raise funds.

The first important friend of her project was Horace Greeley. Soon after Eliza's circular appeared, Greeley published an editorial heartily endorsing her proposal. Many other distinguished men and women, including the famous clergyman Henry Ward Beecher, also endorsed it. The *Tribune* announced that Mrs. Farnham's party would sail on or about April 15, 1849, on the ship *Angelique*.

But in spite of its notable sponsors, Eliza's plan aroused a storm of controversy. Some people might approve, but others vehemently insisted that such an idea could produce no good. They said it would be outrageous for women to leave their "sheltered homes" and go gadding off to California without husbands or fathers to keep them from harm. The women might not be "fallen" when they started, but they would surely tumble down when they got there. The whole scheme was newfangled and un-American.

If these faultfinders had known more about the history of their own country, they would have known that Eliza's plan had been successfully tried before. In the year 1619, a ship came from England to the nearly all-male colony of Jamestown, Virginia, bringing women to become wives of the colonists. In 1704, another ship came into port at Mobile, Alabama. (At that time, the present states of Alabama and Mississippi were part of the French colony of Louisiana.) This ship brought twenty-three young women, chaperoned by two nuns. After they landed, the women lived under care of the nuns until they were married. This was not long, as they were all married within a month. In 1721, another French ship reached Biloxi, Mississippi, bringing eighty-one women, supervised by another group of nuns. A third shipload came to New Orleans in 1727. The second and third groups of these French wives-to-be were called "casket girls" (filles de cassette), because each of them had been given a "casket," or little trunk, holding new clothes for her trousseau.

Eliza's plan was not newfangled and it was not un-American.

In spite of her opponents, Eliza went ahead. But just as the queries were coming in, she was taken ill. She was bedridden for two months. (This is the only time between her birth and death that we hear of her being prevented by illness from doing anything she had set out to do.) By the time she was well again, it was too late. During her long silence, her diehard detractors had had their way. Most of the women who could pay for their own tickets had been scared off. Those who still wanted to go with her but could not pay had to stay behind. The ship on which she had booked passage had waited a month past its intended sailing date, and the captain would wait no longer.

At last, the New York *Herald* of May 20, 1849, reported, "The ship *Angelique,* Capt. Windsor, sailed yesterday morning for San Francisco."

On board the *Angelique* were Eliza and her two little boys, Charlie and Eddie, and a young woman she had engaged as a nurse. Little Eddie, always sickly, needed constant care. Also in her party was a friend, Miss Sampson. The times were more formal than ours, and first names were not used as much as we use them. In describing her journey, Eliza always referred to her friend as "Miss Sampson."

The book on crime and prisons that Eliza had edited during her stay at Sing Sing was written by a man named Marmaduke Blake Sampson. Miss Sampson may have been his sister or some other relative. This is only a guess. But it is certain that Eliza had high regard for her, and Miss Sampson was to prove herself a real friend in the harsh days that lay ahead.

On the ship were two other young women, Mrs. Griswold and Mrs. Barker. They had been among the two hundred who wanted to go west with Eliza and who also could pay for their own tickets. Seven years later, Eliza wrote that in California they both had earned enough money to keep them in comfort as long as they lived and had gone back to New York "with unstained reputations."

Also aboard the *Angelique* were fifteen men going to California for the usual reason of gold. Altogether there were twenty-two passengers.

But there were still some empty berths, because Eliza's illness had made it impossible for her to raise money for the fares of the penniless women she had hoped to take with her to California. Captain Windsor did not like empty berths. This may have been the reason why he tried to save money by breaking his word to the passengers who were now on board the ship.

Before sailing, Captain Windsor had told them that on the way he would make two stops for fresh food and water. One of these would be at the island of Santa Catarina, off the southern coast of Brazil; the other would be at the port of Valparaiso in Chile. They found this an agreeable prospect. Santa Catarina was a picturesque island near the tropic of Capricorn, a favorite watering place for the coastal vessels. They would reach the island in July, the coolest and pleasantest month of the year.

The voyage began well. The *Angelique* was far better than the average vessel that took gold seekers around Cape Horn that year. Most of these others had been built for cargo, and the passengers were crowded into makeshift bunks in the hold. But the *Angelique* was a passenger ship, taken off her regular run because of the sudden need for ships to the gold country. She had staterooms, which gave her passengers the rare boon of privacy. She also had ventilators of the windmill type, which gave them constant currents of fresh air. Captain Windsor was a competent commander; his ship was clean, and the food, while not sumptuous, was adequate. But when they were only a few days out of New York, the passengers began to find fault with the water. Men, women, and children, they said the water was not fit to drink.

In the ships of that day, water was carried in wooden barrels. Travelers knew that after six or eight weeks at sea, even in the best ships, the water would have lost its freshness, but they could still drink it without disgust. However, not all water started the voyage in good condition. If the captain was not careful, he might take water from a supplier who had not made sure his own containers were clean. Or he might take water that had been standing around since long before the sailing date and was already stale when the voyage began. When something like this happened, the water would get stagnant and smelly. The drinkers might find sediment that had to settle in their cups before they could swallow the water without revulsion. Or sometimes, when a barrel was opened, they would see live wiggletails sporting around. It was not often as bad as this, but in any case, stagnant water had a vile taste and was thoroughly unwholesome.

Bad water had long been a hardship of seamen, and they had devised ways of making it seem less horrid than it was. Now the travelers on the *Angelique* took hints from the crew. If they had brought along wine or brandy, they added this to their rations of water. Or they poured in molasses, or vinegar, or rum, or anything else they could get that might disguise the taste and stink of the water and make it easier to swallow. But no matter what they did, the water was still repulsive. Nearly all the passengers, including Eliza, went to Captain Windsor and protested.

Whether the captain had knowingly loaded the water, or whether he had been swindled by some tricky supplier and was ashamed to own it, he did not say. He met their complaints with shrugs. He said they could drink the water or not, as they pleased. He would take on fresh water when they reached Valparaiso.

Valparaiso!

They heard the word with disbelief and dismay. The captain had told every one of them that he would stop twice on the voyage, at Santa Catarina and then at Valparaiso. Now they found that, like so many other captains of Gold Rush vessels, Windsor found it easier to make promises than to keep them.

The time was now the first of June. They could reach Santa Catarina in July. They could not hope to reach Valparaiso before October. To drink this musty water for six weeks more was bad enough; to drink it from now until October—? They would all be sick.

"And I have a frail child," pleaded Eliza. She told the captain Eddie was already sick, and robust little Charlie was showing signs of illness from the foul water; if Eddie had to go on drinking it, by October he might no longer be alive.

Captain Windsor would not yield. A stop meant wasted time and extra expense. He said again that he was going to sail directly to Valparaiso.

The days went on. The ship drew nearer and nearer to Catarina Island. When the passengers begged him to stop for water, Captain Windsor's refusals grew louder, angrier, more profane. He would not.

He had forgotten—maybe nobody had ever told him—that no beast in the jungle will fight as fiercely as one who is a mother defending her helpless cubs. Captain Windsor had made up his mind that he would not stop for fresh water. Eliza had made up her mind that he would.

Taking pen and paper, Eliza retired to her stateroom. While Miss Sampson amused the children, Eliza wrote a petition. "We, the passengers aboard the ship *Angelique* . . ."

The suit brought against Captain Richardson by the *Brooklyn* passengers in San Francisco had not yet taken place. But in New York, nine days before the *Angelique* had sailed, newspaper readers had seen an announcement of the public disgrace of another commander, Captain Tibbets of the ship *Pacific*. This vessel, carrying about sixty men bound for the goldfields, had stopped at Rio de Janeiro for water. Soon after she dropped anchor, a committee chosen by the men aboard had called on the United States minister to Brazil, David Todd, and the consul in Rio, Gorham Parks. The committee members had brought sworn testimony of how, after they had paid for first-class passage, the captain had given them half-rotten food served on dirty plates and had otherwise broken nearly every American law of the sea. Tibbets had been formally tried and deposed, while another commander had taken his place.

Eliza had not actually seen Captain Windsor reading this news item, but it would be surprising if he had not. At any rate, he would certainly hear of it in Valparaiso. He had on board copies of all the New York newspapers up to his day of sailing. A center of commerce, Valparaiso had a thriving colony of American and British traders and their families who eagerly waited for the papers from home.

Eliza wrote in courteous terms. But she made it clear that if Windsor did not keep his promise to stop for water earlier, she and her fellow passengers would make trouble for him when they reached Valparaiso.

She took her petition around the ship. Twenty-one of the twenty-two passengers signed. Charlie Farnham, seven years old, wrote his name. Little Eddie made his mark. The lone holdout may have been a friend of the captain and recipient of special favors, or he may have been a timid soul who feared the captain's power at sea. It was now evening, nearly time for dinner. One of the signers took the paper to the captain's table and laid it beside his plate.

When the captain came to table, he picked up the paper. As he read it, he recognized Eliza's handwriting. Enraged, he glared at her and swore. Eliza did not deny that she had written the petition. The others all knew she had; why should she care if he knew it too? What she cared about was getting clean water for her children.

They were now only two days' sail from Santa Catarina. Profanely and obscenely, the captain said he would stop there. His fury at Eliza increased every hour. He did not like meddling women, he shouted at her, in language that brought shocked reproof from the male passengers. Windsor responded by extending his rage to include the other women as well as Eliza. He yelled at them all, abusing them without distinction.

Eliza kept quiet. She had heard all those dirty words at Sing Sing. They had not hurt her then and would not hurt her now. The ship stopped at Catarina, and the crewmen began to load fresh water. This was what she had wanted to accomplish, and she had done it.

They stayed in port nine days. Captain Windsor continued doing all he could to make life hard for his feminine passengers, but there was not much he could do. They spent most of their time ashore. At Santa Catarina they met a group of Englishmen who had been waiting for a ship to take them around Cape Horn. Several of these men were officers in the British navy; the rest were gold seekers on their way to California. They were happy to learn that the *Angelique* had those empty berths. When they came aboard to book passage, they saw Eliza and her friends and asked to be introduced. Glad to have the company of women who spoke their language, the Englishmen took them sightseeing.

The weather was balmy, the island lush with palms and flowers. The port was busy and colorful. The markets offered melons, bananas, oranges, fresh meat and fish, milk and butter, newly baked bread. And, most gladdening to the visitors from the ship, they had as much fresh water as they wanted. The nine days at Catarina were delightful ones.

When the ship sailed, Eliza was in a happy mood. She had won her fight, and there was enough clean water on board to last all the way to Valparaiso. Already her children's health was better. To be sure, the captain was mad, and he grew madder as their journey went on. But she could ignore his temper and his ugly words.

She did not realize the depth of his hate. She had defied him. She had shown up his cruelty and his littleness of mind. For this, he was not going to forgive her. Eliza had had her way, but Captain Windsor was going to make her pay for it.

14

_____

Eliza had another problem, and the captain found it a pleasant diversion to watch it getting worse. The problem concerned the nursemaid she had engaged to help her take care of the children.

The nurse was a girl about eighteen years old. She was attractive and clever, but she had never been to school. When Eliza had hired her in New York, the girl had been delighted at this chance to see California, and when Eliza had asked her if she would like to learn to read and write during the voyage, she had replied that she certainly would. Eliza and Miss Sampson agreed to set aside part of every day for her lessons. One of them would teach her, while the other would keep the children entertained.

The young nurse set out in high spirits. But she soon found that her voyage to California was not be be a gilded holiday. There were many irksome duties connected with the care of two small boys, cross and restless with the monotony of the days. They had not been long out of New York when the nurse told Eliza that one of the ship's stewards had asked if Mrs. Farnham would let her help him with his work now and then. Among his duties was that of setting the tables for meals. He said he had many tasks every day, and sometimes he had to rush hard if he was to get the tables ready on time. If Mrs. Farnham would let her maid assist him when he was especially hurried, she would be doing him a great favor.

Always ready—sometimes too ready—to give aid, Eliza consented. The girl could help the steward, said Eliza, as long as she did not let it interfere with her care of the children.

This was a major mistake. Already tired of the work she was being paid to do, the girl found it more agreeable to flirt with a young man who kept telling her how pretty she was and how kind she was to help him out. Gradually she began to spend more and more time with him, less and less with the children. Charlie needed games and exercise. When the weather allowed, the nurse was supposed to play with him on deck while Eliza or Miss Sampson told stories to the less vigorous Eddie. But before long, the girl was keeping herself at the steward's disposal, running whenever he called her and enjoying it. She lost interest in learning to read and failed to appear at the hour set for her daily lesson. The steward (described by Eliza as a "lazy, worthless creature") was happy to lounge about while the nurse did his work for him. No reminder of her obligations had any effect. When Eliza told the steward that the nurse had been hired to work for her and not for him, he laughed. Captain Windsor would do nothing. Even before Eliza wrote her petition, her insistence that he stop for fresh water had been making her a nuisance. When she asked the captain to forbid the steward's asking her employee to do his work, Windsor shrugged. He said it was no concern of his.

Shortly before the ship reached Catarina, the so-called nursemaid had told Eliza that the steward had asked her to marry him. Irritated though she was, Eliza still did not want to see the girl bound to a shiftless lout. She strongly objected to the marriage, and at last she persuaded the girl to think it over a while longer.

Now that they were at sea again, Eliza became more and more provoked by the steward's insolence and the girl's lovesick folly. As a nursemaid, the girl was useless. Writing of the voyage later, Eliza said that on the way from Catarina to Valparaiso "almost the whole of her time was spent in the service of the ship." Her lazy lover was still urging her to marry him, and Captain Windsor was heartily approving of their marriage.

"I expostulated very earnestly with her," wrote Eliza, "but the captain, on every occasion when allusion was made to them, encouraged it to the utmost."

It is hardly surprising that the captain favored the marriage. As matters stood, he was getting an extra worker without extra pay, and if the girl deserted Eliza and married the steward, this arrangement would continue. It is possible that the captain was also glad to have another way of annoying Eliza.

The month of August passed, and by September they were nearing Cape Horn.

September in the southern hemisphere corresponds to March in the northern. It is not the coldest month of the year or the most stormy, but it is by no means gentle. The average temperature is not much above freezing. The winds bluster and howl, and a ship is pitched around, with great discomfort to everybody on board. During the weeks when the *Angelique* was doubling Cape Horn and sailing toward Valparaiso, often for days on end, Eliza did not lay eyes on the children's "nurse." Wages she could hold back. But she had paid the fares to San Francisco in advance, and now the girl could do as she pleased.

With the help of Miss Sampson, Eliza took care of the two little boys. The children were scared, wind-tossed, and miserably cold. Captain Windsor had found another way of punishing them, not only Eliza but also the passengers who had put their names to her petition. Though the ship was well stocked with firewood, through all those chilling weeks near Cape Horn, he refused to let them have a fire in the cabin. He allowed the wood to be used for cooking and nothing else.

The Englishmen who had boarded the ship at Catarina might complain all they pleased. They might remind the captain that *they* had not signed Eliza's petition. And the stop at Catarina had brought him good fortune, because there he had acquired them as paying passengers. Windsor would not change his orders. He was going to make Eliza Farnham find out who was boss on this ship. Let such a pest as Eliza start having her way, and there was no telling where it would end.

But at last they doubled the Horn and sailed up the coast of Chile. During the first week of October, 1849, they came in sight of Valparaiso. At this flowery port, latitude 33 degrees south (about the same as the northern latitude of Los Angeles), they could go ashore and enjoy the lustrous Chilean spring.

When the ship dropped anchor, the nursemaid pertly told Eliza that if she wanted a nurse for the rest of the voyage, she could hire one. Because she herself, the girl said, was going to marry the steward there and then. When they sailed for San Francisco, she would go as stewardess on the ship. Eliza still disapproved, but there was nothing she could do. The girl and the steward got married. Eliza set about finding a better nursemaid.

This proved easier than she had expected. During the voyage she had won the respect and liking of the Englishmen who had boarded the ship at Catarina. Those who lived in Valparaiso introduced her to their families and to other members of the English-speaking colony. The domestic workers in their households were nearly all Chilean, and many of them had picked up a fair knowledge of the English language. With the help of her new friends and their native employees, Eliza found a nursemaid. This time she took care not to hire a flighty teenager; instead, the new nurse was a mature woman who had already proved herself dependable.

Wanting no trouble with Captain Windsor, Eliza told him that she expected to bring a Chilean nurse aboard the ship. Captain Windsor said, "Very well," or words to that effect. The American consul was out of town, but Eliza asked the vice-consul, Mr. Samuels, if the nurse would need a passport or any other papers before starting the voyage. Mr. Samuels said no. In Chile, he told her, passports were required only of men.

Names of men who wanted to leave the country were made public, so if they had any unpaid debts, their creditors could take steps to detain them until the debts were paid. But in those days, in Chile and in many other countries, women had no debts. They could not buy anything on credit unless some man—father, husband, lover— made himself responsible for the bill. So Chilean women left the country without passports.

The day before the ship was to sail, Eliza brought the new nurse aboard. The nurse set about getting acquainted with her little charges.

The next morning, the captain summoned the passengers on deck and had them answer to a roll call. When they had answered, he pointed to the Chilean woman and loudly asked who she might be. Eliza replied that she was the new nursemaid.

"Have you a passport for her?" he demanded.

Eliza shook her head. She explained that Mr. Samuels had told her the nurse needed no passport.

The captain shouted that the woman did need a passport and he would be subject to serious penalties if he let her sail without one. He ordered the first mate to take her ashore in one of the ship's boats.

Eliza exclaimed in dismay. She said if Mr. Samuels had been mistaken, she would go ashore and try, at least, to get some official paper giving the captain permission to let the nurse stay on board. She went to her stateroom, put on her bonnet and shawl, and came back on deck. Here, to her immense relief, she met one of the Englishmen who had boarded the ship at Catarina. A lieutenant in the British navy, he had now joined his own vessel but had come aboard with several other Englishmen to say good-bye to the men who were going on to California. He asked Eliza why she was dressed as if to go ashore. When she told him, he exclaimed in surprise, "Chilean women don't need passports!" and added that he would explain this to the captain.

He crossed the deck to where the captain was standing. A moment later, Eliza heard a thunder of oaths from the captain. The Englishman turned and came back to her.

Captain Windsor, he told her, would listen to nothing he said. The woman did not need a passport, but since Windsor was so ill-informed as to think she did, the lieutenant offered to go with Eliza to the consul's office.

Like many other ports at that time, Valparaiso had no wharfs reaching into deep water. Seagoing vessels anchored offshore. Passengers and visitors went from ship to shore in small boats. Eliza and her escort went ashore in the boat he and the other Englishmen had hired to bring them to the ship, and Windsor made the nurse go with them. When they reached the breakwater on the beach, Eliza's friend told the boatmen to wait.

At the consul's office, Mr. Samuels gave them a note, which he told them to take to a Chilean official called the *intendente*. This official received them courteously, read the note, and in fluent English told Eliza the captain was strangely ill-informed. However, he handed the note to the proper functionary and procured the paper she wanted. Eliza thanked him and paid the fee. The price was higher than she had expected, and when she had paid it, she had nothing left in her purse but a Chilean coin worth about an American quarter. But she had the paper, and this was what mattered.

When they returned to their rowboat, the boatmen told them the ship had moved around to the other side of the promontory, where the tide must have seemed more favorable. The men moved the row-boat around the point. From here Eliza could look out to the open sea.

And there, already halfway below the horizon, she saw the *Angelique,* on her way to San Francisco. Miss Sampson and Eliza's two children were on board.

Now she understood what Captain Windsor had done. He was not ill-informed. He knew the Chilean woman did not need a passport. He had sent Eliza on this fake errand because he wanted to leave her behind. She had shamed him by making him stop at Catarina, and now he was taking his revenge. The ship was out to sea, carrying her children and her friend to San Francisco, and San Francisco was six thousand miles away.

What she was going to do now, the captain did not know, nor did he care. He was leaving her alone in a strange city, where most of the people spoke a strange language. She had no money with her but the single coin left after she had paid the *intendente*'s fee, not a garment except the clothes she was wearing. This did not trouble Captain Windsor. He was rid of her. Whether or not she ever saw her children again was no worry of his.

15

Eliza did not faint. But for several minutes she sat staring at the ship, her mind not believing what she saw. She heard the voices of her English friends, and the voices of the boatmen speaking Spanish; but whether English or Spanish, the words were nothing but a meaningless medley. Eliza herself was silent. She simply sat there in the boat, numb with shock.

The *Angelique* was sailing in a fair wind. This small boat could not overtake her. The boatmen started back to shore. When they came to the beach, the English lieutenant gave Eliza a strong supporting arm, and somehow she managed to mount the stone embankment that stood between the city and the sea. The movement began to rouse her senses. As she stood there, out of sight of the ship that was taking her children away from her, she began to understand what her companions were saying.

They were trying to give her hope. They were telling her, over and over, that Captain Windsor could not be serious in a scheme to take the children to San Francisco without their mother. He was playing a joke on her. A bad joke, a cruel joke, but surely he meant only to frighten her. He would go out of sight and stay out of sight, maybe until tomorrow or the next day. Then he would come back, have an ugly laugh at her expense, and take her aboard the ship again. This must be all he meant to do. Now wasn't that likely?

Eliza's mind was clearing. This was not in the least likely, and she knew it. These men were doing their best to encourage her. They wanted her to believe what they were saying; they wanted to believe it themselves. But the more they tried, the more hollow the sound of their words became. She could feel their forced cheerfulness, their efforts to persuade themselves as well as her.

The Chilean woman was wringing her hands. Her clothing and her other possessions were aboard the *Angelique,* and she was standing there destitute. But at least she was in her home city, and she had friends who could help her until she found work. Her situation was by no means as desperate as Eliza's, but she was an unhappy woman as she started back to her former home.

Eliza had nowhere to go. All she wanted was to follow her children. But how could she? When would another California-bound ship come into port? When such a ship did arrive, who would pay her fare to San Francisco? In the meantime, how could she live? And where? The lieutenant could not offer her lodging on a British man-of-war. As it all spun through her head together, she was startled to hear a voice calling her name.

Turning, she saw an elderly gentleman, one of the English residents of Valparaiso who had boarded the *Angelique* at Catarina. Astonished to see Eliza, who he thought had sailed today, he asked if something had gone wrong.

Eliza still could hardly speak, but the lieutenant told him what had happened. Like a father, the elderly man took Eliza's hand in his, drew it gently into the bend of his elbow, and told her she must come with him to see the British consul. The American consul, he reminded her, was out of town, and Mr. Samuels was only acting in his place. But he said he knew the British consul well and knew him to be a man who would give her all the help in his power.

His warmth and sympathy released the terrible tensions that had gripped Eliza ever since the moment she had caught sight of the ship sailing away. She burst into tears. Her friends, knowing the tears were a blessed relief, let her sob until the sobs wore themselves out. When she wiped her eyes and grew calmer, the lieutenant returned to his ship and the older man walked with her to the consulate.

The British consul proved to be as warmhearted as her escort had said he was. Besides offering sympathy, he gave Eliza practical help. He advanced her money for her most pressing needs. He gave her the address of a quiet hotel where she could live while she stayed in Valparaiso. He assured her that though she was in a foreign city, his countrymen and her own would not let her suffer for lack of anything they could provide.

The fatherly Englishman went with her to the hotel. When he

had made sure she had a comfortable room he left her, promising to call again.

One of the loneliest places in the world is a hotel room in a strange town. Eliza walked back and forth across the floor, thinking of her children aboard the *Angelique,* on their way to San Francisco without her. Writing later, she described her anguish.

How were they faring? I knew there were feeling hearts on board that vessel in the bosoms of both men and women, and I knew that, above all, my excellent friend Miss Sampson would devote to them the whole of her little strength; but she was an invalid, requiring care herself. And how could I suppose that a tender and feeble child who had, most of his life, had one person devoted to him, and often two, could receive from her the attention necessary to his health and comfort?

What Eddie's illness was, we do not know. In those days, medical science was fragmentary, and perhaps Eliza herself did not know. When she wrote her memoirs Eddie was no longer living. She continued:

I believe I have never suffered in my own person an injury which remains at this hour unforgiven; but I cannot find in my soul grace to forgive the cruelty which, I fully believe, caused my dear son days and weeks of agony. I cannot forget the paroxysms which brought great drops of sweat upon his brow, and blanched the thin cheeks, and whitened the quivering lips so often.

As for Captain Windsor, she added, "Though I cannot forgive, I can almost pity the wretch."

But as Eliza had just learned how bad a bad man can be, now she was about to learn how good the good people can be. She heard a knock at her door.

The caller was the Reverend Mr. Armstrong, a British clergyman who served the English-speaking colony in Valparaiso. Or the caller may have been a messenger Mr. Armstrong had sent; Eliza's narrative does not make this clear. At any rate, Eliza had been in her lonely room about an hour, and Mr. Armstrong's word was that she was not to stay here an hour longer.

News of what had been done to her had flashed through the colony. Everywhere it was told, the story had roused pity and rage in the people who heard it. They could not ease the pain of her suspense, but they were going to help her as much as they could.

Eliza was to come directly to Mr. Armstrong's home. As long as she stayed in Valparaiso she would be a guest of his family.

She accepted gladly. By the time she reached the Armstrong home,

103

visitors were arriving with packages in their hands. They said they had heard that Mrs. Farnham had been left without a change of clothing. If she could wear this dress, this petticoat, this pair of gloves . . . ? Eliza wrote later, "By noon of the next day I was furnished with a wardrobe bountiful enough to have supplied me for a six months' voyage."

Ships on their way to California were frequent callers at Valparaiso, but most of them had only masculine gold seekers on board, and the captains would not take a woman traveling alone. Eliza had to wait weeks for a vessel that had women passengers. The weeks were long and hard. But at last her friends reported such a vessel. The American ship *Louis-Philippe,* from Baltimore, had come into port. She carried about thirty passengers, among them several married couples. The ship's captain, Mr. Brathane, would be glad to have Eliza with them. On November 9, 1849, exactly a month after the day she had watched the *Angelique* carrying her children away from her, she began her own journey northward to find them.

The *Louis-Philippe* was very unlike the *Angelique*. Captain Brathane was a cultured gentleman. The passengers were friendly. But still, to Eliza, the days were long and the nights were longer. And when they came near San Francisco, she met another hard blow. The Golden Gate was lost behind sheets of rain. The fog was so thick that the captain did not dare try to go into the bay.

San Francisco was in the midst of the coldest, rainiest, most miserable winter it had had within the memory of anybody alive. The native Californios were saying the Forty-niners must have brought their own climate with them, and why hadn't they stayed at home? The Forty-niners, wet and shivering, were wishing they had done just that. But they were here, and they could not go home, no matter how much they might want to. In the bay were three hundred vessels, rocking helplessly at anchor. Their crews had run off to the gold country, and the ships could not get out. At the same time, thirteen more vessels— the *Louis-Philippe* and twelve others—were waiting outside the bay because the fog continued so heavy that they could not get in.

Then, late in the afternoon of Sunday, December 23, the wind blew the clouds away and the sun broke through. Captains, crews, and passengers of the thirteen ships took heart. Now their dreary time of waiting was over. Tomorrow would be Christmas Eve. Tomorrow they would go into port, and they would celebrate Christmas Day on shore.

They rejoiced too soon. Before daybreak on Christmas Eve, they were wakened by shouts from the crews. San Francisco was on fire.

On Kearny Street stood a gambling resort called Denison's Exchange. (It probably belonged to the Lawrence Denison who had been a passenger on the *Falcon*'s first voyage from New Orleans to the isthmus.) Some gambling man had dropped a smoldering cigar or a match still glowing at the tip. Like most other "buildings" on Kearny Street, Denison's was merely a flimsy wooden frame, curtained on the inside with cloth of gaudy colors, and the roof covered with tar to keep out the rain. The fire had ripped through the walls, and the flames were spreading.

This was the first of the great fires that were to devastate San Francisco six times in eighteen months. Eliza could not foresee this, but even if she could have, she would probably not have given much thought to the fires ahead. This fire was here and now, and *where were her children?*

By the next morning, Christmas Day, most of the fire had been put out, but the fog had closed in again. The ships outside the Golden Gate had to stay there two days more.

In body and spirit, Eliza was strong. She lived through the fire and the days after it without breaking. And at last, on December 27, though the rain was falling again, the fog cleared enough for the ships outside the Gate to pass through. They came in, all thirteen of them. In the early winter twilight, the *Louis-Philippe* made her way among the deserted vessels and dropped anchor off North Beach. Through the mist and the gathering dark, Eliza could see nothing but a few blurry lights shining from vessels whose crews were still on duty. Her journey from New York had lasted from May to December–233 days.

It is not likely that Eliza slept much that night. But in the morning, as early as he could, Captain Brathane ascertained that one of the ships in the bay was the *Angelique*. Though the *Angelique* had left Valparaiso a month before the *Louis-Philippe,* she had taken longer to make the voyage and had reached San Francisco only two weeks before.

The rain was still pouring. Eliza did not care. With the captain's aid, shortly after noon that day she set out in a well-manned boat and was taken to the *Angelique.*

To her nearly speechless delight, she found Miss Sampson and the two little boys still on board. Miss Sampson had simply refused to leave the ship until the children's mother came to claim them.

Eliza listened breathlessly as they talked about their voyage. Miss Sampson told her that several of the other passengers, both men and women, had offered to help her with the children. Shocked by Captain Windsor's conduct, they had done all they could to ease the lonely bewilderment they knew the children would feel as they missed their mother.

However, in spite of her joy at being with them again, she was not entirely happy. The older boy, Charlie, was rosy and full of mischief. But little Eddie was thinner, paler, weaker than ever. Separation from his mother had been hard on him. Eliza must have realized by this time that he had not much longer to live.

Eliza stayed in San Francisco six weeks. They were wretched weeks. The wind screamed all day and night, and the rain fell in nearly ceaseless torrents. Half the town had gone down in the fire on Christmas Eve, and what was left stood shakily in a sea of mud.

Eliza had hoped to get some restitution from Captain Windsor. But she soon found that she had little or no chance of doing so. She could not prove that he had not told her the time he expected to sail. Neither could she prove that this experience had caused the worsening of Eddie's health. Convinced that her situation was hopeless, she set about accomplishing the purpose that had brought her to California: to change the ranch from an unused piece of land into an organized business.

While few seagoing vessels could get crews to take them on the long voyage home, the small coastal boats had less trouble. Now in winter the hills were buried in snow, and in most of the placer country, men could not dig gold. They were glad to work on these short voyages and earn their grubstakes for the time when the snow would melt. With Miss Sampson and the boys, Eliza took a boat down to the settlement of Santa Cruz, two miles from the ranch. They reached the ranch on Washington's birthday, 1850.

Tom had died while the property was still almost wholly undeveloped. With her usual energy, Eliza went to work. After six years she had turned the ranch into a thriving enterprise. By this time, little Eddie was gone. Eliza sold the place at a good profit, and with Charlie— now a lad in his teens—she went back to New York.

But not to rest. Working quietly this time, without public attention, she raised enough money to bring two parties of self-respecting but penniless young women to California. She saw them settled there, either as married women with homes of their own or in good employment where they earned the high California wages. She hoped to bring still more, when the outbreak of the Civil War put an end to her plan.

Eliza volunteered as a nurse in an army hospital. Army hospitals then were not the well-organized and supervised places they are today. It is said that during that war, more men in the hospitals died of infection than of battle wounds. Apparently Eliza caught one of these contagious ailments. After a brief illness, on November 17, 1864, she died at the home of a friend in New York. She was forty-nine years old.

In those days, when newspapers had to be printed on expensive rag paper because the process of making paper out of wood pulp was not yet well developed, the papers were much smaller than they are today. But so great was the esteem Eliza had won that, when she died, the New York *Times* interrupted its coverage of the war to give nearly half a column to her life and works.

16

The first two waves of gold seekers came over the isthmus and around the Horn. The third wave came across the plains and the mountain passes.

There were several routes these overlanders might take. Whatever route they chose, they were choosing a journey hard almost past belief.

The overland trek was more toilsome than any other way of getting from the eastern side of the continent to the goldfields, but more Forty-niners took this way than the combined number of those who went over the isthmus and around the Horn. So many of them came overland that today the very word "Forty-niner" calls up a picture of a man driving a covered wagon.

One reason for this is that people who lived in the Mississippi Valley had to make a long and costly journey before they could reach the nearest seaport. If they went overland to California, they could start from where they were. Another reason—probably more important—is that even the most tightly packed vessel can hold only a limited number of travelers at a time. But the great plains had room for them all.

The plains did not have water enough for an unlimited number of thirsty folk, or grass enough for all the mules and oxen who would need it; but few amateur pioneers knew this before they left home. What they did know was that a man with a wagon was his own boss. He could set out from his own home and he did not have to wait for a vacant berth. Once he had packed his outfit, and the grass had appeared on the plains, he could start. And by thousands—men, women, and children—they started.

They suffered tortures. Many of them died on the way. But more of them got there.

Those who got there were men, women, and children. They were all sorts of people. Nobody had ever found any such thing as a typical Forty-niner of the overland trails. In their natures and careers, they had only one detail in common: When they set out for California, they kept going until they got there or they died trying.

In the spring of 1848, before the Gold Rush had begun, the San Francisco *Star* brought out a special edition, intended for Americans who were looking toward the Pacific coast as a place to live. This issue of the *Star* had much to say about the lures of California. But along with these enticements, the paper brought some sober counsel from the young editor, Edward Kemble.

Kemble said he wanted his countrymen to come to California. But he urged them, if they traveled by land, to take the "old road." He told them: Try no shortcuts, listen to nobody who talks about an easier trail. The old road had been proved. Other routes had been tried, and sometimes praised, but the old road was the best.

When Edward Kemble wrote these lines in 1848, he did not know that in another year, every trail on the plains, old and new, would be clogged by a traffic jam—the oxen and pack mules and wagons of the Forty-niners. But his advice was sound. The "old road" was still the road most likely to lead a traveler safely into the gold country.

And what was this road he was writing about?

The "old road" was a trail opened seven years before (in 1841) by a group of pioneers. They had nothing in their favor but their courage and their almost superhuman will to live. These people traveled from Missouri to California (nearly two thousand miles) by a journey that lasted nearly six months. Not one of them had ever been to California. They crossed mountains and deserts they had never seen or heard of. They had no maps except two or three drawings some artist had made up, mostly out of his head. They did not know where California was. They knew only that if they kept moving west, west, west (and if they stayed alive), some day they would get there.

This unbeatable army consisted of thirty-one men and a teen-aged mother who carried in her arms the littlest pioneer of them all.

These people were setting out for California because of the siren-song letters written by an American already there. His name was John Marsh.

When Tom Farnham made his first journey to California, one of the Americans he had met there was John Marsh. Like Thomas and Rachel Larkin, Marsh had talked of his hope that the Americans would gain control of California. He never changed his mind.

John Marsh was a strange character. His behavior of this week so often contradicted his behavior of last week, and both were so different from what he was going to do next week, that he seemed like two or three men living in one body. He could be generous or stingy, wise or witless, sullen or engaging. He had some admirers, but few if any friends. Yet he had great talent for making other people do what he wanted them to do.

Born in Massachusetts, Marsh was a graduate of Harvard and a man of brilliant intellect. He was a loner, who liked to live apart from other people and make his own rules. He also had high ambitions to be rich and powerful.

He had had a spotty career. When he finished Harvard in 1823, his first ambition was to go on to a medical school. But his father, a man of stubborn views, said he could not afford to pack any more learning into that greedy head. He said it was time for his son John to settle down on the farm and work for a living.

John said he would work, but not on the rocky farm and not in rock-minded New England. He would go west. The army officers at Fort Snelling, in the present state of Minnesota (pretty far west in those days), wanted a teacher for their children. Not even waiting for the graduation exercises, John took the job. As he was still hoping to practice medicine, at Fort Snelling he used his free time to study textbooks from the library of the fort physician. With an experienced doctor as his guide, he made good progress.

Here in the West he was more at ease than he had ever been at home, and when he went back to New England to visit his parents, he felt out of place. Though still interested in medicine, he could no longer bear the prospect of spending more years at a strict eastern college. He returned to the frontier. Before long he was keeping a store at Prairie du Chien, in the present state of Wisconsin.

One day in 1832, when he had been nine years on the frontier, his customers brought news of the outbreak of an Indian war.

The war had begun with quarrels between white settlers and the Indians of the Sauk and Fox tribes, led by their chief, Black Hawk. When the Indians attacked the settlers, the United States Army sent troops to the settlers' defense. Another Indian tribe, the Sioux, entered the war on the side of the settlers. Marsh began selling guns to the Sauk and Fox warriors, to be used against the Sioux.

As the Sioux were fighting on the side of the American Army, this meant that Marsh was selling arms to enemies of the United States. It looked mighty like treason. A federal warrant was issued for his arrest.

Nobody knows why such an intelligent man committed such a doltish crime. But it was typical of the self-contradicting nature that he showed all his life. At any rate, he knew he was in trouble. It was time for him to move on. Joining a party of fur traders, in the spring of 1833 John Marsh headed farther west.

When he thought the federal agents had had time to forget about him, he came back—not to Prairie du Chien, this time, but to the busy frontier town of Independence, Missouri. Nine miles east of the present Kansas City (then called Westport Landing), Independence was the meeting place of the fur trappers and the outfitting point of the great trading caravans that went every year to Santa Fe. Here Marsh opened another store. He was doing well when he learned that the federal men were still after him. On June 15, 1835, he headed west again, this time for good. He was now thirty-six years old.

The Santa Fe traders had started their yearly trek only a few weeks before. Marsh caught up with them. He went with the traders to Santa Fe, then down to Chihuahua, Mexico. After many adventures he found himself in the Mexican state of Sonora, at the southern edge of California. He decided to see what California was like.

Early in the year 1836 he went to Los Angeles. Here he told the authorities he was a doctor, and they gave him permission to practice medicine. He went on to the nearly all-American village of Yerba Buena and got a job with a fellow American, Jacob Leese. As only Mexican citizens could own land in California, Marsh became a citizen, bought land, and started a ranch. This was in the spring of 1838. His property lay at the foot of Mount Diablo, about thirty miles east of the modern city of Oakland.

But his funds were running low. To stock his ranch, he became "Doctor" Marsh to the people on ranches nearby and made them pay for his calls with breeding cows. (This was not quite as heartless as it sounds. He did know more about treating the sick than any other man within reach.)

Though he had technically become a Mexican, his change was on paper only. He was still a Yankee with Yankee ideas. He realized how loose was the Mexican hold on California, and he observed that the few Americans living there were doing most of the business of the country. Marsh knew what had happened in Texas, where the

111

American settlers had led a revolt against Mexico, and which was now a republic with Sam Houston as president. Since he did not dare go back to the United States, Marsh asked himself, Why not bring the United States to California? Why not persuade a lot of Yankees to settle here and make this country their own? If they should want to elect John Marsh president of their new republic, he would accept the honor.

The change of government, he was sure, would not be too difficult. Most of the native Californios got along well with the Yanquis. Tom Farnham's article about the Isaac Graham affair had been highly exaggerated, and few of the Californios confused Graham and his drunken cronies with the energetic ranchers and traders from the States. In short, most of the Californios liked the Yanquis, and few of them liked the governors who were sent up from Mexico to rule over them. These governors came in with little or no knowledge of the country, and while some of them did the best they could, as a whole they were a blundering lot. The Californios resented them. Marsh suspected that if California should part from Mexico, most Californios would not mind.

By a little careful hint-dropping, he found that his views were shared by Mr. and Mrs. Larkin and other Americans in California. Whether or not any of these Americans had dreams of becoming president of a California republic, he seems not to have inquired; what he did make sure of was that they wanted California to separate from Mexico and belong to Americans. To further this aim, they wanted more Americans to settle here. Marsh had reached California in the spring of 1836; not long after his arrival, he and Larkin began a campaign of letter-writing.

They wrote to friends they had known in the States, telling them about the rich promise of the West Coast. They entrusted their letters to any fur trader or shipmaster who might have a chance to put them into a United States post office. Some of the letters were lost, of course, but a goodly number did reach the men they were addressed to.

Marsh's letters had more influence than Larkin's. This was not because Larkin was less eager or less determined. The reason was the difference in the natural endowments of the two men. Not only did Larkin lack the advantage of Marsh's Harvard education; even if he had had this, it would not have changed the fact that, though a highly intelligent man, Larkin had no talent for words. His letters were almost dull. He was a shrewd thinker and a zealous patriot, but he simply did not know how to put his thoughts into language that would stir up excitement.

112

John Marsh, on the other hand, was a writer of rare gifts. He wrote mostly to old acquaintances on the Missouri frontier, men he had met while he was running his store in Independence. Only two beaten tracks led westward from the States—the trading route to Santa Fe and the northwesterly track that would later be called the Oregon Trail. Both of these started from Independence. Marsh thought the people on the Missouri frontier, who already knew something about these routes, would be those most likely to be persuaded to blaze the new trail to California. However, he realized that mighty few people in Missouri knew where California was. Even fewer knew how they could get there.

Marsh's problem was that he did not know either. When he had run away from the federal men, he had had no particular destination in mind; he had wandered westward by rambling, spur-of-the-moment routes, often backtracking, stopping here and there and then deciding which way to turn next. If he was going to bring settlers into the West, he knew he had better be more definite than this.

He asked questions of all the frontiersmen he could find. He listened closely to what they said. After putting together all they could tell him, he outlined what he hoped would be a workable guide.

With modern place names added for clarity, his directions went like this:

At the Missouri frontier, turn northwest. Follow the track to Oregon as far as Fort Hall (southeast Idaho). Find the Portneuf River (a little stream south of Fort Hall). Cross the river and go a few miles southeast to the Bear River. Follow the Bear River south until it disappears in the desert (northern Utah). Now turn west and find the Humboldt River. (This river is in the present state of Nevada. When Marsh was writing his letters, it was called Mary's River, but the name was changed shortly afterward, so in this narrative it is called the Humboldt.) Follow this river until it disappears in the Humboldt Sink (a lake with no outlet, in western Nevada). From here go northwest to the Sierra Nevada mountain range.

He told them that in a pass through the Sierras, they would find a stream flowing south. He said this stream emptied into the San Joaquin River, and the second river would lead them into the San Joaquin Valley. In this valley they would sight a lone mountain, Mount Diablo. At the foot of the mountain, on the east side, they would find his ranch.

Marsh had never laid eyes on most of the country through which he was telling his readers to travel. As he had never made the journey himself, he could have formed only a shadowy notion of what he was asking them to achieve. He did not warn them—probably he did not know—that the country they would have to cross included some of the cruelest stretches of land in the world. If Marsh did not know this, his former neighbors in Missouri certainly could not guess it. But as Marsh had expected, the people on the Missouri frontier were receptive readers. They studied his letters eagerly and passed them on to their hometown papers. Other papers reprinted them. The letters were clear, vivid, convincing. To readers along the frontier, California became a shining far country, a land of dreams. Years before Jim Marshall found gold, lively young folk in Missouri were talking about California and wishing they could go there.

One of the spellbound readers of John Marsh's letters was a young man named John Bidwell.

Born in New York State, as a boy John Bidwell had been taken to western Ohio by his parents. They gave him a good education, and in 1839, when he was twenty years old, he began teaching in a country school near Fort Leavenworth, in what was then called Kansas Territory.

Here he met a French-Canadian fur trader named Robidou, who with his five brothers owned a trading post on the river. In his memoirs, Bidwell does not give the first name of the brother he talked to, and historians do not agree on which one it was. Nor do they agree on how the family name should be spelled. Anyway, this fur trader had at one time been engaged in the wagon trade between Independence and Santa Fe. Once he had gone on to California with the traders who brought mules to Santa Fe from Los Angeles. When he came back to Independence, Robidou told such glowing tales of California that John Bidwell and some friends of his were sorely tempted to start for there right away. Then the papers began printing those letters from John Marsh, telling the same story. Bidwell and his friends could wait no longer.

Led by John Bidwell, in 1840 they formed what they called the Western Emigration Society. They drew up a contract that every would-be member had to sign before he could join. Each signer promised to arrange for his own means of travel. He promised to bring his own traveling outfit and enough food to last him until the emigrant train reached buffalo country. He also pledged himself to bring no "spiritous liquors" except for medicinal use. He agreed that on or before May 9, 1841, he would report, equipped and ready to start, at a meeting place called Sapling Grove. This was on the Santa Fe Trail, about nine miles west of the line dividing Missouri from Kansas Territory.

The society members sent copies of their contract to the newspapers. They chose three men to serve as a "committee of correspondence" and answer queries that might come in.

Before a month had passed, the committee of correspondence had received five hundred letters full of questions. Just what should a man include in his outfit? How many animals would be needed to draw covered wagons of various weights? Were mules or oxen the better choice? Could a married man bring his wife? What about children? And so on, and on, and on. The letters came not only from all parts of Missouri but also from Illinois and Kentucky, Arkansas and Louisiana. The committee men found themselves smothering under the storm of paper, and they cried out for help.

But though the members were elated at this surge of interest, their matter-of-fact elders did not like it at all. The leaders of the emigrating group were the most vigorous and enterprising young men of their communities. If they stayed at home, they would prosper and become good customers. They would marry; they would want homes built and wells dug and furniture installed; they would buy supplies for their families; they would give employment to clerks, farmhands, teachers, dressmakers, all sorts of worthy folk. The older solid citizens did not want them drained away.

These citizens gave dire warnings of the distances, the dangers, the uncertainties of this journey. Few of the youngsters would listen. Those old men had never been to California, had they? They didn't know what they were talking about.

And then, just when the excitement was highest, one of the "old men" received a copy of the newspaper containing that anti-California tirade by Tom Farnham.

The "old men" seized upon it. They sent copies of Tom's article to papers in several towns. Now they had a basis for all their warnings. Here was an alarm sounded by a man who *had* been there. He did know what he was talking about, and he was saying, "Beware!" Now would these hotheads change their plans?

Many of them did. The more cautious of the would-be emigrants gave up the whole western idea. Others thought it over and said if they went west at all, they would go to Oregon. The trail to the Northwest, trodden by Indians for hundreds of years, was known to frontiersmen. Already, in the valley of the Willamette River, in the present state of Oregon, there was a small but thriving settlement of farmers, most of them retired employees of the Hudson's Bay Company. Society members who still wanted to go west, but were now afraid of California, said they would rather join this community and be safe.

Some of these would have backed out anyway. In every enterprise there are partakers who start with a rush of enthusiasm and then cool down. Probably some signers of the contract had lost interest before Tom Farnham's warning appeared. But there can be no doubt that the Farnham article did frighten away many who otherwise would have started for the glittering land of John Marsh.

But Bidwell and his stubborn friends did not change their plans. They remembered that John Marsh was not a brief-time visitor in California but a man who had lived there for years. He owned a ranch and nobody was troubling him. His letters had told about other foreigners in California, such as Thomas Larkin and John Cooper, and Marsh's first employer there, Jacob Leese, and the Englishman W.E.P. Hartnell—men who were successful in business and well liked. They proved it could be done. The Western Emigration Society was shrunken but not destroyed. And as usually happens in such cases, the members who kept to their purpose were more determined than ever.

They had already written to Marsh telling him they were preparing for the California journey and would start in May, 1841. Like Marsh and Larkin, they had entrusted their letters to trappers, hunters, traders, sea captains, and anybody else who might deliver them. They were sure some of the letters must have reached him, so he knew when to expect their party at his ranch. Now they waited impatiently for the spring grass to grow on the plains. While they waited, Bidwell was still supporting himself by teaching school. He boarded with the family of a man named Elam Brown.

A kindly fellow who wanted to help, Elam Brown gave Bidwell a map that was supposed to show the country on and near the Pacific coast. Bidwell jubilantly showed the map to his friends. They rummaged in the stores and turned up several more maps. Apparently these maps had been based on descriptions given by returning trappers and traders who had brought their furs—and their tall tales—to Independence. The maps resembled each other but they were not just alike. When the tale-teller had been vague, or when different men had brought different reports, the artist had used his fancy to finish the picture. Bidwell and his friends had to compare the maps and judge for themselves.

All the maps pictured an enormous lake—about 400 miles across—

somewhere near what is now called the Great Salt Lake. Actually, the Great Salt Lake is 80 miles long and 35 miles wide. But though its size was vastly overdrawn, there *is* a lake in this region. The artists had not invented the lake, but in drawing the country west of it they had strayed off into fantasy. Not knowing this, the young men diligently studied their designs.

They found a river—on some maps two rivers—flowing out of the lake westward into the sea. They did not find any mountains between the lake and the coast. But as John Marsh had told them about the Sierra Nevadas, they concluded that the range must have wide openings to let those rivers flow through. They thought one of them must be the river that Marsh had said would lead them into the valley where they would find his ranch.

The helpful Mr. Brown advised them to take along tools for making canoes. Then, he said, if the country west of the mighty lake should prove too rough for their wagons, they could leave the wagons behind and go from the lake to the coast by water. They dutifully packed the tools, so they could paddle their canoes across the present states of Utah and Nevada.

At last spring came. The grass began to grow. As the month of May drew near, the lookouts brought word that the grass was tall enough and thick enough to provide pasturage for all the mules and oxen their party would need to take with them.

Members of the Emigration Society began to gather at Sapling Grove. Every day, two or three wagons came in. Most of the emigrants were single men, but among them were several families with children. Most of the families, and a few of the single men, belonged to the group who had given up the idea of California and were planning to go instead to Oregon by the trail already known. Most of the single men, however, intended pushing their way to California. Also there was a family whose home up to now had been in Missouri. They had lived in Jackson County, famous as the location of the bumptious town of Independence. The family name was Kelsey. Unlike the other family groups, the Kelseys were California bound.

There were three Kelsey brothers, Samuel, Andrew, and Benjamin; Samuel's wife and their five children; Benjamin's wife, Nancy Brown Kelsey, who was to have her eighteenth birthday on the way to California; and baby Nan, about a year old. Samuel and his family were to leave the California-bound party to go to Oregon instead; but Andrew, Ben, and Nancy, with baby Nan, were to go to California. Ben and Nancy and their baby traveled in a stout covered wagon

117

drawn by oxen. They were healthy, full of dash and drive, and eager to get started for that fabled country in the West.

Nobody knows how many sane and sober people had warned Nancy Kelsey that she should not try to make this reckless journey. Nobody knows how many of these sane and sober people had told Ben it would be a crime to take a woman and child into the unknown wilds. But Nancy and Ben wanted to go to California, they wanted to go there together, and they were not scared. Son and daughter of the frontier, they were strong, self-reliant, and as sturdy in character as in body. When they made up their minds to do something, they did it. When they decided to go to California, they asked nobody's permission; they went. And while they had not decided to make history—there is no evidence that any such thought ever occurred to them—they did this too.

Nancy was born in Barren County, Kentucky. When she was three years old, her family moved to Missouri. Nancy and the Kelsey brothers all grew up in or near the town of Independence.

Rough, lusty, boisterous, Independence had a vigor that shared itself with every man, woman, and child who came there. In the spring, the children could watch—and listen to—the prairie traders as they packed their huge covered wagons with the goods they would carry across the plains to Santa Fe. In the fall, the children could watch these men returning, many of them now driving mules from the California ranches. The children could talk with the trappers and mountain men, dressed in their buckskin clothes and flaunting long, wavy hair and beards that sometimes grew down to their belts. All these men brought wondrous tales of the country farther west. It is no wonder that when Ben and Nancy and Ben's brothers heard about the letters from John Marsh, they wanted to start for California. It is not strange that they were part of the company at Sapling Grove. It would have been strange if they had not been there.

Altogether, nearly seventy persons met at Sapling Grove in that month of May, 1841. They organized and elected a president. He was a paunchy fellow about thirty-five years old named John Bartleson. Years later, when John Bidwell wrote his memoirs, he confessed that they had not elected Bartleson because they thought him the best n. for the office but because he was the leader of a party of eight or ten men, and Bartleson said they would not go along unless he could be top man. He could see to it that his party did as they were told, because he was the owner of their wagon.

Bartleson had been one of the first settlers in Independence when the town was founded fourteen years before, in 1827. He had bought land, and traded, and he was now a man of means, but he intended to get richer. For this journey he had provided himself with a large wagon and plenty of oxen to draw it. The other men of his group, younger and less well-to-do, had bought "shares" in his outfit, for the privilege of having the wagon carry their possessions. If Bartleson should decide to stay at home, they would have no way to travel.

So Bidwell and the rest yielded when Bartleson insisted that he be made president. They knew they had a perilous journey ahead of them, and the larger their party was, the stronger it would be.

Now they were ready to start. Or, they asked each other, were they truly ready? Courageous as they were, they could not help feeling shaky as they faced the fact that not one of them knew the region they were about to cross.

Then, all unforeseen, came a stupendous blast of good fortune.

17

A stranger rode into the camp at Sapling Grove. He said he had been sent by a man named Thomas Fitzpatrick. Maybe they had heard of this man?

Yes, they had heard of him! Thomas Fitzpatrick was one of the most famous scouts of the western trails. He did not know everything about the West—nobody could know that much—but there were few if any men who knew more than he did. Now he had sent this messenger to offer his skill and experience to the greenhorns brought together by John Marsh.

The messenger explained. A group of Jesuit priests, on their way to the Oregon Country to teach the Flathead Indians, had engaged Fitzpatrick as their guide. But in their group were only eleven men, not enough to go safely through such a wild region. Before they left St. Louis, they had heard of two parties that were expected to go from Missouri to Oregon this summer. One of these was to be made up of trappers employed by John Jacob Astor's American Fur Company. The other, they had been told, would be an exploring expedition sent out by the War Department. This party was to be led by a well-known French pathfinder named Jean-Nicolas Nicollet.

The priests had planned to travel with one of these groups. But the trappers' journey had been postponed. As for the exploring expedition, nobody in this neighborhood seemed to know anything about it. A year or two earlier, the Frenchman, Nicollet, had been commissioned by the War Department to map the country between the upper reaches of the Mississippi and Missouri rivers. He had done this. But the expedition to Oregon—if it had ever been planned—seemed to have been canceled. Now the priests found themselves at the starting point of the trail, ready to start but not able to do so. When they learned that a large westbound party was camped nearby, it had seemed like the intervention of Providence.

The messenger said if the emigrant party would wait a day or two, the missionaries would join them. John Bidwell, with Ben and Nancy Kelsey and most of the others, agreed that being led by such a guide as Fitzpatrick was well worth a few days' patience. John Bartleson, however, said he wanted to get going right now. He did not want to wait for any slowpoke missionaries. One of Bartleson's companions, a man who gave his name as Talbot H. Green, also insisted that they start now.

Talbot H. Green had good reason for urging haste. Bartleson did not know it, but Green's right name was Paul Geddes, and in his baggage was a pack of gold and silver coins he had stolen from a bank in Philadelphia. He was eager to get into the unknown country before the bank could trace him. (As it happened, he did get safely to California. He set himself up in business with his plunder and became a prominent citizen of San Francisco. But alas for Talbot Green, the Gold Rush brought in thousands of new people, some of whom came from Philadelphia. In the spring of 1851, ten years after he had joined the emigrant train, he was recognized by some old acquaintances who knew his record. He hurried away from California and spent the rest of his life as a roaming fugitive.)

Bartleson had not stolen anything and had no special reason to be in a hurry, but he liked to make his voice heard on all occasions. With Green and his other cronies, Bartleson set out on May 9. He airily said the others would have to catch up with him later, if they could.

Bidwell and the Kelseys, and the other more sober-minded emigrants, told the messenger they would wait for Fitzpatrick and the missionaries. Writing in later years, Bidwell said this decision had proved to be a choice between life and death, not only for those who waited for the guide but for those who had been in too much of a hurry to wait. The group who waited for Fitzpatrick, once they started, had moved faster than the men with Bartleson and had soon caught up with their hasty companions. This was not to be the last of their troubles with Bartleson, but it did give the members of both groups a chance to learn from an expert guide. In his narrative, Bidwell said frankly that without what they all learned from Fitzpatrick, none of them would have lived to reach California.

Fitzpatrick was a striking figure. Forty-two years old, he had been a rover among the mountains and deserts for most of his life. He was lean and tough, darkly tanned. When he pulled off his hat to let the wind cool his head, onlookers were often startled to see that, in contrast to his leathery face, his hair was white. If he had used his left hand to take off his hat, they would notice that the hand, though he used it deftly, had been mutilated.

His hair was whitened when he had been tracked through a forest day and night for many weeks by a party of Blackfeet Indians. The Blackfeet tribe, always at war with white men, had tried to kill him and were still trying. One of a group of trappers camped in the present state of Wyoming, Fitzpatrick had gone to meet a pack train bringing supplies. When the pack train reached the camp, and the men reported that Fitzpatrick had set out for camp ahead of them and should have been here by now, his friends were frightened for his safety. They sent rescuers to look for him.

After a long search the rescuers found Fitzpatrick lying in a helpless huddle on the ground, so nearly dead from hunger and exhaustion that he could not stand without help. Though he was just past his thirtieth birthday, his hair was turning white.

Usually, however, Fitzpatrick was able to make friends with Indians. They called him Broken Hand. Early in his trail-blazing days, a rifle in his left hand had exploded, blowing off one finger and part of another and breaking several bones. But his fellow frontiersmen said Fitz could do more with a hand and a half than most men could do with two hands whole. They gave him the respect he deserved.

At Sapling Grove, he began by telling the emigrants what lay ahead. If any of them were going to drop out, he wanted them to do it now.

At this time, the so-called "Oregon Country" included the present states of Washington and Oregon, most of Idaho, and parts of Montana and Wyoming. Fitzpatrick knew the country and he knew the trail that led there. He told them frankly that they would have a rough journey. But, he said, if they would do what he ordered, they would have a good chance of reaching the trail's end without mishap. Any man—or any woman—who did not obey him exactly would find the journey dangerous and might not reach the trail's end at all.

They promised to heed everything he said. Those who were still frightened by Tom Farnham's anti-California outburst told Fitzpatrick they would follow him all the way to Oregon. One of those who had begun to be doubtful about California was Samuel Kelsey. Concerned for his wife and five children, he thought a journey to Oregon would be easier and safer for them all. But Bidwell, along with Ben and Andrew Kelsey and others, told Fitzpatrick they would go with him only as far as Fort Hall. This was where Marsh's instructions had said they were to turn southwest, toward California. They would change their minds, Fitzpatrick told them, when they had more understanding of what they would be getting into.

Fitzpatrick knew all about greenhorns on the trail. He knew how much they thought they knew, and how half-learned they really were. He knew how often they ignored advice and then had to be rescued from trouble they had made for themselves. But guiding greenhorns was his business, and he was a hardy soul. With no qualms, he set about his work. Under his direction, they began their journey. It was now May 19, 1841.

On their fourth day out, a group of six men, well equipped with wagons and work animals, caught up with them. The leader of this group was Joseph Ballinger Chiles (pronounced to rhyme with miles), who was to become an outstanding citizen of California. Several days later, May 26, while they were cooking supper around their campfires, a grave-faced gentleman in his sixties rode horseback into the camp, bringing his supplies on a pack horse. He proved to be the Reverend Joseph Williams, a Methodist clergyman on his way to join one of the missions of his church in Oregon. They made him welcome. The Jesuit leader, Reverend Pierre-Jean De Smet, invited him to have supper with his group. The next morning, Father De Smet gave Mr. Williams a slice of venison to start the day.

They all liked Father De Smet. He was forty years old, a learned man, chubby and pink-cheeked and cheerful. A native of Belgium, he had received much of his education in this country and was as much at home in the English language as in his native French. Mr. Williams, who kept a diary of his journey, wrote that Father De Smet was "very kind" to him and added, "He seems like a very fine man."

A few days after this, under Fitzpatrick's guidance, they caught up with Bartleson and his pals.

Mr. Williams was constantly being shocked by the shameless language of his guide, but he had to admire Fitzpatrick's competence in his work. Mr. Williams was himself in many ways a notable man. When he first heard of the party gathering at Sapling Grove, he was living in southeast Indiana. He announced that he had decided to go with them to Oregon. His friends and neighbors warned him that a man more than sixty years old could not endure such a journey. They urged that there were sinful people right here at home who needed his teaching as much as the Indians. They protested in vain. Stubbornly, Mr. Williams mounted his horse and rode across Indiana, Illinois, and Missouri to the rendezvous. When he got there, he found that the emigrants had already left.

Undaunted, he went after them. He rode alone. He followed the tracks of the wagon wheels. He cooked his meals outdoors and slept on the ground wherever he happened to find himself at nightfall. After joining the wagon train, he went with it all the way to Oregon. All that way, he kept his journal, and though he was probably the oldest person in the party, he never recorded that he was finding the journey too much for his strength.

Altogether in the train there were now about eighty persons. Sixty-nine of these—men, women, and children—made up the party brought together by the letters of John Marsh. The first group to leave the frontier of the United States with the express purpose of making their homes on the Pacific coast, whether Oregon or California, they were the vanguard of the Great Migration that came after them.

Fitzpatrick told them about the route they were going to take. This route, soon to be called the Oregon Trail, had long been traveled by Indians but was known to few white people other than the mountain men. Those who traveled this way went up the west bank of the Missouri River into the present state of Nebraska. They crossed Nebraska westward and went on to a trading post of John Jacob Astor's fur company, Fort William, in the present state of Wyoming. Here they usually paused to rest and buy supplies. Then they crossed Wyoming to South Pass, a mountain gap that leads travelers over the Great Divide.

West of the Great Divide the mountain men would go past the site of the present city of Pocatello, Idaho, to Fort Hall. This fort belonged to the Hudson's Bay Company, Astor's great rival in the fur business.

Over and over, when the words "Fort Hall" were spoken, Fitzpatrick told his followers that they must *not* follow John Marsh's directions and turn there toward California. If they said they would do so in spite of him, he shrugged and told them again that they would change their minds.

At any rate, they were on their way.

Fitzpatrick was a born leader. He spoke and acted with confident authority. With the skill of long experience, he organized these assorted people into a functional unit. They had quarrels, of course, and upsets, but he kept them safe and he kept them moving. Every day they were nearer the West Coast than they had been the day before.

They started early in the morning. They stopped at noon for a rest and stopped again, well before sundown, to cook their evening meal and make camp for the night. Fitzpatrick made them do their cooking in the daytime and douse the fires before dark. This was done so they would draw as little attention as possible from Indians. Most of the Indians hereabouts were not murder-minded, he said, but they were exceedingly covetous. They wanted the fine horses and mules and oxen these strangers brought with them, as well as their guns and supplies. And if the white men objected, the Indians were likely to shoot. The emigrants listened, and shivered, and doused the fires.

When they camped for the night, they turned the wagons into a corral for the animals. With ropes or chains, they linked the tongue of each wagon to the back of the one ahead, forming a hollow square, and picketed the animals inside. This protected the animals from thieves and kept them from wandering away and getting lost. The men took turns at guard duty.

For these first few weeks, as they moved up the Missouri River, the journey was almost like an outing. The prairie was green and starred with flowers. There was plenty of grass for the animals and plenty of game. They were going toward the point where the Platte River meets the Missouri, just south of the modern city of Omaha, Nebraska. Near this junction, about two weeks out of Sapling Grove, they had their first adventure.

The company had halted for one of their regular rest periods. A venturesome young fellow named Nicholas Dawson, ignoring Fitzpatrick's warning, rode his mule out of camp for a hunt.

At the campsite, men were cleaning their rifles, women cooking and mending, children playing games, when all of a sudden they heard screams of terror. Up rushed a man, half wild and nearly naked— their overbold comrade Dawson, scared almost out of his head. To the first man who laid hold of him, Dawson gasped that he had met a troop of Indians on the warpath. They had surrounded him, taken his mule and gun and hunting knife, and nearly killed him. There were at least a thousand of them and they were riding this way.

While the terrified emigrants were preparing for battle, the Indians appeared. Instead of attacking, they calmly set about making camp of their own, in plain sight and not far away. Instead of a thousand, there were about forty. They were Cheyennes who, as Fitzpatrick had said before, were not a bloodthirsty lot. Fitzpatrick, who knew the Indian sign language, went to have a powwow with the leaders.

What had happened was that while Dawson was tracking an antelope, he had heard what he thought was a war whoop and had caught sight of an approaching Indian party. (What he had heard was merely a routine signal that the leaders of the party had seen a stranger.) Frightened, Dawson had tried to turn his mule back toward camp, but the mule, being contrary, galloped straight toward the Indians. With visions of being scalped, Dawson shouted orders to the mule, waved his gun over his head, and in general behaved like a fierce attacker. The mule paid no attention to him or to the startled Cheyennes, who by now were all around him.

Nearly as scared as he was, they forced Dawson off his mule and took mule and weapons away from him. In the scuffle, they also tore the clothes off his back. When they saw him running away from them, they drew a sigh of relief.

Hearing all this, Dawson's friends argued about whether they should tie him up, so he could get into no more trouble, or merely laugh at him.

But for poor Dawson, the episode was not over. From that day on, his traveling companions forgot that his parents had named him Nicholas. They renamed him "Cheyenne." All the way to California, as long as he stayed there, and any time thereafter, when he met an old-timer who had been with him on the journey, his name was Cheyenne Dawson. To this day, it is by the name Cheyenne Dawson that he is known to history.

18

The next morning they started again. When they came to the Platte River they turned west and followed the river to the fork where the North and South Platte rivers join. They crossed the south fork. This was no easy feat. Now in the month of June, the melted snows had brought the water almost to flood height and made the current so swift that some of the wagons were barely saved from being carried downstream. The travelers not driving wagons had to mount their horses and let the horses swim them to the far bank. It was a fearsome way to cross a river.

However, they all got across without mishap. That evening they made camp in the fork, on the land where the rivers divided, near the site of the present town of North Platte, Wyoming. The next day they went on westward, between the rivers.

On June 12, four days after the crossing, they had a tragedy. A well-liked young man, who bore the ominous name of George Shotwell, while handling a rifle, by accident gave himself a fatal wound. He lived several hours longer and died bravely. The Reverend Mr. Williams conducted his funeral service. Shotwell was lowered into the grave his friends had dug for him, and the wagons moved on.

Shortly after this they came to Astor's trading post, Fort William, on the North Platte River. They managed to buy some food supplies here, but not much. Fort William was not a large post, but the men stationed here told them that when they had gone a little farther they would come to the new post the company was building, Fort Laramie. Larger and stronger than this one, the new fort stood on high ground overlooking the spot where the Sweetwater River joined the North Platte. (A few months later, Fort Laramie was finished. It became a noted stopping-place for emigrants going west.)

At a point near the present town of Casper, Wyoming, they crossed the North Platte River. They had as much fright and trouble as they had had when crossing the south fork, but they got over safely. They went on, toward Fort Laramie and the Sweetwater.

The Sweetwater River joins the North Platte at the site of the modern Pathfinder Reservoir in Wyoming. The travelers reached this point early in July. A few miles farther west they came to Independence Rock. This rock, which was to become one of the most famous landmarks of the western trails, is a vast lump of granite, with a mass of more than 300 million cubic feet. One of the first groups of exploring frontiersmen sighted the rock on a Fourth of July. They stopped here to celebrate the Declaration of Independence and gave the rock its name.

The train paused here and camped. Most of the men made haste to follow what had already become a custom among the hunters and trappers—they painted their names on the great rock to show later visitors that they had been here. Fitzpatrick had put his name on the rock years before. Now he touched up some of the letters, which had been blurred since then by the winter storms.

They moved on, and on, and on, toward South Pass, so called because it lies at the southern end of the Wind River Mountains in Frémont County, Wyoming. This was where Fitzpatrick had told them they would cross the Great Divide.

Every day they had more reason to be glad they had such a man as Fitzpatrick to guide them over the trail. It was not really a trail. A better word for it would be *track*. Fitzpatrick could carry maps in his head, but even he sometimes missed the way and had to lead his followers back several miles to start again. But he knew what to do and he was teaching them how to do it.

From the first, driving wagons over the rough ground had been a wearisome task. But as they moved westward, it became harder and harder. John Bidwell and his company were working as most of them had never worked before. Fitzpatrick, who well knew how to boss men around, made them all work. He was too tough to allow anybody to be lazy, and he set the example by working as hard as any of them.

They would meet great splits in the earth and would have to dig up stones and clods to fill these gullies before they could drive their wagons across. Or they would come to places where last winter's storms had scattered rocks, ranging in size from tennis balls to water-melons. The rocks were strewn so thickly that often the men had to work for hours to clear them away and make passage. Or they would meet boulders so large that it took the efforts of four or five men to push them aside. But they had either to move the boulder or take axes and clear a way around it. They never did agree on which job was harder. Or they met ground so bumpy that they had to gather hundreds of pebbles and fill the depressions, so the wagons would not turn over. One night a raging storm blew down their sleeping tents, threw the sleepers into the mud, and mired the wagons. Mr. Williams expressed his horror at the language they would use at such times, but they went right on using it.

But even then, in spite of the rough going, their life was not an unbroken series of hardships.

The country around them was beautiful. Wild flowers made the air rich with fragrance, and along the riverbanks were willow groves that gave them cooling shade. Game animals provided adequate meat. After the day's march they rested and spun yarns by starlight. Nancy had other women to chat with, and playmates for baby Nan. Mr. Williams and Father De Smet conducted religious services for all who cared to attend. They even had two weddings in the train, one in the Platte River country, the other west of South Pass. Mr. Williams performed the first ceremony, writing in his journal, "Perhaps this was the first marriage in all these plains among white people." The second ceremony was performed by Father De Smet.

Of course the travelers were not always in good humor. For both men and women the days were harsh. Tired folk lose their tempers easily and quarrel over matters of no importance. And it was inevitable that there should be some doctrinal disputes between Mr. Williams and Father De Smet. But in general, their life was peaceful enough as the wagons moved toward the Wind River Mountains.

These mountains are part of the Rocky Mountain Range. The wagons were moving uphill. Though the month was July, the women in the wagons were unpacking their heavy blankets. The mornings were frosty, the nights were cold and getting colder. But the rise toward South Pass was so gradual that the emigrants did not realize how high they were getting until they came close and had a good look at the even higher mountains they would have to cross. When they saw these heights, even the most stouthearted began to feel qualms of fear.

Few of them had ever seen peaks that even in midsummer were covered with snow. And they had to cross this mighty range? *Could*

129

they cross it? With these heavy wagons? The mountains were not only cold and rugged, they looked deadly.

Fitzpatrick assured them that they could cross. Fitzpatrick himself had been one of the first white men ever to go through this pass. That had been seventeen years before, when he had been one of a party that had included some of the greatest of the mountain scouts. He had gone through the pass several times since then, and he knew the way.

Still tremulous, they cooked supper, and that night they camped near the pass. In the morning they found ice on their drinking water.

South Pass is a short way above the 42nd parallel. This is almost the same latitude as that of Detroit. But the summer weather of South Pass and that of Detroit are not alike. In Detroit, midsummer days are swelteringly hot. In South Pass, the howling wind piles up the snow, and the air is finger-numbing cold. In July and August, people familiar with South Pass are not surprised by an ice storm.

When they woke that morning, they were shaky-scared, but they hitched the mules and oxen to the wagons and started, because there was nothing else they could do. The air was frigid, but by good fortune they had no storm today. The sky was clear and the sunlight glittered on the snow.

They found South Pass to be an opening about twenty miles wide between two walls of impassable mountains. It was not smooth going for the wagons, but to the astonishment of the emigrants—though not Fitzpatrick—it was not steep. The climb over this great mountain range was so gentle that the wagon drivers actually did not know when they were definitely across the highest ridge and had passed the Great Divide. They knew it only when they glimpsed a little stream trickling west.

Fitzpatrick said this stream was called Little Sandy Creek. Pretty soon it would be joined by Big Sandy Creek, and then they would be going downhill until they came to the Green River. And undoubtedly he shrugged and said, "I told you so."

As they came down from the heights, the weather grew warmer. On July 23 they saw the Green River, flowing through a valley of trees and grass and flowers. Fitzpatrick was leading them to a stopping place on the riverbank, where hunting and trapping parties liked to pause for a rest as they went eastward with their winter's catch of furs and buffalo robes. When the wagon train stopped to camp, Bartleson astonished the company by going to his wagon and bringing out a keg of alcohol.

130

Fitzpatrick was not only astonished, he was dismayed. There had been no drinking among the emigrants since they had begun their journey. The last problem he wanted now was to be responsible for a lot of men on a spree.

John Bidwell was shocked and thoroughly angry. Hadn't Bartleson signed the same contract as the rest of them before they left Sapling Grove? he demanded. And wasn't there a pledge in this contract that the signer would bring along no strong drink except for medicinal · purposes?

(Bidwell's opposition to liquor was no passing fancy. Years later, when he had become rich and prominent, he was to run for President on the Prohibition ticket. This was in 1892, the year Grover Cleveland was elected for his second term.)

Bartleson was not impressed by Bidwell, or by Fitzpatrick either. He retorted that he had not brought this alcohol to drink. He had brought it to sell. Like other people who had lived in the town of Independence, he had known many hunters and trappers who came there to trade. He knew they camped on the Green River every summer, and he had thought it likely that after months of hard work in the wilds they would be glad to pay for such a civilized comfort as liquor.

Very well, said Fitzpatrick. Eager to get rid of Bartleson's stock as soon as possible, he sent a scout named John Gray to look for a party of returning trappers and bring them in. John Gray was a professional guide, engaged by a young man who had joined the party for the adventure of it. Born on the frontier, son of an Indian mother and a white father, Gray knew his way around.

As Gray started off, one or two other men brought alcohol from their wagons. Apparently they had had the same bright idea as Bartleson. This brotherhood now proceeded to make what they called whiskey—that is, they diluted each gallon of alcohol with about three gallons of water—and settled down to wait for customers.

They did not have to wait long. An expert tracker, John Gray found footprints and followed them. He caught up with a party led by Henry Fraeb, a man known to both him and Fitzpatrick. When he told them his errand, they happily went with him to the emigrant camp. Only a day or two after leaving his own companions, Gray was able to rejoin them, bringing the trappers with their usual following of squaws and half-breed papooses. As Bartleson had foreseen, they bought all—or nearly all—of the so-called whiskey.

Whatever the rest of the emigrants thought of this transaction,

131

they were glad of the chance to trade for goods the trappers were carrying: buckskin suits, moccasins, ropes, buffalo robes. In exchange the emigrants gave flour and molasses and store-bought clothes, and perhaps some of the tools they had brought on the advice of Elam Brown for making canoes.

After the two groups parted, the emigrants made a safe journey to their next stopping place. The trappers, however, met with trouble. Before they had gone many miles, they were attacked by Indians who tried to take their rich stores of skins and furs. The Indians did not succeed in getting the booty, but in the fight, Henry Fraeb, leader of the trapping party, and four other men were killed. When John Bidwell heard of this, he felt sure the trappers could have beaten off the Indians without tragedy if they had not been drinking Bartleson's firewater. When he wrote his memoirs, forty-nine years later, he was still sure, and he may have been right.

When the travelers broke camp at the Green River, their number was lessened by three. Two men who had come along for the adventure said they were ready to quit. With the guide, John Gray, they turned back. This left sixty-four grown people in the train besides Fitzpatrick and the missionaries. Some of these sixty-four had been planning all the time to go with Fitzpatrick to Oregon; others, who had set out for California, had heeded his warnings and changed their minds. But there was still a band of blockheads (as he thought they were) who would not change. They said they had started for California, and this was where they meant to go.

Now that the wagons were rolling again, at every noon pause and every overnight camp, Fitzpatrick gave them more reasons why he believed they would not live to get there.

He told them a favorite rendezvous of the trapping parties was a woodland called Cache Valley. (It is now Cache County, in the state of Utah.) Long ago, the French-Canadian trappers had named it Cache, the French word for hiding place, because this was where they hid the furs they had already caught while they went to look at traps they had set elsewhere. In the years since then, the trappers had explored the country around and beyond Cache Valley, hoping to find streams that held beavers. They had found instead that a great part of this country was utterly desolate.

Fitzpatrick had already told the emigrants their maps were worthless. The map Elam Brown had given John Bidwell, showing a river flowing from the lake to the Pacific Ocean, was a picture of sheer nonsense. True, there was a lake in that general area, though not nearly as large as the lake shown on the map. But it was a *salt* lake. They could not drink the water, nor could their mules and oxen. And no rivers flowed *out* of this lake. Like the Dead Sea of the Bible, it lost water only by evaporation.

He reminded them that they had never felt real hunger or real thirst. The country south and west of the Salt Lake, he told them, was a desert. Nothing could live there. He meant *nothing*. No plant or animal could find sustenance in that empty waste. The country north of the lake was not quite a desert, but they would find it harsh and dry, with little water and almost no grass. And rough, cut with canyons, bare of landmarks. Men with years of experience sometimes got lost there and never came back.

As they listened, the emigrants looked at each other with foreboding. Some of the keenest advocates of California felt their zeal going limp. One after another they told Fitzpatrick they had changed their minds. They would go with him to Oregon.

Fitzpatrick cordially approved. He hoped the rest would show sense enough to do the same. Fitzpatrick was no coward. But he said he had never made any journey to California, and he had no plans to do so.

(Maybe it was fortunate that Fitzpatrick could not look into the future. Two years later, he had to go from Oregon to California in midwinter with an army expedition commanded by the reckless explorer Frémont. The men managed to reach Sutter's Fort, but they nearly died on the way.)

The Oregon-bound emigrants were vehement when they talked to Nancy Kelsey. They said it would be a crime for her to take a child into that country west of Salt Lake. If her husband was so demented as to insist on going to California, wouldn't she at least bring baby Nan to Oregon? If Ben should reach California after all, maybe next summer he could board some trading ship bound for Fort Vancouver and come for his wife and child.

Nancy gave them the same answer she had given her neighbors in Missouri when they asked her why she wanted to start on this wild escapade with Ben. She smiled and said, "I'd rather go with him than worry about him." Her hearers did not have to be very bright to realize that Nancy wanted to go to California as much as Ben did, and nobody was going to stop her.

Nancy was not a great talker. Her traveling companions, writing their memoirs in later years, paid tribute to her endurance and her courage. Not one of them says she had a habit of complaint or nervous chatter. When Nancy said something, she said it simply, plainly, and with conviction. She made up her own mind about what she ought to do. Then she did it.

If Nancy and Ben and the rest of them had known as much about the subject as they were to know later, maybe they would have yielded. But they did not know. With suicidal stubbornness—as Fitzpatrick regarded it—they still said "California." Seeing that his case was hopeless, Fitzpatrick told them there was no reason for them to take John Marsh's suggestion to go as far as Fort Hall before they turned southwest. The fort would be out of their way. They would save some valuable miles by turning toward California when they reached the Bear River. He planned to stop by the Bear River for a few days. There was abundant game in that vicinity, and abundant fish in the river, so it was a good place to talk things over again.

The two factions were not reconciled. As they traveled there were some heated arguments and, the Reverend Mr. Williams wrote in his journal, "such swearing I never heard in my life before."

The second week in August they reached the Bear River. This is a very crooked stream near the point where the three states of Utah, Wyoming, and Idaho touch each other. The river rises in Utah, flows northeast into Wyoming, then northwest into Idaho. Here it flows north, makes a hairpin turn and flows south, back into Utah, where it empties into the Great Salt Lake. As they drew near the hairpin turn, the travelers came to a brilliant pageant of waters called Soda Springs. They were now in Caribou County, Idaho, not far from the site of the modern town of Pocatello.

Set among spendid mountains, the springs bubble and spurt with endless vigor. The water is clear, a refreshing drink; put into dough, it makes the bread rise. Here at Soda Springs, about August 15, 1841, the party split.

Mr. and Mrs. Samuel Kelsey and their children turned toward Oregon. All the other children except baby Nan Kelsey were also taken to Oregon by their parents. In the California group were Nancy, baby Nan, and thirty-one men.

Nancy wanted to go to California with Ben and his brother Andrew, and baby Nan had no opinion about it. The men who were independent—such as John Bidwell, Joseph Chiles, and others—had made their own decisions. But it may be that not all the thirty-one men really wanted to undertake this journey. After hearing Fitzpatrick's dire warnings, some of the men in Bartleson's group might have

134

preferred to go to Oregon. But they had no choice. They had bought shares in Bartleson's wagon, the mules that drew it, and his spare saddle horses. In that big wagon were their food supplies, their blankets, clothing, extra guns and ammunition, and goods they were bringing for Indian trade. Bartleson had refused to take Fitzpatrick's orders. He did not like to take advice from anybody. He had chosen to go to California, and his messmates had to go with him.

Fitzpatrick gave them the best directions he could. He said, "Go down the west bank of the Bear River. When the water starts tasting salty, you will know you are near the lake. Turn west, go around the north side of the lake, and go on west."

He added a warning.

"Be on the lookout for Blackfeet Indians. They sometimes go hunting here along the river."

They promised to be careful, and the two parties went their separate ways. Four men of the Bidwell-Kelsey group followed Fitzpatrick as far as Fort Hall. Here they hoped to meet hunters and traders who could tell them more about the way ahead. Fitzpatrick said they could probably learn something from Captain James Grant, who commanded the fort for the Hudson's Bay Company. The four scouts, riding horseback, would have no trouble catching up with the slower-moving wagons.

The rest of the California group went down the west bank of the Bear River. They would stop later and catch some of those abundant fish for their evening meal.

Now they were really on their way to the fabled land of California. They knew a great deal more about pioneer traveling than they had known when they left home three months ago. Fitzpatrick had taught them how to track buffalo. He had taught them how to cut the meat into long thin strips and hang them to dry on a scaffolding before a fire. They had learned how to make the night corral that kept the animals safe. They knew they must hoard coffee beans like precious jewels. This was because they might come to places where the only water they could find would be stale and bad-tasting, and coffee would make it easier to drink. And they knew a thousand other small details that would make their journey less dangerous—details they had not known before.

There was much they did not know. They did not know how many miles they would have to travel before they reached John Marsh's ranch. Nor how long it would take to travel them. They had no guide and no real map. Not one of them had any knowledge of the country they would have to cross, and there was no trail for them to follow. They had never seen a desert. As Fitzpatrick had warned them, they had never felt real hunger or thirst. They had no idea of what hazards might lie ahead.

But as they rode along the riverbank, they were a merry group. They were young, they were vigorous, they were on their way, and the world was opening before them.

19

They went on, following the Bear River south toward the Great Salt Lake. They met no enemies, but after the first day or two they found that their journey was not going to be pleasant. Hour after hour, they had to make their way through clouds of smoke so thick that sometimes they could hardly recognize each other.

The smoke came from Indian fires among the mountains. While most of the Indians here were not hostile, they were cautious. When their lookouts observed something unusual taking place, they started slow fires, to send up smoke signals to their fellows. Such a signal was a warning. The approach of strange conveyances, bringing palefaces into their hunting grounds, might mean danger. It was wise to be on guard.

Meanwhile, the palefaces were coughing till their throats were sore and wiping away the tears that streamed out of their smarting eyes. The mules and oxen were suffering as much as their owners. To spare the animals, most of the travelers walked. When a gust of wind scattered the smoke, they dried their eyes and drew long, grateful breaths of clean air; when the smoke covered them again, they stumbled along as best they could.

Still they had much to be thankful for. The Indians were keeping away from them. They had all the water they needed, plenty of grass for the mules and oxen, and, for themselves, plenty of fresh fish, sometimes varied by jackrabbits. It could have been worse.

And worse it got, soon.

About a hundred miles south, along the riverbank, the scouts who had gone with Fitzpatrick to Fort Hall caught up with the wagon train. Captain Grant had told them as much as he knew about the way ahead. They now repeated his directions.

As Fitzpatrick had said, when the river water began to taste salty they would know they were coming close to the lake, where the water would be undrinkable. When they tasted salt, they were to turn west. The scouts said they were nearing this point now.

Captain Grant had said they were to travel not due west but southwest. The Salt Lake had a big bulge at its northwest side. If they went southwest from here, they could move in a fairly straight line. Thus they would avoid most of the north shore, which had a lot of dips and turns that would add needless miles to the journey. When they reached the bulge, they should go around it and then go west, west, west and find the Humboldt River. Captain Grant could not give them any directions about finding the river. But they must find it, to give them water as they went on.

Captain Grant had said that before they left the Bear River they should fill their water casks, as they would be going through a dry country. And they should start early every morning. Turn the animals out to graze at three hours after midnight, he said, and get going no later than four. Then the animals could rest through the hottest hours and start again when the day began to cool.

The travelers made ready. They realized that their journey was reaching the serious stage. They filled the casks and packed the wagons. From now on, they would have to live mostly on game. They still had the coffee they had hoarded for times of bad water, but the food supplies they had brought from Missouri, or bought on the way, were nearly gone.

The next morning they turned southwest. As they moved away from the river, the landscape speedily changed. By the time they ended the first day's march, from the looks of things they might have come a hundred miles. They were now in a country of sand and sagebrush, where everything seemed the same color of grayish tan. In places the sagebrush was so tall and tough that the men had to take axes and cut a road so the wagons could get through. The ground was bumpy. Now and then a wagon would topple over, scattering the baggage of the owners right and left. They would have to stop and repack and then catch up with the wagons ahead.

But along with the bother it gave them, this ugly sagebrush also gave them a savory food supply. The brush was the home of jackrabbits and sage hens. They both made good eating; and the heavy, dry sticks of the brush made good fires for cooking them. There were so many jackrabbits that during the midday rest periods the emigrants could dry some strips of leftover meat for hungry times that might lie ahead.

But nothing about this route was easy. All day the sun beat mercilessly down upon their heads; when the sun went down they shivered in the sudden desert cold. They did not lack food, but they sorely needed more water. The water in the casks lasted only a day or two, and then they had to look for water holes—the depressions that caught and held rainfall—of which there was none too much in this region. Here again the little dwellers in the sagebrush were useful. They knew where the water holes were. The travelers followed their tracks, and the tracks led to water holes. The water often had a brackish taste from long standing, but they drank it because they had nothing else to drink. As before, they took turns driving the wagons. Between turns they walked.

And from the very beginning, they discovered those desert tortures, the mirages.

Panting under the glare of the sun, they would see ahead of them a lake with bushes in bloom on its bank. No matter how hot and tired they were, they would find strength to go toward it; but as they came near the lake, it was not there any more. All they saw was the same dull brown earth, and the same sagebrush, which they had mistaken for clusters of bloom. Even the bravest of them would groan and exclaim, "Oh, God, why does the earth tease us so cruelly?"

But they pushed on, through a country getting hotter and drier as they went, until one morning they stopped the wagons in an area where they could find no water at all. The most diligent search through the sagebrush gave them not one water hole, nor could they find any jackrabbit tracks to guide them. The sun went higher and higher, and its scorching heat was making their heads ache and their throats burn. They started the wagons again and as they kept moving ahead, looking in every direction for some sign of water, they caught sight of an oasis on the far horizon. A fair stretch of grass it was, with a river flowing under tall, waving trees. Shouts of joy went up from their parched throats. Hot, tired, nearly choking, they walked toward the oasis all the rest of the day, without water, and kept on walking after the dark had closed in.

The night was cold. A high wind was blowing, lashing them with the rough chill of the desert. They walked and walked. It was nearly midnight when they realized that they were walking over a plain, flat and featureless, which looked as if it were covered with snow. But this was not snow. It was a hard crust of salt. By the dim light of stars and a faint moon they could see that in places their wagon wheels had broken the crust, and fragments were rolling about in the wind. As they walked, they were crushing these fragments under their feet.

Now they realized and had to admit that they had fallen victims to another mirage. They had spent all day and half the night without water. The animals were staggering, and so were the people who depended on them. As they helplessly stared at that crust of salt, they knew—for the first time in their lives—how it felt to be *really* thirsty.

Their mouths were so dry that it was hard for them to talk, but they managed a few words. In bitter defeat, they confessed to each other what they all knew. They could not cross that plain of salt. Not tonight.

Fitzpatrick had warned them that something of this sort would happen. They had not listened.

The animals were still trying to plod along. Now the men could see that the crust of salt was softening, and the hoofs of the mules and oxen were sinking into the mush. If it grew much softer, or if their hoofs sank much deeper, they would not be able to move at all. The men looked at each other in fear. They did not know how many more miles the salt plain extended, but they did know that if they tried to go much farther on it, or if they stayed here in the midst of it, people and animals alike would fall and die. And it would be a hideous death.

They had to have water. They knew of only one place where they could get it. They had to do what they had declared they would never do. They had to turn away from California and go back to the Bear River.

It had taken them some days to come this far, but they had been traveling southwest. If they turned here and went due east they would have a much shorter journey back to the river. They would reach it a good way south of the spot where they had left it, but no matter. The river would have water in it.

And then?

They did not know. They could think no farther ahead. Animals so tired they could hardly draw the wagons, men so tired they could hardly walk, they turned their backs on California and started eastward. Ben Kelsey drove his wagon, with Nancy beside him, and the baby asleep in her arms. Baby Nan was the only emigrant in the wagon train who had any sleep that night.

140

20

Through the night they struggled on. They could make no plans, short of getting to the river and having water to drink. They would still be alive when they got there, because the return journey was so much shorter than their journey to the lake had been. It was like following one of the short sides of a right-angled triangle instead of the long side that faced the right angle itself. And so, in the bright sunshine of the next day, they caught sight of the Bear River ahead of them.

This was no mirage. The river splashed and murmured in the sun, and on the banks the grass twinkled as if with a million drops of dew. To these water-famished wanderers it seemed the most beautiful landscape they had ever looked upon. Running, stumbling, shaking with joy as much as with fatigue, they rushed to the water's edge and flung themselves on the ground beside it. Some of them dipped up water with their tin cups, others made cups of their hands and began to lap up the water, ox fashion. Then from all their throats rose a groan of frustration and despair.

The water was like brine. As for the grass, the twinkling that they had thought was sun on a million dewdrops was really sun on a million crystals of salt.

At this point on the river, miles south of where they had left it, they were so near the Salt Lake that the salt had seeped into the river and made it nearly as briny as the lake. Last night, though they had not known it, they had been going straight toward the northwestern bulge that Captain Grant had spoken of at Fort Hall, They had, in fact, almost reached it. (This was why the salt plain had begun to get mushy. In spring, the high-water time, much of this plain was part of the lake bed.) And now, after their exhausting journey back to the river, all they could find was salt and more salt. Through lips parched and cracked with dryness, they mumbled that they could *not* drink this water.

But they did drink it. Before long, to their own astonishment, they found themselves gulping it down, salt and all. Nature was asserting itself. For days now, they had been living on a meager supply of water, and they had just passed a day and night with no water at all. Their bodies were demanding water, no matter how it tasted. They drank the water because they could not help it.

"It would not quench thirst," Bidwell said in his memoirs, "but it did save life."

The horses and mules and oxen were drinking the water too. The animals had behaved like their owners—they had rushed to the river, had drawn back from the water with loathing, and then, pushed by their imperative need, had returned to drink. But they would not eat the salt-crusted grass. They flopped into the grass to rest, but famished though they were, graze they would not.

The party spent a day here by the river, sleeping the heavy sodden sleep of exhaustion, eating such scraps as they could get down with the help of the salt water. The next day they started again. They did not follow the long southwesterly course they had taken before; by following a new route, they had at least a chance of finding new water holes instead of those they had already emptied. This time they moved northwest. They crossed their own tracks on the salt plain, and, always tired, always thirsty, they pushed on through a dry and nearly barren land. They spent another day and night without water. And then, just as they were wondering how much longer they were going to live, one of the men gave a joyful shout. He had seen the tracks of an antelope.

Tracks meant water. As they had followed the jackrabbits through the sagebrush, now they followed the antelope. The tracks led them north, to a real oasis, a beautiful patch of green in the brown desert, with a clear spring and abundant grass.

Here they stopped to rest. Their animals were half starved and nearly worn out, and the men were not much better. While the animals feasted on the lush grass, the men hunted and dried the meat and wondered how near they were to the Humboldt River.

John Marsh had said they must find and follow this river or they would never reach California. At Fort Hall, Captain Grant had said the same thing. Now Bartleson announced that as he and one of his followers, Charles Hopper, had the best horses, they would go out and find the river. They had gone as scouts to Fort Hall, and they would again scout for the company. This was an important mission, and Bartleson liked to feel important.

The others agreed—or, more precisely, they yielded. There was no reason why Bartleson and his friend Hopper should not be the scouts again. They did have the strongest horses. While Hopper had never been as far west as this, he had more experience of western living and hunting than the rest of them. But Bartleson was making himself more and more unpopular with his fellow emigrants. Now that Fitzpatrick was no longer leading the train, Bartleson was constantly reminding them that they had chosen him captain before they left Missouri. He talked and gave orders as if this election had endowed him with superior knowledge about what the other men ought to do. However, though there was some mild grumbling about Bartleson's blustering ways, none of the others made any real objection to his going out to look for the river. He and Hopper rode off together.

Behind them in the oasis, the animals ate and rested, the men dried meat, while Nancy washed and mended clothes and looked after her child. She took good care of baby Nan. She knew how. Nancy was not highly educated in the schoolbook sense, but she had a fund of knowledge ready for hard times. Women like her, bred on the frontier, were rich in folk-learning. They knew that even in the depth of winter, pine needles simmered in warm water would make a brew to ward off scurvy. They knew that when there was no soft food for a child still half toothless, the toughest jerky could be shredded between two stones and cooked in water, which could then be strained through a rag and leave a nourishing broth. They knew the uses of wild plants, and they were always ready to share their skills.

It is not by chance that of all the letters and memoirs of the men who were with Nancy on this trek, not one of them says that baby Nan was ever sick.

After having been gone five or six days, Bartleson and Hopper came back. They reported that they had found the river. They had found it only after going around the Salt Lake by way of a harsh country that would be hard to cross with the wagons, but the river was there. Filling their water casks and packing their dried meat, the people of the emigrant train started again. It was time for them to move. Smoke signals in the mountains reminded them that Indians were still watching. Besides, the summer was turning into autumn, and winter was not far ahead. Between the columns of smoke they could see the peaks of more distant mountains. These looked higher than those near at hand. The travelers knew if they were going to cross, they had to do it before the passes were blocked with snow.

Using their food and water supplies as sparingly as they could, they made their way around the northwestern side of the Great Salt Lake. The going grew harder and harder, the animals leaner and more weary. After several days, the Kelsey brothers said they could take their wagons no farther. Their oxen were not strong enough to draw them. Ben said Nancy would ride a horse, holding baby Nan in front of her, while he and his brother Andrew would take turns walking, to spare the other horses as much as they could. A few days later, the rest of the men said they would follow the Kelsey's example. Abandoning all the wagons, they would pack the animals with the supplies they could not possibly do without and throw away the rest.

Packing the animals proved to be a frightful task. The men found that they did not know how it ought to be done. During the earlier part of their journey they had met parties of hunters and trappers loading pack animals. The emigrants had watched those men at work and had seen nothing about it that looked too difficult. But those men had been packers made expert by years of learning how to do it right, and those animals had been trained to carry packs.

These greenhorns tried and tried. They cut up the wagon beds to make pack-holders, and tore the tents into strips to twist ropes for tying the packs on the animals. The animals were tired and weakened, but they found strength enough to make vigorous protests. They stamped and kicked; they tried to run away; they shook off the packs, sent the goods flying in all directions, and had to be packed all over again. Most of the men had used mules for drawing their wagons, but the Kelseys and John Bidwell had chosen oxen. Oxen moved more slowly than mules but they were not so strong-minded and therefore were easier to manage. But now, when it came to carrying packs, they were even less docile than the mules. They had no idea of what was being done to them, but they fought as hard as they could to keep the men from doing it. (If there were any men in the party who had followed Bartleson unwillingly toward California instead of Oregon, they certainly said so now.)

But at last, the men got the creatures loaded somehow and began the journey again. Now that they were using so many of the horses and mules to carry their supplies, at all times at least half the travelers had to walk. They tried to cheer themselves with the reminder that every step across this land of dry torment was bringing them nearer the Humboldt River. Another gladdening thought was that the eigh-

144

teen or twenty oxen owned by Bidwell and Ben Kelsey, no longer needed for drawing wagons, could now be killed for beef. The travelers were all so hungry that almost any hardship was welcome if it meant more food.

The animals gnawed at the sparse growth around them—sagebrush, dry bushes, a little bunchgrass. As for the people, the food supplies they had brought with them had given out, and in this desolate country there was no game. Until they could find game they would have to live on the oxen. They killed one ox at a time. The only water they had was what they could find in the water holes or in the beds of creeks nearly emptied by the summer dryness. Sometimes, if they dug in the earth around the water holes, they would find a little more water underground. The water was far from clean and the taste was disagreeable, but they were too desperate to be fastidious. With their other supplies, their coffee had given out. They boiled the water and got it down.

They met Indians, well armed with bows and arrows, but as the white men had guns and were ready to use them, the Indians did not make trouble. However, the smoke signals on the mountains still warned the white men to take care. Their tempers grew shorter. Bidwell and Bartleson began to quarrel. Most of the other men liked Bidwell better and took his side. The mood of the party grew more and more tense.

The journey from the oasis seemed endless, though it took only seven or eight days. But at last, one afternoon, in what is now Elko County, Nevada, they came to the Humboldt River.

It was not a beautiful river and it did not flow through a beautiful country. The time was now late September, and through the past summer the country had received very little rain. The river had shrunk till it was not much more than a creek. Along its banks were willows and clumps of grass, but the growth could hardly be called verdant. The country around was bleak and dusty.

No matter. This was a river, it had water in it, the water was clean and wholesome, and the bunchgrass was good food for the animals. Right now this was all anybody in the train was asking for. Scooping up water, they drank and they drank and they drank. They made fires and cooked the beef from one of the oxen still left. The ox had been so lean that the meat was tough and stringy, but the travelers were too hungry to care. The living oxen, and the horses and mules, lapped up the water and cropped the grass. It was a time of feasting.

The next morning they started again. Day after day, wearily and

145

doggedly, they trudged along the bank of the river. The ground was bumpy, and sometimes they had to go over patches of sharp gravel, nearly as hard to walk on as crushed glass would have been. To spare her horse, Nancy walked with the rest of them, carrying her baby and usually barefoot, to save her last pair of shoes for walking that might be even harder than this. She walked until her feet were so sore and blistered that she could walk no longer. Then she had to ride her weary horse, holding baby Nan in front of her, until her feet healed enough for her to start walking again.

Nancy and the others were a rugged lot. In spite of all their troubles they were moving eighteen miles a day.

This rate of progress, for people always tired and always hungry, is almost awe-inspiring. They probably did not know it, but they were outdoing the magnificent Roman legions of history. At the time when the Roman Empire was conquering most of the known world, the standard day's march for the soldiers was fourteen miles. These sturdy pioneers were marching four miles farther.

The Humboldt River flows in a crooked course, turning this way and that. A traveler who follows it has to go many more miles than would be necessary if the river did less meandering. But these travelers had to stay near the riverbank because they needed the water. The river was dwindling as it flowed toward the Sink, a low spot occurring at a point where a river has shrunk almost to nothing, and the scant water accumulates in a stagnant pool that loses moisture only by evaporation. The more sensitive among them complained that the water was beginning to have a bitter taste. The tougher ones said, "Be thankful it's water," and pushed on.

In this bare country there was no game but a few antelope, so swift and agile that they were hard to kill. The travelers were living almost wholly on the oxen. To keep the oxen as fat as possible, the men shifted their loads to the mules and horses. When they killed an ox, they made it last as long as they could. But in a company of thirty-two adults and a child, all except baby Nan walking most of the day, an ox would seldom last longer than two days. They were hungry all the time.

Bartleson was growing impatient. They were living on such skimpy rations that his paunch had shrunk to about half its former size. He yearned for the spacious green ranches John Marsh had written about. Oxen moved more slowly than mules or horses, he said; why not abandon the oxen and hurry on to California? The men who had traveled with him from the start were inclined to agree with him.

146

But the others refused. Led by Bidwell and Ben Kelsey (who owned all the oxen anyway), they reminded Bartleson and his messmates that the oxen were their only sure source of food. If they left the oxen behind, they might go miles without finding game and have to eat the mules and horses. Then what would become of the goods they could not live without—guns, ammunition, hunting knives, blankets, water casks?

Bartleson exclaimed that there was plenty of beef in California.

Yes, retorted Ben and John Bidwell, but how far away was California? How long would it take them to get there? Nobody in the train could answer.

But the dispute continued. Then one day, an ox had been killed and for some reason—perhaps at Bartleson's suggestion—most of the meat had been packed on a horse of Bartleson's. The men of his group mounted their horses. The others were mounting, loading their pack mules, and in general making ready to resume the march. All of a sudden these others heard some shouted words from Bartleson. He said something like, "We're on our way to California. If you can keep up with us, do it. If you can't, go to hell."

Nobody could be sure of his exact words, because by the time he had finished his speech, Bartleson was dashing off, with his pals (nine men in all), their pack animals, and the horse carrying the meat. But those left behind had no trouble understanding what he meant.

21

The emigrant party was now on the north side of the Humboldt River, heading west toward a vast range of mountains. Because of that quick and sudden start, Bartleson and his comrades had managed to ride across the shallow river and get out of sight before the rest of the party could mount and go after them. The men he left behind followed as soon as they could, not because they wanted more of Bartleson's companionship but because they wanted their share of the meat. If they were going to cross that mountain range ahead, they needed all the food they could get.

Believing that Bartleson would not dare to go far from the river, they followed his tracks for two or three days, until they came to a stretch where the wind had blown off all traces of the runaways. The pursuers gave up. They killed another of their precious oxen and went on down the bank of the Humboldt. The stream grew smaller, and steadily more bitter with alkali, but the water was still drinkable. After a day or two they came to the place where the river ended. This was the Humboldt Sink.

The sink lies a short way north of the present town of Fallon, Nevada, about fifty miles east of Reno. At high-water time, it is a narrow body of water about twenty by eight miles. In October, the emigrants found it shrunken and the water, not freshened by rain for many weeks, stagnant and discolored, almost slimy. But they had to drink something, and this was all they had. They boiled the water, and in spite of its nasty taste they managed to swallow it.

By this time, nearly all of them were walking all day. They took the best care they could of the horses and mules, but the poor creatures were nearly exhausted. From the Humboldt Sink the train struggled on westward, toward those forbidding mountains. After two more weary days, they caught a blessed glimpse of trees ahead. Another mirage? Hardly. They were no longer traveling under a summer sun. Their pitiful animals caught the scent of water and managed to move faster as they dragged themselves toward it. They reached a stream flowing between grassy banks. Men and beasts alike, they sank down beside it.

The party spent one night by the river, but they did not dare pause here long enough to give themselves and the animals a real rest. Those mountains were looking down on them, a constant reminder that winter was near. In the morning they filled their water casks with as much water as they thought the animals could carry and went on. To their joyful surprise, after a short march they came to another river, smaller but just as welcome as the former one had been. Now they had water and grass again.

(At that time, these two rivers had no names. Later, when John Charles Frémont came this way, he named them Carson and Walker for two famous mountain scouts, Kit Carson and Joseph Reddeford Walker. This is what the rivers are called today.)

The emigrants had now almost reached the present eastern border of California, but they did not know it. They did know that they were facing a terrifying range of mountains, and for food they had only two oxen left. Two oxen, lean and half starved.

These mountains were the Sierra Nevada, the stupendous range that for uncounted centuries had stood like a wall between the Pacific coast and the rest of the continent. Some Indians had gone through the passes, but very few white men, and these few were the hardiest and most experienced mountaineers. No non-Indian women had ever crossed this range. Nancy held her baby tight as the party followed the Walker River to the spot where it flowed down the mountainside.

If they were going to cross the mountains, they would have to start here, and they knew they had better do it fast. They would have to follow the river upward. Into what dangers it might lead them, they could not tell.

Fearfully, they asked each other, "Can we get across or can't we?"

Everybody asked. Nobody answered.

Since they had parted with Fitzpatrick, Ben Kelsey and John Bidwell had come to be recognized as the leaders of the party. Neither of them had asked for leadership, and there had been no election, not even after their so-called captain, Bartleson, had deserted the train. It was simply that the dangers and hardships of the journey had scraped off the veneer of formalized living and laid bare the real characters of them all. Some people are durable. Their inner strength takes them through the hardest knocks of life and keeps them going, not weakened but stronger than before. Ben and Bidwell were this sort. Ben, with an almost flawless sense of direction, was the best pathfinder among them. John Bidwell had the dependable moral fiber that wins confidence anywhere. When these two spoke, the others listened.

Now Ben and Bidwell suggested that they camp here by the river. They would have supper, get a night's rest, and in the morning they would send out scouts to look for a pass through which the party might cross the mountains. If the scouts could find a way, good; if they came back and said they could find no sort of opening and believed the crossing was impossible, the party would have to consider where to go from here.

The others agreed, though there were some among them who were already sure they could not get across. These men wanted to turn around and go back, toward the Bear River and Fort Hall. But they could not turn back that night. With the rest, they made camp, ate a scanty meal of dried beef, and stretched out to sleep. The night was cold.

In the morning, a brave man of the party named Josiah Belden volunteered to go exploring. He chose two other men to go with him. The names of these two seem not to have been recorded, but Josiah Belden was one of the most capable and highly respected men in the train. He had already shown himself to be a man utterly trustworthy. On this uneasy day at the foot of the mountains, Belden's fellow emigrants knew they could count on him to make careful observations and bring back a clear report. With his two aides, he set out on the scouting expedition not long after daybreak, October 16, 1841.

While they were gone, the other men killed the ox that appeared to be the fatter of the remaining two and dried the beef. Few if any of them were in a cheerful mood. Their situation was desperate and they knew it.

Late in the afternoon the scouts returned. The rest of the party crowded around them to hear what they had to say.

They reported that crossing the range would be a hard, hard task, but they believed it could be done. All three of them agreed on this. But not all their hearers concurred. Several men still insisted that it could *not* be done. They had said so last night, and nothing the scouts could say would persuade them to change. They wanted to go back, toward the Bear River and Fort Hall.

Others—Bidwell and Ben Kelsey among them—urged that they brave the mountains and go forward. John Marsh had told them California was a rich and beautiful country. Bidwell's French-Canadian friend, Robidou, had said the same thing. Now, if the party dared attempt the crossing, they stood at least a chance of getting there. They had been traveling for five months. Was all this long, hard journey to be for nothing?

It was fearfully dangerous, insisted those who wanted to go back.

Yes, replied those who wanted to go forward. But turning back, and facing starvation in the desert, was dangerous too.

It was the time for decision. Somebody suggested that they take a vote. Should they go forward? Yes or no?

By a majority of one, the vote was yes.

Ben Kelsey and John Bidwell, Josiah Belden and his scouting companions, and maybe others, voted yes because they had made up their minds to go to California and they meant to do it. Other yes-voters said candidly—some now, some later—that they had been prompted by neither courage nor strength of purpose. They had voted yes because they felt they had reached what we now call the point of no return. They wished they had never started. But with winter just ahead, and no certain food but their few staggering animals, they did not believe they could get back to Fort Hall alive.

Again the party had a supper of beef and spread blankets for the chilly night. Shortly after daybreak they began their climb, following Josiah Belden and his fellow scouts up a mountain on the north side of the Walker River. At first the climb was not too difficult. Nancy was riding, holding the baby in front of her, but nearly all the men had to walk and lead the animals. One of the men happened to look back, toward the open country below the mountain range. He caught his breath. "Indians!" he exclaimed.

At this, the others stopped and looked down too. The early morning mists blurred the landscape, but there could be no doubt that a group of horsemen was riding toward them.

Indians? They might be. They were still too far away, and too indistinct, for the onlookers to be sure. They did not look like a large party, but the men put their hands on their guns, to be ready. Those in charge of the beef and the pack animals and their one precious ox tried to conceal them behind the bushes. Roaming Indians always wanted food.

But as the riders came nearer, one of them raised his arm in a gesture of recognition. And one of the climbers, perhaps more keen-eyed than the rest, burst out, "Hey, boys—it's the Bartleson bunch!"

It was easier to forgive Bartleson's companions than to forgive Bartleson. Their blankets and spare guns and other equipment, at first packed in his wagon, were now loaded on Bartleson's horses. Without him they would have had no supplies with which to get to California. It must have been a great temptation for the mountain climbers to tell Bartleson he was a pompous blunderhead and give him nothing to eat. But the men of the emigrant train were not a vindictive lot. With exasperation, a certain wry humor, and no doubt some blistering words, they greeted him as they greeted the others who had come back.

The runaways were tired and they were hungry and they looked sick. Bartleson had lost still more weight. Now he was saying plaintively, "Boys, if I ever get back to Missouri I'll be glad to eat out of the trough with my hogs." The Bidwell-Kelsey group gave him and his cronies a meal, then told them to start climbing. Nobody asked them to vote. They had no choice.

As they trudged along, the returned prodigals told what had happened to them.

The meat they had taken had not proved to be much when divided among hungry men on the move. It soon gave out. The best hunter among them, Charles Hopper, had tracked and killed a deer, but the deer had vanished in one meal. Just when they had thought they were going to have to throw away their outfits and start eating the pack horses, an Indian had wandered into their camp. Hopper, well versed in the Indian sign language, had given him some trifles out of the packs and asked him to guide them to a place where they could barter for food. The Indian had led them to a lake, probably the sink where the Carson River went underground.

A short way past the sink, the Indian had taken them to a village. In exchange for some hunting knives, the Indians of the village had provided a basket of pine nuts. They harvested these every fall from the cones of a pine tree that grows in the southwestern United States and Mexico, still called by the Spanish name, piñon. The pine nuts were good, but when they were gone, the white men had still been hungry. They had demanded more to eat. The Indians had given them some fish.

But the water near the Carson Sink was as stale and bad as that near the Humboldt Sink. The fish had made some of the men violently sick.

(It may be that the Indians knew the fish were not fit to eat and handed them out on purpose to get rid of these ravenous strangers. Or it may be that not all the fish were polluted, as not all the white men were made sick.)

When the sick men were well enough to ride again, they offered their Indian guide more presents if he would help them find the tracks of their former associates. He had consented and had brought them here, to the Walker River.

As the hours passed and the climbers went upward, the air grew colder and the wind blew harder. The next morning they reached the snow. Stubbornly they draped their blankets around them and pushed on. In two days of hard going, they reached the top of the mountain. The terrain was so rough and rocky that they did not know they had reached the top, and passed it, until they saw a stream gushing out of the rocks and flowing downhill toward the west. This was the source of what they later learned was the Stanislaus River, named by early Spanish missionaries who had seen it in the country below. The emigrants had climbed by way of what is now known as Sonora Pass, which at the summit is nearly ten thousand feet high.

Standing on this mountaintop, they were actually standing in the land of their dreams, California. They had come into what is now called Alpine County. But they did not know where they were. They could only hope they were somewhere near the western shore.

But tired as they were, they felt a cheerful triumph. Reaching the summit must surely have been the hardest part of their undertaking. Now, they told each other, their route, like that of the river, would be downhill. Going down would be easier than going up.

But it was not. The way grew worse and worse and worse. They dragged themselves along, more and more slowly. They stumbled over loose stones, forced their way around boulders, trembled with hunger. They found a little game, but not much. And they had only one ox left. Soon, they said wearily, they would have to start eating the pack animals. And what would they do when they had no more mules and horses?

While they were dreading these prospects, they came to a slope where they saw a grove of magnificent oak trees. Under the trees, the ground was covered with freshly ripened acorns.

Acorns—food! Indians ate roasted acorns. Why should not acorns be good food for palefaces too?

When they came to the grove, the time was earlier than their usual camping time, but they were so hungry that they could not resist the promise of a meal. They halted where they were, started fires, pulled off the acorn hulls, and had a feast.

These hungry people left no record to tell us what sort of oak the acorns came from. It was probably the same species that was to help save John Charles Frémont and his party from starvation two years later. This was during the expedition for which Frémont, ignoring the advice of Kit Carson and Tom Fitzpatrick, had ordered his men to move from northern Oregon to Sutter's Fort in the depth of winter. After months of frightful hardships, the men had reached central California. They were following the stream that Sutter had named the American River.

As Frémont's men went through the woods, tired and half starved, they began to notice a type of live-oak tree they had not seen before. They would have been glad to eat acorns, but the month was February and the trees provided none. After a time, the men came to a group of Indian huts, from which the Indians, frightened by the strange footsteps, had just run away. The men went into one of the huts, desperately hoping they would find something to eat.

Find it they did. In the hut were five or six big boxes made of woven twigs, all full of raw acorns, and several baskets full of acorns already roasted. These acorns were long and slender, and surprisingly large, some of them two and a half inches long and nearly an inch wide. Grabbing them by handfuls, the men began to eat. Of these acorns, Frémont wrote later, "They were sweet and agreeably flavored." They tasted so good that the men helped themselves to about half a bushel for later meals and, in payment, left a shirt, a kerchief, and some knickknacks.

They made the acorns last until they reached Sutter's Fort. Sutter welcomed them and gave them all the food they wanted.

Acorns were a staple food of the Indians on the Pacific side of the continent, as important to them as corn was to the Atlantic Indians. They gathered the ripe acorns in the fall and stored them for use throughout the year. Not all the acorns were the same. Those from the oaks near the coast had a high tannic-acid content, which made them unfit for food in their natural state. The Indian women ground them up with stone mortars and pestles and used sand and water to leach out the acid.

Evidently these acorns from the mountain oaks contained so little tannic acid that, in general, Indians and white people alike could eat them with no harm. For Frémont and his men, and for most members of the emigrant party, the acorns proved to be a wholesome food. But they made Ben Kelsey gravely ill. That evening, while everybody else was enjoying the almost forgotten sensation of feeling well fed, Ben was attacked by fierce abdominal pains. He was sick all night. In the morning he still lay on his blanket, groaning. Nancy sat on the ground beside him, giving him all the help she could.

Nancy did not know why Ben was so stricken, and neither did anyone else. At that time the word allergy had not been invented, but it may have been that Ben was allergic to tannic acid. Perhaps his allergy was so acute that even the tiny bit in these acorns made him ill, though it troubled nobody else in the party.

While Nancy sat beside him, with one arm around baby Nan, two or three of the other men approached. They told her the train must move on. They had no time to wait for Ben to get well. As she had seen higher up, the winter snows had already begun. Nancy and baby Nan should come with the train, leaving Ben, and he would try to catch up later.

They thought this was a reasonable idea, but Nancy raised her head and looked at them in astonishment.

Nancy had grown up in a sturdy Bible-quoting family who believed in, and practiced, the unpretentious loyalties of the frontier. When Nancy had spoken her marriage vows, she had meant exactly what she said. Now, when these men suggested that she leave her husband alone, hoping he would get well somehow and somehow manage to find the train again, she answered without vehemence, but clearly.

"I will never do that."

Every man who heard her understood. It was no use to urge her. Again, Nancy had meant exactly what she said.

The party waited another day.

22

The day under the oaks was not wasted. The pack animals were better for the chance to rest and graze; the travelers had bountiful meals of acorns, and roasted more acorns to take with them. Not Ben, of course. Ben had discovered that as far as he was concerned, mule meat was a more savory tidbit than the finest acorns ever roasted by an Indian gourmet.

Thanks to Nancy's care and his own tough constitution, Ben was up and ready to go with the train early on the second morning. We are not told that he was ever sick again on this journey.

They pushed along through the mountains all day. About sunset they came to a crisscrossing of canyons that looked like a blockade Nature had cruelly set in their way. The riverbed had become a deep ravine, so deep that the men could not possibly have taken pails and climbed down to the water level and then with full pails, climbed up again. A smaller stream ran into the river here, but this too was flowing between high rock walls. Standing on a point of rock jutting out at the meeting place of the rivers, the thirsty travelers could look down and see water in plenty below them, but they could not reach it. Nor, in this dark place of rocks and shadows, could they find any grass for the animals.

They had been walking since dawn. Horses, mules, and people, they were all so tired they could do no more that night. They went to sleep. In the morning they tackled the seemingly impossible task of finding a way to go on.

The mountainsides were cut with so many canyons that the view was bewildering. The party divided into several groups, one to take charge of the animals and look for some sheltered spot where they

156

might find grass, the others to go in different directions and look for some gap by which they could get through. Describing her journey years later, Nancy said that while she was crossing the mountains, she spent half a day alone, sitting on her horse with baby Nan. This was probably the day.

She stayed on horseback, she said, because she was afraid of Indians. The emigrants had seen occasional Indians in the mountains; the train had, in fact, several times been guided for short distances by Indians who were rewarded with shirts and trinkets. So far, no Indians had troubled them, but this might have been because the red men had seen that the white men were well armed. Today, however, with the men scattered, the Indians might be more daring. Nancy felt safer on her horse, which she said was "a fine animal."

Cold, tired, hungry, scared, she sat there waiting, soothing the whimpers of her baby, hearing nothing but the wind.

Bidwell and a friend of his, named James Johns and usually called Jimmy-John, had undertaken to explore a small canyon that they thought might be crossed. Bidwell decided that no crossing could be made here; Jimmy-John insisted that it could be done. Most of the party, believing that Bidwell had the more practical head of the two, agreed to take his advice and look farther, but Bartleson announced that he was going to attempt the crossing. He did attempt it, and the men whose supplies were packed on his horses had to attempt it with him. The horses were so worn with hunger, thirst, and fatigue that by the time they had made the difficult descent into the canyon, they could do no more. To rest them, the men had to stay in the canyon all that day and all night. They looked for water and found a tiny rivulet at the bottom of a split in the rock. The horses could not reach it, so the men had to scramble down and bring up water in cups, kettles, even in their own shoes, to keep the horses from dying of thirst. Then they had to start over, and bring up handfuls of the sparse blades of grass that grew by the water's edge.

When they finally got out of the canyon, by the same route they had used to get in, they found that the rest of the party had gone ahead of them, through a gap that one of the exploring groups had found. Again they had the task of catching up.

They rejoined the train. But somehow, in the confusion, Jimmy-John had disappeared. This brought genuine distress to his comrades. Jimmy-John had been reckless, mischievous, and likable. Many times he had given them something to laugh about when they needed it most. They missed him.

But they could not think of him much. Not now. They were struggling too hard to keep themselves alive.

Hour after hour they slogged on, leading their animals. They were always hungry. Now and then one of the men would sight and kill a wild animal, but it was never enough. Four days after they found the stream flowing downhill to the west, they killed the last ox.

About this time an Indian wandered into their camp. He wore no clothes at all, but he was a good-natured fellow and seemed to know his way about, so they gave him some clothes and ornaments and engaged him to guide them farther down the mountain. He led them along an old Indian trail.

It was a terrifying march. They had to walk along the rims of almost countless canyons. Sometimes they had to follow ledges so narrow that a single misstep would have sent the animals, or the people leading them, falling to their deaths on the rocks below. One day, four animals did go down, taking with them the supplies on their backs, supplies the travelers so desperately needed. Sometimes an exhausted horse or mule would fall where it was and be too weak to get up. When this happened, they killed the poor creature with a blow on the head and cut up the body for meat. When this meat was gone, they had to kill one of the stronger animals and throw away whatever he had been carrying.

These horrible days in the Sierra Nevada gave them little that they wanted to remember. Gaunt with hunger and sore in every joint, leading their precious pack animals along the ledges, they simply put one foot ahead of another, over and over and over, thousands of times a day, walking to California.

23

With the last ox gone, and hardly daring to kill a pack animal unless it had grown too weak to carry a load, the emigrants ate whatever they could shoot among the rocks—crows, coyotes, a wildcat. Once when Bidwell had gone ahead, scouting, he came back to find that one of his messmates had shot a coyote, but the starving men had devoured it all except the lungs and windpipe. Thankful that they had left anything, Bidwell sat down and finished up this remainder.

The party no longer made any effort to travel as a unit. The strongest of them went ahead; the others came along as they could. The foremost were sometimes three or four miles ahead of those farthest behind. They were all so tired that, when darkness fell, each one flopped down and went to sleep where he was. They did not even try to tether their animals now. The poor beasts had not strength enough to run away. Ben and Nancy, encumbered not only by their stumbling animals but by a child who now must have weighed more than twenty-five pounds, were among those who moved slowly.

But Ben and Nancy had found a good friend for these harsh days. He was Joseph Chiles, who had joined the emigrants when they were four days out of Sapling Grove. One day Chiles came to her and said, "Let me help you, Mrs. Kelsey," and lifted baby Nan out of Nancy's tired arms. Himself a father and a loving one, Chiles knew how to take care of a child, unlike the young bachelors who made up most of the company. He had recently lost his wife, and, leaving his children with relatives, he had joined the emigrant party to see if California would be a good place to make a home for them. Meanwhile, he was glad to help Ben and Nancy with their baby. After that first approach, he often carried baby Nan.

159

Chiles was concerned for Nancy, and perhaps he was also concerned for Ben. Ben had a good deal to worry about just now. His brother Andrew, and a friend of Andrew's named Tom Jones, had not been seen for several days. Ben was afraid they had strayed from the party and were lost somewhere among the rocks and underbrush. But this was no time to stop and worry. There was nothing for him to do but keep going.

The trail became easier as they moved down toward the valley at the foot of the mountain. Ahead of them they could see another mountain range, and they wondered if they would have to cross this one too.

At last, about the end of October, the party straggled into the San Joaquin Valley in central California. Here at the foot of the mountain, the country was brown and bleak, with a few scrubby trees and no water in sight. However, toward the north, several miles away, they could see a grove. This must mean water somewhere nearby. Water should mean game. But the sun was setting, and they were too tired to go any farther. Those who had any scraps of food ate them; those who had none did without, and they rolled up in their blankets for the night.

The next morning they started toward the grove. A few were riding, but most of them had to walk because they had so few animals left to carry their supplies. Ben and Nancy were walking. Joseph Chiles or one of the other men was carrying baby Nan so Ben could put his arm around Nancy and support her as she struggled along. After walking for a time, Nancy stumbled and fell.

Ben leaned over her and took her hands in his to help her back to her feet. Nancy murmured, "I can't get up, Ben."

He tried to raise her. Nancy's knees gave way.

She repeated, "I can't get up, Ben."

She lay there where she had fallen, like one of those worn-out mules that was no longer of any use and so was killed for food.

Ben had not forgotten the day when Nancy had refused to abandon him as he lay sick under the oak trees. Now it was his turn.

Leaving Nancy in the care of the friend who was carrying baby Nan that day, Ben forced his own weariness out of his mind and set out for the grove. When she told about this episode years later, Nancy did not say how he got there. Probably he took off the load one of his horses was carrying and rode the horse. Nancy lay where she was, on the ground, because there was nowhere else for her to lie. She did not know how long she lay there, dozing and waking and dozing again, but she was roused by a jubilant shout. Ben was coming back, and he was bringing water and a deer he had shot. They had a feast of venison, and Nancy felt stronger.

Ben was feeling more cheerful on his own account. In the grove or near it, he had sighted the tracks of two men. The tracks looked as if they had been made several days ago, and he was sure he had recognized one set as having been made by his brother Andrew. Apparently Andrew and Tom Jones were all right.

In the meantime, the other members of the party, whether walking or riding, had reached the grove. To their weary eyes, it looked like paradise. The trees stood on both sides of a river, and grass was growing along the banks. They learned later that this river was the Stanislaus, which they had last seen flowing through that deep gorge in the mountains. Today they did not care about the river's name. What they did care about was that this blessed grove provided ample water for them all. And not only water but deer and antelope and, besides these, a luscious extra treat, vines heavy with ripe wild grapes.

They killed two antelope that afternoon and had a regal banquet: all the meat they wanted, and dripping clusters of fresh grapes, the first fruit they had tasted in many weeks. They were a happy group as they spread their blankets on the grass and went to sleep.

The next day, while Nancy rested and played with her little girl, the men shot fifteen deer and antelope, made fires, and dried the meat. The game was so abundant here that the hunt was easy, and when they had finished drying the meat, an hour or two of daylight was still left. Bidwell and Ben Kelsey suggested that they would do well to start moving now. They could travel several miles before dark. The month of November was beginning, and if they were going to cross that mountain range ahead of them, they had better move as fast as they could, to reach the range before snow blocked the passes. Between their present camp and the range was an isolated mountain, and beyond this mountain the most clear-sighted of them could see what looked like a gap through which they might cross the range.

Most of the other men agreed with Bidwell and Kelsey, and began to load their animals. But Bartleson declined.

Bartleson said he and his messmates would stay here a few days more. They would stay, he said, until they had packed enough meat to last them all the way to California. Bidwell and Ben demurred. If California was a hundred miles away, or maybe even farther, wouldn't that be a mighty lot of meat? Could their horses carry so much?

161

Bartleson reminded them that he and his followers had the strongest horses in the party. The others had spoken of this often, with envy.

Still, not all Bartleson's friends would consent to his proposal. One or two, remembering their unhappy adventure in the canyon, said they would go with the main party. Bartleson, with half a dozen cronies, stayed in the grove. The others went ahead. They were traveling northwest, toward the gap that lay beyond the lone mountain.

About sunset they made camp, and in the morning they had started going ahead in good spirits when they heard men behind them, shouting their names and begging them to stop. Those farthest back in the train looked around and saw Bartleson and company.

They were astonished to see that the men of the Bartleson group were walking. They were carrying their guns and as many of their possessions as they could hold in their arms or strap on their backs. Their fine horses were not with them. The group ahead waited, full of curiosity. When the Bartleson party reached them, the Bidwell-Kelsey group exclaimed as one man, "What's wrong *this* time?"

When the Bartleson company had caught their breath and rested their aching legs, they told their tale. During the night, a band of Indians, far outnumbering them, had crept into the grove and raided their camp. The Indians had galloped away with all their horses.

These Indians belonged to what the Californios called the Horse-thief Tribe, and they were a costly nuisance to the ranchers. In a land rich with cattle and game, their favorite food was horse meat. They would choose the poorest horse over the finest elk. Probably they had been lurking near the grove ever since one of them had spied the white men coming up. When they had seen most of the white men going away, leaving a group too small to defend itself, they had swooped upon the horses. While the Bartleson company was tagging after the main group, the Horsethief Indians were dining in luxury.

Now for the third time there was nothing anybody could do about the Bartleson bunch but give them food—and hope they would not get themselves into any more trouble.

The party took the usual noon rest and went on until it was time to make camp. They unloaded the animals and had another meal of dried meat. Twilight was gathering when they saw two men riding toward the camp. Hands on their guns, the men in the camp watched cautiously until one of them exclaimed, "Why, that looks like Tom Jones!"

The speaker was right. The man approaching was Tom Jones, who

162

had wandered away with Andrew Kelsey. With him was an Indian. Ben hurried to meet them and asked about his brother. With a grin and a twinkle Tom Jones replied, "I left him at John Marsh's ranch."

With disbelief changing to ecstatic belief, the wayworn travelers found that they had come actually in sight of their journey's end. The lone mountain they could see ahead of them was Mount Diablo, and at the foot of that mountain was the ranch of John Marsh. They did not have to cross those mountains farther west. Those were the mountains of the Coast Range, which sweep down to the Pacific Ocean.

Tom Jones told them he and Andrew, tired of the slow progress of the train, had gone ahead, scouting to see what they could find. They had pushed west until one day they had met an Indian on horseback, dressed in a cloth jacket (and nothing else). Seeing the two white men, the Indian had begun to talk. He said the same word over and over, and what he said was "Marsh! Marsh! Marsh!" As he said it, he kept pointing westward, and making gestures indicating that he wanted them to follow him.

Tom and Andrew began to understand that he wanted to lead them to a man named Marsh. Almost certainly, the only man of this name in California was the John Marsh whose letters had brought them here. Hardly daring to believe their good fortune, they followed the Indian. He guided them to Marsh's ranch at the foot of Mount Diablo.

Marsh had sent the Indian to find the emigrants, because he had calculated that by this time they should be somewhere near the ranch. The Indian spoke no English, but Marsh, who had a rare talent for languages, had no trouble giving him clear directions about where the emigrants were likely to be found.

Andrew had stayed at the ranch, while Tom Jones, with another Indian, had come to guide the emigrant train. He said they could start tomorrow. Two days' traveling would bring them to the ranch.

When he had spoken this far, Tom stepped aside and beckoned to Ben Kelsey. He handed Ben a package. "For Mrs. Kelsey," he said.

He and Andrew had told Marsh how much Nancy and her little girl needed some nourishing food. Except for the acorns and wild grapes, for weeks past they had had nothing to eat but meat and such broth as Nancy could make of it, and most of the meat had been the flesh of animals who had collapsed from fatigue and starvation. Marsh had sent Nancy a package of farina.

Farina at that time was a favorite food for the captain's table on long voyages. One of the best-known packers was the firm of Hecker and Brother, whose office was at 201 Cherry Street, New York. A cereal grain finely ground, often flavored with arrowroot, farina was put up in sealed containers and would keep for months if the seal was not broken. The sea cooks used it to make porridge, or mixed it with chopped dried fruit to be served as a pudding for dessert. To Nancy and her little girl, a bowl of hot cereal was like a royal repast. Fifty-two years later, when she was telling a young friend about this journey, Nancy spoke with gratitude of that box of farina John Marsh had sent her, long ago.

The emigrants were in a happy mood as they set out for John Marsh's ranch. Their toilsome journey was about to end. As they went along, they talked about what a joy it would be to get back into civilization, to see neat white farmhouses with wells and chicken runs, cows grazing in the meadows, barns full of hay and grain, plowed fields stretching into the distance. And to eat some homelike food again: ham and corn and apples, bread and butter—*butter*! They sighed with joyous anticipation.

They were all hungry for food with fat in it. The meat from their starving mules had no fat, and most game is lean. They were no longer suffering from empty stomachs, for they had plenty of elk and antelope meat. But people need fat in their meals, and lack of it produces a craving as much as lack of water results in thirst. Any soul in the party would gladly have exchanged the finest cut of antelope for a plate of fried eggs.

Their Indian guide led them away from the Stanislaus River toward another river called the San Joaquin. This river was not much more than a creek, but it provided as much water as they needed. Riding or walking, they followed the banks in good cheer. Every step was bringing them nearer the ranch, with its safety and shelter and buttered bread.

They traveled all that day and most of the next, as usual the strongest men and horses foremost, the less vigorous scattered behind them. In the afternoon of the second day—November 4, 1841—they crossed a ford on the river, near the lone mountain. The Indian pointed, and the men first in line saw the ranch of John Marsh.

But where were the neat barns and farmhouses, the meadows and the plowed fields?

The travelers saw a great stretch of bare brown earth. They saw a few scattered little houses that seemed to have been built of lumps of the same brown earth. They saw a stingy trickle of water, some naked and half-naked Indian children playing about, and some skinny cattle foraging for grass that wasn't there. And this was the glorious California? This barren vista was the land of fruit and flowers and perpetual spring? This was the climax of their six months' journey, the goal they had struggled so hard to reach, the reward of their hunger and exhaustion, their hours of desperation and despair?

Yes, this was California. They wished they were back where they had come from. They said so, and they used some strong words to say it.

But here they were, and here they had to stay until they could get out.

The Indian sent some of the children scampering to find Marsh, and several of the new arrivals went toward the largest of the earthy buildings, which they rightly assumed to be the dwelling of their host. The door was swinging open, and they went in. Inside, they looked around with disgust. Marsh's home was as ugly as the outdoors. The house was made of what they later learned were adobe bricks. These were flat chunks of earth, about eighteen inches long and twelve inches wide and two or three inches thick, dried in the sun. They were piled up without mortar. The roof was thatched with bulrushes of a sort native to California, called tules.

There was no floor; they stood on hard, bare earth. The "windows" were nothing but holes in the walls, with no glass, merely ill-fitting wooden shutters. The house had only three rooms, and its furniture consisted of a rough table and several clumsily made benches to serve as seats or beds.

While the newcomers were mumbling angrily about their dashed hopes, from outside they heard a man's voice shout a greeting. They went out to get acquainted with the master of this graceless domicile.

At this time John Marsh was forty-two years old. He was six feet two inches tall; he was tough and sunburned and, according to those who knew him, not handsome. We are not told what sort of clothes he was wearing that day, but after five years in California he was probably dressed like any other rancher. This meant he wore wide trousers slit halfway up the sides, open-collared shirt with big sleeves rolled above his elbows, bright-colored sash with tasseled ends hanging to his knees, broad-brimmed sombrero, and boots with star-shaped spurs. If this is what he had on, these men from Missouri would have found him fantastic. They would have wished again that they were back home among men of good sense.

But he gave them a welcome cordial enough to cheer the most

downcast visitor. As he had run a store in Independence for two years (1833–35), he already knew several members of the party. These he greeted like old friends. He genially shook hands with the rest and told them he hoped they would be as happy in California as he was. He called his Indian servants to unload the horses and bring fresh water and otherwise make his friends comfortable. Now at last they could rest, he said, and he would serve them dinner as soon as it could be prepared. What would they like to eat?

With one voice they exclaimed, "Something with fat in it!"

Marsh answered with an understanding laugh. Their wish would certainly be granted. He had some fine, fat pigs. A pair of these would be killed and roasted, and they would have all the pork they could eat. Would his friends like to wait in the house, or, since they had been living outdoors for so long, would they like to stay outdoors while dinner was being prepared?

As there was nothing in the house that made it worth while to stay indoors, most of them chose to walk outside. When Marsh came back after giving orders to his cook, they began asking him questions about California. He gave clear and graphic answers. Later, Bidwell said he had never met anyone who had a better command of the English language than John Marsh.

Marsh explained why the look of the country was so dismal. This year 1841 had been one of the driest years California had ever known. There had been no rain for months. In normal times, during these weeks of late autumn, the hills and plains would be covered with wild oats that came up to a man's thigh and made succulent pasturage. But the wild oats had withered away; the crops had failed utterly; the streams were almost or quite dry; the cattle were dying of thirst and starvation. The staple foods of the Californios were beef, beans, and the big pancakes called tortillas, made of corn or wheat flour. But now, only the richest families had any flour left, or beans, or other vegetable food. Most of the people were living on beef, poor stringy beef from half-starved animals, not much better than the meat the emigrants had been forced to eat on their way here.

He was sorry their first glimpse of California had shown them the place when it looked so dreary. He promised them that as soon as the rains began, the country would burst into bloom. It would be just as fair and fruitful as he had told them it was.

Marsh was in high good humor that afternoon. His dream of glory was beginning to come true. He had brought thirty-two Americans to California. And two men of the party, Elias Barnett and Michael

166

Nye, had brought him letters from a leading citizen of Missouri. The letters said the people of Missouri were greatly interested in California. If Marsh would send more information about the route, the writer believed two or three hundred families would leave Missouri for California next spring. They talked about the prospect. Next spring, and the next spring after that, and the next—why, soon there might be thousands of Yankees in California!

As Marsh talked with them, and the emigrants listened to his eloquent answers to their questions, they felt better about the desolation around them. They knew a long drought could lay waste the richest fields. Marsh was telling them to look at that miserable dribble of water flowing past his own home. This was all that was left of the San Joaquin river. In ordinary times the San Joaquin was a *river*; now it was nothing but a brooklet. When the rains began, he said again, everything would be different. He spoke with convincing assurance.

Their spirits were rising. They had a feeling of conquest. They were *here*. They had defied Tom Fitzpatrick. One of the greatest of the western scouts, he had been wrong and they had proved it. Now they could laugh at those people who had started for California with them and had lost their nerve. The emigrants could hardly wait to write letters and tell the folks back home what they had achieved. And the odor of roasting pork that drifted from the cooking fires did nothing to make them feel depressed.

They began to ask for suggestions about finding work.

They asked about work because they needed it. The journey from Missouri to California had been a costly undertaking. Those great covered wagons, with the tools and spare parts to keep them in repair, were staggeringly expensive. So were the horses and mules and oxen that pulled them along. So were the supplies they had to carry: blankets and guns, ammunition to last five or six months, clothes and shoes to replace those that wore out on the way, hundreds of whistles and mirrors and bright ornaments for trade with the Indians. In short, an outfit for crossing the continent cost a lot of money. Most of the men in the party had spent all, or nearly all, they had, just to get here. Now that they were here, they had to start earning a livelihood.

Work? said John Marsh. They could find all the work they could do, anywhere they wanted to look for it. There was an abundance of otter on the San Joaquin River. Otter skins brought good prices. They could go to Monterey and help unload the vessels that brought goods to be exchanged for cattle hides. Or to the pueblo of San José, a thriving little town that needed a store to sell these goods to the ranchers round about. Or to Sutter's settlement. The energetic Yankees could always get employment in California. The Californios, pleasant and charming though they were, had found life too easy. With Nature in most years providing endless pasturage for the cattle, leaving their owners nothing to do but round them up for beef and hides (and Indians doing most of this work anyway), the Californios had never formed the habit of making much effort. Yankees, with Yankee dash and drive, were the sort of people this country needed. And now, dinner was ready.

The servants brought piles of sizzling pork, and red wine from the California vineyards, and then—surprise!—the delicacy they had not seen for months, except in their dreams: bread.

There were thirty-two adult guests. John Marsh had told the cook to make thirty-two tortillas, one for each of them. The cook had had no flour. Marsh had dipped into his priceless store of seed wheat and had told the cook to grind it into flour and make the tortillas of this.

When they learned of this gesture of welcome, these hard-fisted men were ready to cry. California was a beautiful place.

But there was no butter to go with the bread. The Californios had no use for milk or anything made of milk. To them, cattle meant beef and hides. John Marsh could not be sure, of course, but he doubted that his friends would find a churn anywhere this side of the Bear River.

24

The emigrants were so grateful for Marsh's generosity that after dinner they opened their packs and rummaged for something they could give him, such as a hunting knife or powder for his gun. Marsh received these gladly. There were no factories in California, and sometimes such items as these were hard to find.

Host and guests, for a long time they sat around under the stars, while the new arrivals asked more and more questions about California. Marsh answered in detail. The newcomers began to gain confidence. They felt less like outsiders and more like men who would have no trouble getting along.

But at last the time came when even the most eager of them could stay awake no longer. Marsh had told them that most folk in California slept outdoors, unless a hard rain was coming down. When this happened, they would spread hides or blankets on the dirt floors of their houses and sleep there. Like them, he said, he usually slept outdoors. His visitors could do as they pleased.

By this time the visitors were used to spending their nights outdoors. Most of them spread their blankets on the ground as usual. But the night air had a nip, and several men said they would rather sleep inside. Those who made this latter choice, however, speedily changed their minds. They found that Marsh's house, like most ranch houses in California, was a regular hatchery of fleas.

The cattle were quite wild; they roamed about with no supervision, and in every one of their valuable hides nestled thousands of fleas. In fact, one land grant was candidly named Rancho de las Pulgas— Flea Ranch. When the cattle were slaughtered and the hides stretched out to dry, the fleas sought other victims to feast upon. Over and over, the Americans who left records of life in California during these early days tell the same story. They say that, on the ranches, the Californios were so used to the fleas that they slept with them peacefully. But the strangers could sleep peacefully nowhere but out of doors.

But though the fleas were not much of a pest outside, tonight many of the newcomers had another problem. They had been so starved for fat that when the roast pork was served they had eaten too much of the fatty part, and now they were sick. Several men were awake half the night with stomach cramps and nausea.

However, when they woke in the morning, they were not depressed. There were here, they were safe, and the drought could not last forever. They looked forward to another talk with Marsh. A few more questions, a few days' rest for their horses, and they would set out to look for the jobs he had assured them they could find so readily.

But when they approached Marsh, they received a shock.

Since last night he had undergone one of his bewildering turnabouts of mood. Yesterday he had been open-handed, jovial, a welcoming host. This morning he was cross, churlish, stingy, thoroughly dislikable. Yesterday, like the most liberal of men, he had killed the fatted pigs and used part of his precious seed wheat to give them the bread they had missed so keenly. This morning he begrudged them the leftover scraps. He growled that they had already cost him more than he could afford. Fattening animals for meat was hard and costly in these bad times. And their horses were eating the fodder he needed for his own. He spoke as if they were a pack of loafers who had come to California with the purpose of living at his expense.

The emigrants resented this. They had good reason. They had been brought to California by his urgings, he had sent an Indian to meet them and bring them to his ranch, and one of their first questions had been, "Where do we find work?"

The men held a conference. They agreed that they would leave as soon as they possibly could. They could not set out at once. The horses were not strong enough, and the Bartleson group had no horses at all. For a few days they would have to depend on Marsh's reluctant bounty, but they would take it no longer than they had to. They told him so.

But in another day or two Marsh had switched back into good humor. He told Ben Kelsey that he would be happy to have Nancy and baby Nan stay at the ranch until Ben had found steady work and could give them a home. He told all the men they could leave their tools and other possessions with him, and he asked John Bidwell

170

to stay behind and protect their goods from night-prowling Indians. In his free time, said Marsh, Bidwell could ride around and get familiar with the country. He was so urgent, and so friendly again, that both Nancy and Bidwell accepted. It seems that after his first tantrum, Marsh had found that he liked to be with his fellow Americans.

The other men scattered. About half of them went up the San Joaquin River to trap otter. The rest set out for the pueblo of San José, about thirty miles from the ranch, to look for work.

It all seemed like a good arrangement. However, they were not to have peace just yet.

Halfway between the ranch and the pueblo stood the mission of San José. When the job seekers came near the mission, they were arrested and put in jail. This was done by order of the governor of California, Juan Bautista Alvarado.

The governor was blustering with rage. He was stormily telling his supporters that John Marsh, in spite of his now being a citizen of Mexico, had let a band of armed Yanquis invade the country. Though winter was at hand, Alvarado was making threats to order them back across the mountains. One of the men arrested, Michael Nye, was told to go back to the ranch and tell Marsh to report at once to Alvarado. The governor also decreed that the men who had gone to trap otter return to the ranch at once and await his pleasure. He shouted that he wanted no more Yanquis around. They were dangerous people.

Bidwell, riding about and exploring, met Michael Nye on his way back to the ranch. They went on together, and Nye delivered Alvarado's ultimatum. Marsh acted quickly. He sent an Indian to find the trappers and bring them in. He told Bidwell to list the names of all the party members. Taking the list with him, the day after Nye reached the ranch, Marsh set out on an errand of his own.

He called on Mariano Vallejo, commander of the troops who had arrested the Americans. A Californio born, Vallejo was one of the richest men in the country. He was also one of the most respected. Vallejo had no objection to Yanquis. His own daughter was married to one, Thomas Larkin's half-brother, John Cooper. His sister was married to another, Jacob Leese, who had been John Marsh's employer when Marsh first came to California. Vallejo well remembered the imbroglio the year before—1840—when Alvarado had arrested the boozy braggarts from Isaac Graham's distillery and had tried to turn their bar talk into evidence of an international plot. Like most other leading Californios, Vallejo had scant respect for Alvarado, or for the general type of official tolerated by the Mexican government. As Marsh was

171

to write Senator Lewis Cass of Michigan, a few years later, "They [the Californios] care about as much for the government of Mexico as for that of Japan."

Vallejo told Marsh how matters stood.

He said the Mexican officials were growing more and more afraid of American encroachment. Not long ago they had sent an order to their consuls and other envoys in the United States. This was: They should give public notice that any foreigners who wanted to come to California must get written consent from some Mexican diplomat in their own country. If they came to California without this, they did so at their own risk.

But this order, said Vallejo, had been issued *after* the Bidwell-Kelsey people had left Missouri. If they had never heard of it, how could they be held guilty for not obeying it? When Alvarado had ordered him to arrest these Americans, Vallejo had obeyed. However, with translations by an American who had been living here for years, Vallejo had explained the situation to the prisoners. He had told them he was sure they would not be long in jail. Now, said Vallejo, he and Marsh would call on the governor.

Three days later, Marsh came back to the ranch, bringing passports that gave the newcomers the right to stay in California as long as they pleased. He said the men in jail had been released and had gone on toward the pueblo to look for jobs. He would distribute the passports to the rest of them now. The cost of each passport was five dollars.

Five dollars! Few of them had so much money. They had invested what they had in their outfits, expecting to go to work as soon as they reached California.

Very well, said Marsh, if a man could not pay for his passport in cash, he could turn over five dollars' worth of tools or other goods from his pack. If he had nothing that Marsh could make use of, he must give an IOU. One by one he read the names. The men paid in whatever way they could.

But when all the others had received their passports, Bidwell found that Marsh had brought none for him. Where was it? Marsh replied that its lack was no doubt due to a mistake or an oversight. But Bidwell suspected—and when he wrote about the incident many years later, he still suspected—that Marsh had not procured a passport for him because Marsh wanted to make him stay on the ranch as a worker.

Bidwell had no intention of staying there any longer. He left at once for the mission of San José. Here, after some inconvenience and language trouble, he found an American named Thomas Bowen, probably the same man who had translated for Vallejo and the prisoners. Bowen spoke to Vallejo for him, and Bidwell was issued a passport. When he held out five dollars to pay for it, Bowen and Vallejo were both startled. There was no charge, they said. There never was. When Bidwell told them Marsh had charged each of his companions five dollars, his hearers shook their heads in disapproving wonder. Why on earth should he have done that?

They did not know, as Bidwell did, that now Marsh had been paid for two fat pigs and thirty-two tortillas.

Passport in his pocket, Bidwell joined a group of three other young men who were about to start for Sutter's settlement, New Helvetia, to ask for work. They mounted their horses and set out November 20, 1841, expecting to get there in two or three days, but they had a harder ride than they had expected.

The people of California had been yearning for rain. Now, all of a sudden, they got it—a howling storm that flooded the countryside, poured torrents into the dry creekbeds, and turned the earth into mud so deep that the horses stumbled and sometimes were mired to their knees. Instead of three days, the men were eight days on the way. But for Bidwell, at least, the arrival was worth all the trouble it had cost.

When Bidwell called on Sutter and gave his name, Sutter responded with a hearty handshake. "I'm glad to meet you, Mr. Bidwell!" he exclaimed. "I've been expecting you."

But how, Bidwell asked in astonishment, could Sutter have known to expect him?

All very simple, Sutter replied. A friend of Bidwell's, named James Johns and called Jimmy-John, had reached New Helvetia several weeks ago and was now in Sutter's employ. He had told Sutter about the emigrants on their way to California. Jimmy-John had also said his friend John Bidwell was an energetic youth who, when he heard there was a lot of work to be done in New Helvetia, would be likely to turn up, looking for a job.

And here he was. Sutter gave him a job, and also gave work to his three companions, not at all bothered by the fact that one of them was a runaway sailor who ought to be turned over to the law.

When he heard that Bidwell was here, Jimmy-John sought him out. He laughingly answered Bidwell's eager queries about how on earth he had reached California.

Somehow—Bidwell never did understand just how—Jimmy-John

173

had managed to get through that dreadful canyon in the Sierra Nevada. Jimmy-John could hardly explain it himself. Separated from the rest of the party, he and his horse had wandered until they saw light ahead and found that it came from a gap they could get through. Jimmy-John gave most of the credit to his horse. They went out into daylight, and after wandering a while longer, they caught up with a group of Indians riding westward. The Indians were friendly and let Jimmy-John ride with them and share their food. They brought him right into California. Either they used a route more direct than the one Bidwell and his friends had taken, or they had traveled faster because their animals were less worn than those of the emigrant party. At any rate, they had arrived about two weeks ahead of the party and had left Jimmy-John at Sutter's settlement.

So Jimmy-John was alive and well and as perky as ever. This meant that every member of the group who had left Soda Springs for California had safely completed the journey. They had had no leader, no guidebook, nothing but that rocklike will to keep going. Theirs was one of the most remarkable achievements in the history of our country.

Their influence on that history was profound. They had proved that crossing the continent to California could be done not just by hunters and trappers and other mountain men seasoned by long experience. It could also be done by people less flamboyant—teachers, farmers, storekeepers, and others engaged in such everyday pursuits. And they had proved more than this. Ben and Nancy and baby Nan had shown that a *family* could make the journey together. Nancy Kelsey was the first non-Indian woman to cross the Sierra Nevada, but she was not the last. With her child in her arms, she had beaten a trail that hundreds of other pioneer women were to follow in the years to come.

25

It is no wonder that the Mexican officials wished they could make the Yanquis stay home. On March 3, 1841, while John Bidwell and his friends were packing their wagons, the New Orleans *Picayune* published this news:

Yesterday, the second of March, was the fifth anniversary of Texan independence. In honor of the occasion, the lone-starred banner was floating all day from the office of the consul of the young Republic in this city.

The Mexican consul in New Orleans would almost certainly have sent this paragraph to his government. Texas was flaunting her independence. This had been brought about by the influx of Yanquis while Texas was part of Mexico, and the Americans were frankly showing that they were proud of it. No wonder the Mexican authorities were worried about California.

But though they might fume all they pleased, they could not keep the Yanquis out. Not while the native Californios were so glad to see them. More than once in records of the time we read that the young señores complained because, they said, so many of the most attractive señoritas were marrying Yanquis.

They kept coming in, the Californios kept making them welcome, and they kept staying. In the Bidwell party, a few young fellows had come west only for the adventure of it and expected to go back. But most members of the party had come to California expecting to stay for good. One of these was Joseph Chiles.

Chiles did not marry a señorita, but during the winter after his arrival he traveled many miles through California, getting familiar with the country, talking with Americans who already lived there, and making sure he wanted to choose this as his permanent residence with his children. He decided that he did.

But not just yet. He wanted first to set up a home where they could be happy and comfortable. To this end he made his plans. He decided to go back to Missouri and organize a second group of pioneers. He had crossed the continent once, and on the way he had learned a great deal. To this knowledge he had added more by talking with trappers and mountain men in California. He felt confident that he could cross again. In spite of Alvarado's swaggering talk, Chiles seems to have had no doubt that when he brought his party into California, they would stay there as long as they pleased. For himself, he planned to become a citizen of the country and ask for a grant of land.

He spread the word that as soon as the coming of spring made the journey feasible, he was going to lead a party to Missouri. Anybody who wanted to go along was to join him at Sutter's Fort in April, 1842, equipped with supplies and ready to start.

Hearing that the return party was gathering, John Bidwell came to see Chiles. Bidwell had become as enthusiastic about California as Marsh and Larkin. Like them he wanted to bring more Americans to live here. He gave Chiles a copy of a diary he had kept on the journey and asked him to give it to a newspaper. Chiles agreed to do so and stowed the diary in one of his packs.

And so, in April, 1842, Chiles and twelve other men set out on horseback, with pack mules carrying their baggage. Several of the men were young adventurers who had come west with the Bidwell party and were now ready to go home and settle down. Four were mountain men going only as far as Fort Hall. Another was Charles Hopper. Like Chiles, Hopper had decided that California would be a good place to live. He had left his wife and children in Lexington, Missouri, and now he was heading homeward so he could bring them back with him.

Also in the group—and probably the most eager of them all to go home—was John Bartleson. Some people might think California was a fair and pleasing land, but John Bartleson most positively did not. Bartleson's idea was that he had given himself a lot of expensive trouble and he wanted to end it as soon as he could. He yearned for his farm in Missouri. We can safely assume that the men who had come west with him were prompt to ask him if he was looking forward with joy to the day when he would eat out of the trough with his hogs.

At any rate, he went back to Missouri. Here he must have been content, for here he seems to have faded out of history.

Chiles and his companions reached Missouri in September. Chiles found his children healthy and happy, so he left them where they were while he went back to California to ask for his land grant. By this time Bidwell's California diary had been published and had roused a clamor of interest, so Chiles had no trouble assembling a company to go with him. Among these emigrants were the two daughters of George Yount (an old friend of Chiles's who had gone to California some years before), with the husband and children of the older daughter; and another couple, Mr. and Mrs. Julius Martin, with their children.

The party started westward in May, 1843. They had plenty of company as they rode along. On May 31 they met a party led by John Charles Frémont, sent out by the United States government to map the route from South Pass to the Pacific Coast. The two parties camped together at a spot called Elm Grove, and for several days they traveled together. This was Frémont's second expedition into the West, and with him were some seasoned frontiersmen. Chiles and his followers asked many questions. Before they said good-bye, Chiles had learned much more about the country ahead.

A few miles farther on they caught up with a long train of wagons bound for Oregon. The emigrants in this train had chosen as their captain a lawyer from Nashville, thirty-five years old, named Peter H. Burnett. They had made a wise choice. Peter Burnett was a natural leader. In 1848 he was to be captain of the first party that came from Oregon to the gold country, and the next year the voters of California were to elect him their first civilian governor.

For eight weeks the two groups traveled in company. When they had gone a few miles west of Fort Laramie, the group headed by Chiles had a turn of good fortune like that of the Bidwell party when they gained Thomas Fitzpatrick. Chiles met one of the greatest of the mountain scouts, Joseph Reddeford Walker.

There were two Walker brothers, Joseph and Joel, and their names are bright lights in the history of the American West. Joseph Walker had been into California nine years before. He had gone with a party headed by Captain Benjamin de Bonneville of the United States Army, sent to explore the Sierra Nevada. While on this expedition, Walker had discovered a pass through the southern end of the range. It is now called Walker Pass in his honor. He was as well qualified as any man alive to guide a party to this pass and through it. Chiles went into conference with Joseph Walker, and before they parted, Walker had been engaged to lead Chiles's company the rest of the way to California.

No doubt Walker took this job because he was being paid for it, but there may have been another reason too. His brother Joel was already in California. This was a chance for them to see each other. Back in Missouri, Joel Walker had married a girl named Mary Young, and he was now the father of five children. Apparently he had thought it was time he settled down with his family, and California was a good place for it. In the summer of 1840 he and Mary, with their children, had crossed Canada to Fort Vancouver on the Pacific Coast. They spent the winter in the settlement around the fort. In the spring of the next year, 1841, while Ben and Nancy Kelsey were moving west, Joel and Mary Walker came south into California, Mary bringing baby Six in her arms. When Nancy was seventy years old, she told a newspaper reporter that she and Ben had met Joel and Mary Walker at Sutter's Fort on a Christmas Day. How much the four of them must have had to talk about!

The Chiles and Burnett wagon trains stayed together as far as Fort Hall. Here they parted, the Burnett train going toward Oregon and the Chiles-Walker party toward California. In spite of the expert leadership of Joseph Walker, the Chiles party found their journey hard. But by January, 1844, they were in the San Joaquin Valley of California, among ranches and villages, talking about where they would like to settle. Some of them stopped in Monterey, others went on northward to the Santa Clara Valley, still others to Sutter's Fort.

Chiles went to George Yount's ranch, bringing Yount's daughters and grandchildren. He stayed at the ranch several weeks, resting from the journey and applying to the California officials for a land grant.

They gave him just what he asked for, a tract in the Napa Valley near Sutter's Fort. One day in March, 1844, he went to the fort to buy supplies. There, to his astonishment, he again met Frémont, who had just come down from Oregon.

The two men swapped anecdotes about the rigors and hazards they had been through since they had last seen each other. Frémont found Chiles's adventures so interesting that he included these along with his own in the report he gave the army. His report was published in book form in 1845, and as the book was read by thousands of people all over the country, it prompted many more venturesome youths to start making plans for California.

Chiles went back to his land grant and Frémont back to Washington. They were destined to meet again. But this time it would be in surroundings far less agreeable than those of their friendly chat at Sutter's Fort.

Frémont was one of those men who can command but cannot obey. As long as he was giving orders to his exploring parties, he did well. True, he took more risks than he should have, but in general he was competent and successful.

But he was so used to being a king that he could not bring himself to be a subject. In 1846, when the war between the United States and Mexico began, Frémont was in California on a third exploring trip. As an army officer, he undertook to raise a battalion. The nucleus would be the men of his exploring party; the rest would be volunteers. Commodore Robert Stockton of the USS *Congress*, who was to command both land and sea forces until an army unit arrived, approved of the plan. He urged the Americans in California to join. Hundreds of them did. One of them was Joseph Chiles. Stockton sent them south to occupy Los Angeles.

In December, 1846, troops under Brigadier General Stephen Kearny reached California. After a brief stay in the south, General Kearny led his men to Monterey and set up his headquarters there. At intervals he sent letters by army couriers to Frémont, giving orders. Frémont ignored the orders and went on doing as he pleased.

He had been doing as he pleased for so long that he seemed to have forgotten that a soldier obeys orders, whether he likes them or not. At this time Colonel Mason, who had reached California only a few weeks after General Kearny, was serving as one of the general's chief aides. Kearny sent him to Los Angeles to investigate Frémont's behavior. Frémont was so defiant that at one point Mason threatened to put him in irons. Raging, Frémont challenged the colonel to a duel. Before this could take place, General Kearny himself came south, intending to see to it that Frémont did as he was told.

What he told Frémont was, "You will come to Monterey, attended by an army guard, and report to my headquarters."

Frémont and his guard left Los Angeles May 12, 1847. On the last day of May, Kearny and an army escort began an overland march to Fort Leavenworth on the Missouri River. With them were Frémont and the members of his exploring party; also with them were numerous men who had been ordered to go east with General Kearny. One of these was Chiles.

The army men in California, and those in the marching party, felt sure that Frémont was being taken east to face court-martial. They were right. There was a court-martial, in which Chiles and the other men of the battalion were important witnesses. They did not know what Kearny had ordered Frémont to do in certain situations. But they did know, and were required to tell under oath, what he had actually done. Their testimony played an important part in the trial.

There can be little doubt that Chiles testified with regret and reluctance. He and Frémont had not been close friends, but they had had much in common. They had met the same dangers and the same troubles. Chiles felt a genuine liking for his fellow chance-taker of the trails. He was not the sort of man who would enjoy seeing his colleague get hurt.

Frémont's court-martial took place in Washington in the fall of 1847. Frémont was found guilty of mutiny, disobedience, and other charges. He was dismissed from the military service. President Polk remitted the dismissal, but Frémont resigned. He went back to California and got rich.

Chiles also went back to California. After his return, he built the comfortable home he had been wanting to build on his land grant. When everything was ready, he went back to Missouri again and led still another wagon train west, and among the emigrants this time were his children. After this he settled down as an affable and prosperous rancher on his own acres. He lived in California the rest of his life, a well-respected citizen. Descendants of his live there today.

26

When Jim Marshall picked up those bright grains at Sutter's mill, and Jenny Wimmer tested them in her soap kettle, they were both astonished. Nobody had told them a fortune lay in the California sands. They chanced on it themselves. But once the news had spread to the ends of the earth, an astonishing number of other people came forward, yawning, to say, "News? Not to me. I could have told you long ago."

These lookers-back remembered now that they had known about California gold for years, but for one reason or another they hadn't mentioned it. They recalled references in dusty old books, or letters from emigrants, or samples of gold dust brought east from California years ago. But, they said, it just hadn't seemed important at the time.

Reports of gold in California did exist in books written long before Jim and Jenny were born. Some early residents of California did know a few bits of gold had been found near Los Angeles back in 1842, when the ranch hand Francisco Lopez had pulled up some wild onions and seen gold specks on the roots. But nobody had recognized these incidents as events brimming with promise until Sam Brannan made his run through San Francisco. Then, all sorts of people found their memories suddenly refreshed. They had known it all the time.

One of the most prominent of these was James Gordon Bennett, owner and editor of the New York *Herald*.

Gold fever had struck New York December 8, 1848. That was the day the New York papers published President Polk's Message to Congress, along with Colonel Mason's letter describing what he had seen at the mines. When the fever had been raging in New York for six weeks, Bennett published an editorial on the front page of his paper.

181

This appeared January 22, 1849. In part, the editorial said (like most other editors, Bennett used the editorial "we" when he meant "I"):

Are you going to California? We are not. Almost everybody is going to California. We are going to remain behind, for the purpose of giving a correct, faithful history of all the movements that are being made by the California emigrants. We have a clear, undoubted right to write a history of these movements, for our record would commence some years ago. We knew all about this gold as early as June, 1844.

In that month we saw, in the secretary of state's office at Washington City, samples of gold brought by Captain Stephen R. Smith, who was then purchasing goods to take out to Upper California in the ship belonging to him, then lying at New Bedford. Captain Smith proposed to us that we should then go out with him.

We did not accept the proposition of Captain Smith, and regret that we did not. But we have nothing to do with the past. We will endeavor to give some idea of the revolution that is going on in our midst, caused by this thirst after gold.

The secretary of state in June, 1844, was John C. Calhoun of South Carolina. The gold Bennett had seen on display in his office had probably been picked up in 1842 on the ranch near Los Angeles. A specimen of this had been sent to the United States Mint by a California trader who had come from Massachusetts. His name was Abel Stearns.

Abel Stearns was the Pacific Coast agent of an American trading firm. He was the most prominent merchant in Los Angeles, and like other Yanquis who brought forth complaints from the young señores, he had married a señorita, Arcadia Bandini, daughter of a leading California family. When he heard that gold had been found so close to Los Angeles, Stearns went to see for himself. He saw that there was not much to be found. But as he was one of the first to come looking for it, he brought home more than most of the other men— about twenty ounces.

At that time, the principal merchant of the nearby town of Santa Barbara was another man from Massachusetts, Alfred Robinson. Like Stearns, he represented an American trading company and, like Stearns, he had married a señorita, Ana María de la Guerra. In the fall, after he had picked up the gold, Stearns learned that Robinson was about to sail for the States on a trading vessel. Stearns asked him to take the gold to the Mint, so it would be tested and he could know what the value was. Robinson promised to comply.

Robinson sailed in November, 1842. He delivered Stearns's gold to the Mint in July, 1843. In August of that year, the officers of the Mint sent Stearns a check for $344.75, which represented the value of his gold, less the fee they had paid some sea captain to take the check to California. In due course, the check arrived and Stearns cashed it.

The amount of the check suggests that this gold was of unusually pure quality, like the gold that Beale and Loeser were to bring to Washington in 1848. In those days, the standard value of gold was $16 an ounce. Beale and Loeser's superfine samples were valued by the Mint at $18 an ounce. The payment of $344.75 for about twenty ounces would mean payment of over $17 an ounce, after deduction of the cost of sending the check.

Anyway, James Gordon Bennett could and did tell his New York readers that he had known it all the time.

But not Bennett, or Stearns, or Lopez was first to know there was gold in California.

Probably the earliest printed mention of California gold appeared in a book published in London during the reign of the first Queen Elizabeth. Its title page said *Divers Voyages Touching the Discovery of America and the Islands Adjacent, Collected and Published by Richard Hakluyt.* Not surprisingly, people who read the book called it simply *Hakluyt's Voyages.*

The first issue, dated 1582, was dedicated to "Master Philip Sidney." In his dedication essay, Hakluyt called California "the back side of America." He did not say much about the place. Captain (later Sir) Francis Drake had just returned from a voyage around the world, during which he had stopped for several weeks on the California coast. But he had come home so recently that Hakluyt had been able to get only a brief summary of his voyage. Later, however, Hakluyt produced a greatly expanded edition of his book, in three thick volumes. In the third volume, published in 1650, he included accounts of the California landing, written by men who had been members of Drake's company. These narratives do not agree on all details—eyewitness accounts rarely do—but they give us vivid pictures of what took place. It was in this third volume that his readers found the reference to California gold.

Captain Drake had asked Queen Elizabeth for permission to explore the Pacific Coast of the little-known Western world. Of course, he said, he could attack every ship he saw flying the flag of England's great rival, Spain. These vessels would be laden with plunder the Spaniards were bringing from the rich lands of the Orient. They would be sailing along with no idea that an English vessel had dared to enter

183

what they considered their own private looting space. Drake promised that he would bring back their cargoes to enrich her Majesty's treasury. As he had already proved himself a patriotic pirate, the queen granted his request and helped finance his enterprise.

The chaplain of the expedition, the Reverend Francis Fletcher, was the record keeper. He wrote in his journal that Captain Drake sailed from Plymouth, England, in December, 1577, "with one hundred and sixty-four men, gentlemen, and sailors." (In this quotation, and others following, the spelling has been modernized.) They had five vessels: the *Pelican,* "commanded by Captain-General Francis Drake," and four smaller ships commanded by lesser officers. Through many dangers, they crossed the Atlantic and sailed down toward the Antarctic Sea.

Eight months after leaving England, they came to the Strait of Magellan at the tip of South America. Here Drake changed the name of his flagship from *Pelican* to *Golden Hind.* He made the change in honor of Sir Christopher Hatton, one of his companions, on whose coat of arms was a figure of the female red deer, called a hind, pictured in gold.

This new name was sheer prophetic chance. Drake had no premonition that the *Golden Hind* was going to take him to a golden land. (Many observers have commented on how often the words *gold* and *golden* were used in connection with California before Jim Marshall's discovery.)

The *Golden Hind* went safely through the Strait of Magellan and turned north. By this time she was sailing alone. Before reaching the strait, Drake had found that two of his five vessels were unseaworthy. He had abandoned them and distributed their crews and supplies among his own ship and the other ships remaining. These other two, commanded by Captain William Wynter, had shortly afterward turned back to England.

Drake ordered his men to sail up the west coasts of the two Americas. Below the equator and for some distance above it, the voyage prospered. The Englishmen captured several Spanish vessels and loaded the *Golden Hind* with treasures for the queen. By the time they were off the upper coast of Mexico, they were using bales of silk and velvet, and chests of gold and silver artifacts, as ballast in the hold of the *Golden Hind.*

But as they went farther north, the fog along the coast was so blinding that they passed the harbor of San Francisco without seeing it. At last, in April, 1579, Drake ordered the men to turn back. They went southward, eagerly scanning the fog banks for some harbor where they could rest and get warm. At last, on or about June 17, 1579, one of the lookouts caught sight of "a fair and goodly haven." Joyously the men landed on a coast where the weather was mild and the grass was thick.

There was plenty of game here, and the Indians were friendly. Drake told the men they would stay in this "goodly haven" long enough to put their ship into repair and build up their spirits with rest and fresh food.

It was almost like a vacation. The men hunted and fished, explored the land, feasted on fruit and venison. One day, the chaplain held a religious service for the Indians, with Bible reading, prayers, and hymns sung by the sailors, accompanied by music of the viols and trumpets they used for their own services at sea. How much the Indians understood is open to question, but they were enchanted by the music. By signs and clamor they demanded more, and more, and more, until the sailors, husky fellows though they were, had grown too tired and hoarse to play and sing any longer. The chaplain pronounced a benediction and the Indians reluctantly scattered.

This was the first religious service of any sort ever conducted in the English language on the soil of what is now the United States.

Drake spent about six weeks in his "goodly haven." Most geographers agree that he had anchored in one of the coves north of San Francisco Bay. They are not of one mind about which cove it was. The majority believe it was an inlet east of Point Reyes in Marin County, now called Drake's Bay.

Before he left, Drake conducted a ceremony on the beach by which he formally claimed possession of this country in the name of Her Majesty Queen Elizabeth. He called it New Albion. "Albion" was the original name of England. The word went back to Roman times and was probably based on *albus,* the Latin word for white, referring to the chalk cliffs of Dover. Drake chose this name for California, says his chronicler, "in respect of the white banks and cliffs, which lie toward the sea."

The Englishmen had explored the country for a long way inland and had made notes of what they saw. Everywhere they stepped, said their notes, they saw signs of gold or silver. When they sailed away, they sailed west into the Pacific. On June 15, 1580, almost exactly a year after the lookout had sighted the California coast, the *Golden Hind* doubled the Cape of Good Hope at the southern tip of Africa. Three months later, in September, she entered the harbor of Plymouth, from which she had sailed nearly two years before.

She had completed the first around-the-world voyage ever accomplished by Englishmen; she had brought back vast treasure from the Spanish vessels and much news about the dim far places of the world. But the greatest news she had brought, Francis Drake did not perceive, nor did Queen Elizabeth when she dubbed him Sir Francis in recognition of his achievement. This great news was in the day-by-day record kept by the Reverend Mr. Fletcher and his helpers and later published in Hakluyt's history. These recorders told the world about the vast mineral resources of New Albion. They said, for instance, "There is no part of earth here to be taken up, wherein there is not some special likelihood of gold or silver."

But in the world of Queen Elizabeth and Sir Francis Drake and the gorgeous galleons of Spain, plunder was more enticing than the blistering, backbreaking work of digging. Neither then nor later did England make any attempt to occupy New Albion.

But in 1848, when some real workers did start digging there, many a scholar who had read Hakluyt could (and did) say proudly, "I knew it all the time."

Throughout the 1600s, the Pacific coast of what is now the United States continued remote and almost unknown. The Spaniards built towns in South America and Mexico, but they penetrated very little into California. The English established colonies along the Atlantic seaboard, but they seemed to have forgotten New Albion.

Then, in the year 1719, another English buccaneer, Captain George Shelvocke, went out with royal approval to rove the seas and bring back treasures to lay at the feet of the sovereign, this time King George I. He went up the North American coast to California, where his men stopped for water at a port that Shelvocke (in the account of his voyage that he wrote later) called Puerto Seguro (Safe Harbor). From here they went across the Pacific to China.

Shelvocke did not have a pleasant time in China. There were endless complications in dealing with Chinese officialdom. He was not too much surprised to find that many a functionary in China held his office because he was somebody's nephew and not because he knew anything about the work he was supposed to be doing. It was a situation not unknown in Shelvocke's England; nor is it unknown today in other countries, including our own. Shelvocke thought himself a lucky man when at last he could resume his voyage with his ship intact and his crew in good health.

186

During all his adventures—which were many—Shelvocke and his assistants kept a record of day-by-day events. He had this record with him when he re-entered his home port. This was in 1722, three years after he had sailed. In 1726 he published a book based on his daily records. The book, published in London, was called *Voyage Around the World by Way of the Great South Sea.*

In his book Captain Shelvocke described his stop at Puerto Seguro on the California coast. He said:

The soil about Puerto Seguro (and very likely in most of the valleys) is a rich black mold, which, as you turn it fresh up to the sun, appears as if intermingled with gold dust, some of which we endeavored to wash and purify from the dirt, but though we were a little prejudiced against the thought that this metal should be so promiscuously and universally mingled with common earth, yet we endeavored to cleanse and wash the earth from some of it, and the more we did, the more it appeared like gold; but in order to be farther satisfied, I brought away some of it, which we lost in our confusions in China. But be that as it will, it is very probable that this country abounds in metals of all sorts.

This was published 122 years before Jim Marshall picked up gold at Sutter's mill. The book was read then and for years afterward. It was still around in 1848. The readers remembered the part about California gold. They had known it all the time. But they had remembered it too late to change history.

By 1849, California gold was the talk of the world. The boasting of the lookers-back who had merely read about it in advance was received with disdainful smiles by certain other people, who said they had not merely read about it but had seen and touched the gold long before either Lopez or Jim Marshall had seen and touched it. In this latter group were some gentlemen who belonged to the Royal Horticultural Society of London.

The Royal Horticultural Society was an honored circle. The members were learned men concerned with the science of botany. Organized in 1804, they had gathered an impressive body of knowledge about the world of plants, and they were eager to learn of useful or beautiful foreign species that might be transplanted to their own country. By the 1820s they agreed to send the brilliant young Scots naturalist, David Douglas, to the wilds of western North America. His mission would be to collect plants not known in the Old World and send seeds and specimens to the society's headquarters in London.

A lover of every sprig and sprout that grew, David Douglas ac-

187

cepted the offer with gusto. He made his first voyage across the Atlantic in 1824, when he was twenty-six years old. With a party of fur trappers he went to the main office of the Hudson's Bay Company, Fort Vancouver. Reaching the fort in April, 1825, he set to work gathering plants there in the Oregon country.

After sending numerous plant and seed collections to the society's headquarters in London, Douglas returned in 1828 to make his official report. He brought with him another hoard of botanical finds and a carefully kept journal of what he had observed.

Some of his shipments had been lost on the way. But enough of them had reached their destination to convince the most doubtful society members that they had engaged a dedicated researcher. To his delight, they sent Douglas back to America. This time he was to look for plants in California.

Douglas went back to Fort Vancouver and took a trading vessel for Monterey. In April, 1831, the Mexican governor, Manuel Victoria, signed a paper allowing him to roam the country for six months. Aglow with interest, he roamed. When his allotted time was up, he returned to Monterey, bringing plants nobody in England or Scotland had ever seen. He sent these to London. This done, he went on to Hawaii to seek further.

Most of Douglas's California collections reached London safely. But to the endless regret of plant lovers from that day to this, his California journal, written with as much care as the journal he had kept in Oregon, was lost in a shipwreck on the Fraser River in British Columbia. David Douglas's account of his California tour is gone.

His California plant specimens reached London in 1832. By this time Douglas was in Hawaii. There, when he was thirty-six years old, his life was cut short by an attack from a wild bull.

Nobody questioned the value of Douglas's work. He had introduced into Great Britain a fortune in trees, shrubs, flowers, and other vegetation. Apparently nobody had thought he might have enriched his native island in any other way.

But in 1849, when the world was all astir about California gold, somebody, or several somebodies, recalled an incident concerning the learned men of the Horticultural Society. Like the other hindsighters, they said it had seemed such a trivial occurrence that they had forgotten it. But now they remembered. When they had opened one of the chests that David Douglas had sent from California, they had taken out some little pine trees of a sort that grew to vast size in the American woods. In their laboratory, the learned men had examined the trees, and in the soil clinging to the roots they had seen some shining dots of gold.

The story spread fast. California gold had really been discovered, not in California, but in London! It had been discovered in London ten years before Francisco Lopez had found golden specks clinging to the onion roots!

Had it really? Or was this only somebody's dream?

We do not know. In 1849, when the tale was going around, David Douglas was no longer alive. His California journal, where he might have left some record of gold, if he had seen any, had been swept down the Fraser River to the sea. An anonymous writer in the *British Quarterly Review* for August, 1850, refers to the rumor and scoffs at it. Some writers have accepted it as a fact of history.

There is room for doubt. Nobody seems to know which botanist, or botanists, saw the golden dots on the pine roots. And though they were men of science, the discoverers (if there were any) seem to have made no tests to prove whether these shiny bits were gold or something else. If they did make sure the bits were gold, they were mighty quiet about it for a mighty long time.

But perhaps they did see bits of gold, or believed they had. Perhaps the find did not seem of much importance. Perhaps the episode roused an hour's chat in the laboratory, and then the scientists turned their attention to more serious matters and thought no more about it until the real gold fever stirred their memories. Maybe it did happen like this. Maybe it didn't. At this late date, how can we be sure?

Another man who knew about gold in pre-Lopez days, but did not think it worth mentioning at the time, was Richard Henry Dana, author of the world-famous book *Two Years Before the Mast*.

A Harvard student who had strained his eyes with too much studying by candlelight, young Dana welcomed this chance for an adventure he had long been dreaming of. Working as an ordinary seaman, he left Boston for California in 1834. He shipped on the brig *Pilgrim*, one of the vessels that made regular journeys to get cattle hides from the California ranches and take them to the leather factories on the Atlantic seaboard. Two years later he came back to Boston on another hide ship, the *Alert*, and when he reached home he wrote his famous book. Published in 1840, it is one of the finest books ever written about a seaman's life at sea. Also, it gives a priceless description of California in pre-Yanqui times. But nowhere in his book does Dana mention gold.

189

Twenty years after the book was published, Dana went to California again. When he came home, he wrote an account of the amazing changes that had taken place between his visits. This was added to a new edition of his book, published in 1869. For the new edition, Dana also added footnotes to his original narrative. One of these footnotes appears in Chapter Nineteen.

In the earlier book, this chapter had told about the cargo the *Alert* had been carrying when she left California in 1836—hides, cattle horns, and otter and beaver pelts. In the new footnote, Dana added that the ship had also carried a shipment of gold. He said the vessels that went to California for hides in those days often brought back packets of gold dust, but nobody had paid much attention to this. He had not thought California gold important enough to be mentioned when he wrote the first edition of his book.

But like so many others, he had known about it all the time.

Another man who said he had known about California gold long before Lopez and Jim Marshall was neither an adventurer nor a scientist. He was one of the most practical businessmen of his day. His name was William Heath Davis.

Davis was born in Honolulu in 1822, son of an American father and a native Hawaiian mother. An energetic young fellow, before he was sixteen he had several times worked his way to California and back on trading vessels. Then he decided he wanted to stay in California. He made his home there until he died in 1909, at the age of eighty-seven, one of the most successful men in the country.

He had seen so much history as it was happening that his friends often urged him to write his memoirs. This he at length consented to do, and in 1889 he published a book called *Sixty Years in California*.

In his book he tells about his friendships with priests in the Franciscan missions, during his early trading years when he was making frequent visits to deliver supplies. In 1843 or 1844, says Davis, Father Muro, a priest at the mission of San José, in an unguarded moment told him that the mission priests knew there was a lot of gold to be found in the Sacramento Valley. Father Muro said the Indians had brought in many specimens. But then, apparently shocked that he had said something he was not supposed to say, Father Muro told Davis this was a great secret. He begged Davis not to tell anyone about it.

Prospering in his own affairs, Davis was not greatly tempted by this whisper of gold. But he could not help being curious about such an interesting subject. He made inquiries of another friend of his, a priest at the mission of Santa Clara, Father Jesus María Vásquez del Mercado.

Father Mercado was not, like Father Muro, a reticent man. He was affable, outgoing, talkative. He was also a bon vivant who enjoyed good food and wine and liked to have his friends join him at his bountiful table. Asked about gold in the Sacramento Valley, he said why yes, he knew it was there. In fact, he had a good deal to say on the subject; but like Father Muro, he urged Davis to keep quiet about it.

Davis promised not to divulge the secret, but being a man of Yanqui verve, he asked why it should be a secret. If the priests would only let the news be known, said Davis, Americans would flock into California. With their skill and vigor, they would put up factories, build cities, open the harbors to worldwide commerce, and, in general, make California a rich and bustling country. Father Mercado replied that this was exactly what the Spanish priests did not want to happen. If the Yanquis came in, he said, they would soon control everything. They would take over the whole region.

Considering the carefree indolence of the native Californios, Davis felt pretty sure that this was going to happen anyway. However, he kept his own counsel, went about his own business, and held his peace. But when he wrote his book, he could not forbear telling the world that he too belonged to that group of enlightened elite who had known it all the time.

There were many other claimants to foreknowledge of gold. But among this profusion of lookers-back who knew it all the time, there are others who deserve a different sort of acclaim. These are the narrators brave enough to admit that though they were right on the spot all the time, they had never heard of California gold or even thought about such a thing until after Jim Marshall picked up his nuggets at the sawmill. One of these was a young naval officer named Joseph Revere.

Joseph Revere was a grandson of Paul Revere who, in 1775, is said to have made the famous ride calling his neighbors to arms the night before the battle of Concord. A lieutenant in the Pacific squadron commanded by Commodore John Drake Sloat, Joseph Revere was one of the officers on duty when the American flag was first raised in Monterey, July 7, 1846.

After the flag was raised, but before Marshall had picked up any nuggets at Sutter's mill, Revere was ordered back to the Atlantic side of the continent. He reached Boston in the spring of 1848, before the first news of gold was published in the States. But when the Gold Rush actually began, every literate person who had ever seen California was besieged by eager publishers begging, "Please write a book!"

Joseph Revere wrote a book. Unlike most of the amateur authors pushed into print at that dizzy time, he wrote a good book. His book, published in 1849, was clear and dependable history. But perhaps its most notable feature was the calm confession by the author that during the whole time he had spent in California, nobody had told him there was gold in the hills, and he had never suspected that there might be any. He says, "I had traveled over the richest placers a hundred times, but it had never occurred to me to wash the golden sands over which I traveled and upon which I often slept."

What rare and shining candor! It is refreshing now and then to meet the people who were courageous enough to make public the fact that they had *not* known it all the time.

27

The gold exodus from San Francisco had started that day in May, 1848, when Sam Brannan made his thunderous run. Already, at that time, a good many Americans were living in California and had no plan to live anywhere else.

According to the most reliable estimates, in 1848 the non-Indian population of California was about fourteen thousand persons. Seven thousand of these were people of Mexican or Spanish descent. A few hundred had come from France, Germany, and other European countries. Six thousand, or nearly half, were Americans.

These Americans had traveled to California before they heard of gold. They had come there because they wanted to live there. Some, like the New York Volunteers, had sailed around Cape Horn on military transports, but most of them had fought their own way across the plains and deserts and mountains. They were a hardy folk, used to fighting for what they wanted. Now, when they found themselves facing another fight, they were not scared. They were simply *mad*. They were mad because the issue at stake was so preposterous that at first they could not believe it was real. The battle this time was for their right to be received by their own country.

On August 11, 1848, when the people of San Francisco had heard the news that Mexico had ratified the treaty and California was now part of the United States, they had reacted with delight. The New York Volunteers had paraded through resounding streets. When Robert Semple thanked Providence that he was standing on American soil again, his hearers had cheered themselves hoarse.

Their joy was not prompted entirely by patriotism. By that time word of the gold find had spread to nearby ports, and new people were pouring into California. These new people were men and women of all sorts. Some were sterling characters; others were riffraff that a dozen nations were glad to be rid of. The Californians badly needed a strong means of dealing with this second class, and now they thought they were about to get it. They were taking it for granted that Congress would give them the same efficient government it had given other new lands acquired as the country grew.

A new area was organized as a territory. The governor and judges were appointed by Congress; the lesser officers were elected by the people. The people also elected a delegate to Congress, who spoke for their interests. Then, when the territory had reached a certain stage of development, the people asked for admission to the Union.

There was nothing dark or baffling about the road to statehood. It was the road already followed by every state that had joined the original thirteen. There were now thirty states. The thirtieth, Wisconsin, had been admitted May 29, 1848. The Californians were expecting that, at some time not far distant, they would make California the thirty-first.

But to their angry amazement, they found their countrymen in Congress would not have them.

Congress would not accept California as a territory or give it any other sort of government. Congress would not accept California as anything at all, except as a payer of taxes.

The block in the road was slavery.

Up to now, the territorial form of government had been provided simply to ensure law and order while the territory was developing. When the people of the territory believed they were ready to become a state, they voted on the various issues of the day, including slavery, and decided on the state laws they wanted. Then they asked for admission to the Union. The members of Congress could, and sometimes did, debate the issues for a long time. But while the debates were going on, the people of the territory had laws, policemen, courts of justice, and other taken-for-granted elements of civilized life. California had none of these. California was drifting into utter lawlessness, and Congress was doing nothing to stop it.

This was the fault of two minority groups, so violently opposed to each other that neither group would yield to any suggestion from the other side, no matter how trivial. Between these two extremes stood the men of more reasonable minds. These men merely wanted the Americans in California to be treated like the other Americans who had settled in areas that belonged to the United States but had not yet developed their new homes to meet all the requirements of statehood. News reporters, with their usual irreverence, called the middle faction the "soberheads." They called the men on both sides of the middle the "ultras." Today we should probably refer to them as the "moderates" and the "extremists."

California was caught in the fiercest conflict that has ever threatened the United States, a conflict that was resolved only by the Civil War. But the soberheads, many of whom felt as strongly on the subject of slavery as the extremists, realized that shouting matches were not going to end the quarrel. They urged that the duty of Congress now was to give California the safeguard of an organized government. It might be a long time, said the soberheads, before California would have fulfilled all the requirements for statehood. When this did take place, like the people of the other territories they could draw up a constitution and ask for admission to the Union. Then, before accepting California as a state, the different parties in Congress could debate as long as they thought needful on that constitution. But in the meantime, it was the duty of the men in Congress to protect the lives and property of their fellow Americans on the Pacific coast.

The ultras said *no!* Each side insisted that before any government be given to California, the question of slavery must be decided to the satisfaction of the side arguing. It was useless for some of the finest legal experts on Capitol Hill to express their opinion that the United States Constitution did not give Congress the power to enforce or prohibit slavery in a territory. The moderates, trying to give California a government, were constantly outshouted. Tempers were flaring. On both sides the extremists wanted to defeat each other. But together, for a long time they defeated everybody else.

And while the extremists argued and wasted time, hooligans were hurrying toward the land of gold and the Californians were finding their lives in more peril every day.

Colonel Mason and other army officers, foreseeing that this might happen, had not been altogether happy when they learned that Mexico had ratified the treaty of peace. Before this, the Californians had at least had a military government. But now that the war was officially over, the men of the New York Volunteer Regiment had to be mustered out.

The regular army had already been dangerously reduced by the loss of men who had deserted to the mines. Some of the New York Volunteers had also deserted, but most of them had not. Their loyalty had been caused partly by a sense of duty but also by shrewd sense.

Their terms of enlistment had required them to serve only for the duration of the war. The day the war was known to be over, each man would receive an honorable discharge and his pay. The volunteers would be free to go where they pleased, without the taint of desertion on their records and with money in their pockets to buy the supplies they needed for the gold country.

Fine for them, yes. But now, who was left to defend the citizens—all those men and women and children who had cheered so joyfully because they were Americans again?

As the summer of 1848 changed into fall, these citizens felt more and more uneasy. They had good reason for it.

As the guardians of the peace became fewer, the disturbers began to emerge more boldly. At first their misdeeds were the ordinary sort: a store burglarized, a fellow relieved of his gold pouch in a barroom. But as the weeks passed, the crimes grew more frequent and more serious. Before long, these crimes included murder.

One of the first murders took place about October 1, at Sutter's sawmill. With Sutter's permission, several miners were sleeping in the building that housed the mill. One night, a drunken man made his way inside and fatally stabbed one of them, against whom he had some real or imagined grievance. The newspaper account said he was now locked up at Sutter's Fort. But what sort of justice could be given him? California had no courts of law.

After reporting the incident, Editor Kemble made a comment of his own: "This affair brings forcibly to mind the present condition of California, without law . . . and yet holding out unparalleled inducements to desperadoes, escaped convicts, and the scum of the Pacific."

Shortly after this, another news item told about two men who had left Fort Sacramento with their gold dust. When they were found, they had been robbed and murdered. Again Kemble had an angry comment: "Shall we ever have a government? . . . We are now virtually *without* law."

Such reports came again, and again, and again. Then, about December 1, people learned of the most shocking crime that had yet taken place among them. This was the mass butchery of a whole family—father, mother, small children, and servants—ten persons in all.

The father, William Reed, was an Englishman. He had been living in California for about ten years and had married a native señorita. Two years earlier, he had received a grant of land for a ranch, near the coast town of Santa Barbara.

After a prosperous summer in the placer country, the Reeds were on the way back to the ranch. They were close to home when they were set upon by four men, who killed every member of the party and made off with their gold dust. Some other men who had camped in the neighborhood—probably another group of returning miners—roused by the shots and screams, rode to give help. Too late to save the victims, they rode after the attackers. In the pursuit, they shot one man and captured the other three. These three they took to Santa Barbara.

The evidence was heard before an impromptu jury in an improvised but serious trial presided over by the alcalde of Santa Barbara. (This Spanish title, meaning the chief magistrate of a town, continued to be used in California long after the American occupation.) The three men were convicted. The alcalde could settle minor local disputes, but he did not feel that he had authority to pass sentence on men convicted of a major crime, so he held them in jail while the case was reported to Colonel Mason. The colonel promptly ordered that the men be executed.

His quick action probably made the trails safer, but he, as well as everybody else, knew that the men who captured the killers were men who had just happened to be nearby at the time. If they had not been there, or if they had been less willing to risk their own lives, the murderers would have gone free. With no courts of law, there was no real shield for anybody's life. By this time, only a man of rare recklessness walked around without at least one gun at his belt.

At the gold camps, the miners held kangaroo courts under the trees and administered their own justice. Many a ruffian was hanged from a tree or lashed out of camp with a warning that if he ever came back he would find a tree waiting for him. Several years later, the editor of the San Francisco *Bulletin* (who signed his name "James King of William" in memory of his father, so he would not be mistaken for any other man named James King) wrote an article about the wild disorder of those early Gold Rush days. He had been in the gold country at the time, and he recalled that he had actually heard men around their campfires discussing the question of whether or not murder was really a crime in California, as the word *crime* meant the breaking of a law, and with no government there were no laws to break.

Colonel Mason was doing everything possible. But he had an impossible task.

He had been sent to take command of a quiet little nook where his men's chief complaint was that nothing ever happened. Now he had suddenly found himself expected to keep order in a savage carnival.

197

Every day he was called on to make decisions on matters no man had ever dealt with before, to answer questions nobody up to now had ever asked. He had to do this and, at the same time, keep within army orders issued to him long before these problems existed. No wonder he felt himself breaking under the strain.

In November, 1848, Mason had written to Adjutant General Roger Jones in Washington, asking to be ordered home. He had left the United States two years before (November 12, 1846), bound for California. After two years of service outside the States, he was eligible to ask for a change. He could not expect a replacement to reach him for several months, and he had grimly made up his mind to hold out that long. But Colonel Mason was a mighty tired man.

However, in spite of the present chaos, the spirits of the Californians were buoyed by their confidence that they were about to get a government from Washington.

Few if any of them were childish enough to expect that their new officials would turn California all at once into an island of peace and harmony. But they did believe that a stable government could, and would, tend to calm the turmoil. They looked eagerly for an arrival from the States who could tell them what Congress had done.

Their time of waiting was long and wearisome. Not until December, 1848—four months after they had heard news of the treaty—did they know whether or not their country had given them a government. When at last they heard the answer, it was curt and clear. No.

The United States ship *St. Mary's* reached Monterey during the first week of December. On board she had newspapers which told the people of Monterey the bad news. After several days in port she sailed up the coast, and on December 12 she brought the bad news to San Francisco. California still had no government except what could be enforced by the few soldiers left in Colonel Mason's shrinking army. However, the gentlemen in Congress had decreed that the Californians must pay customs duties on imports.

The Californians were blazing mad. Import duties had two purposes. First, they were meant to encourage the people to buy goods made in their own country and thus protect the home factories from too much outside competition. Second, like other taxes, they were meant to raise revenue for the cost of government.

But California had no factories. In California, every cup and spoon, every shovel and pickax and blanket, every spool of thread and yard of cloth had to be brought in from outside. Usually these goods came in foreign vessels, from Pacific ports: Mazatlán, Valparaiso, Hong Kong. Every one of these articles was to be taxed, with no benefit to the Californians. And as for raising revenue for the cost of government— California had no government.

They were enraged. They had been denied the most fundamental means of protecting their lives and property. As residents of a territory they would have been able to send a delegate to Congress, not to vote on the affairs of states already admitted, but as an envoy to keep Congress informed about the interests of California. Now they would not be allowed to do this. But they must pay taxes to the country that had refused to let them have these safeguards. Who was it, anyway, that had gone to war over taxation without representation? They said the editor of the *Alta California* was right when he wrote of the men in Congress, "They have dared to say, in effect, that the principle of 'no taxation with representation' is a fallacy, an unmeaning jingle of words."

This was written by Edward Gilbert. A former lieutenant in the New York Volunteers, Gilbert had joined Kemble in the newspaper business. He was an outspoken young man, the sort most wanted by the Californians of his time.

These Californians were not a meek sort of people. Men and women who had lived through such a trek as that made by the Bidwell-Kelsey party (and there had been many others since then) were tough in mind as well as in body. They might not be likable folk. They might not be the coziest of next-door neighbors. For when they got mad, they were not afraid to talk back.

As the *St. Mary's* had made her first stop at Monterey, the people of Monterey, San José, and other towns south of San Francisco had received the bad news first. In these towns, the law-abiding citizens— or rather, those who would have been law-abiding if they had had any laws to abide by—got busy at once.

December 11, the day before the ship reached San Francisco, the leading citizens of San José held a meeting. They agreed that the people of California should wait for Congress no longer. They should elect delegates to a general convention which would draw up a constitution for California. Word of their decision was sent to San Francisco and other towns.

By the time the messenger reached San Francisco, the citizens there were holding protest meetings of their own. They gathered in the little redwood schoolhouse—the only public building in town— and passed resolutions calling for the people to form a government

199

for themselves. The gatherings were large and stormy.

News of these meetings spread fast. Others soon followed. During January and February, 1849, indignant residents met in Sacramento, Santa Cruz, Monterey, Sonoma, and elsewhere. Like the patriots of the Thirteen Colonies, and the pioneers of John Bidwell's Emigration Society, they chose "committees of correspondence" to keep in touch with each other.

In Sacramento, they elected as their president Peter H. Burnett, leader of the Oregon-bound wagon train overtaken by Joseph Chiles in 1843. Burnett had liked Oregon, but when Jim Marshall found gold, Burnett had led the first party of gold seekers who came into California from Oregon. Now he was again proving his gift of leadership.

On the other side of the continent, Congress was in session again. By letters from their California friends, and from officers of army and navy, the men in Congress had been told all about the near-anarchy in California. They still had time to set it right before the Californians defied them. The soberheads from both North and South did their best. But each one in turn was shouted down, by men from his own section as well as by his so-called opponents.

A northern soberhead, Senator Stephen Arnold Douglas of Illinois, urged that California be made a territory without further delay. He said the decision on slavery should be left to the people who lived there. Loudly and vehemently, the ultras of both sides said *no!*

A southern soberhead, Senator Henry Stuart Foote of Mississippi, reminded his colleagues that the Americans who had gone to California were still Americans. They were not used to being governed by some remote authority. Why not make California a territory now? When the Californians were ready to ask for admission to the Union, they could draw up a state constitution for themselves. (He did not know they were about to do just this.) Like other territories, he said, they could say in their constitution whether they wanted their state to be slave or free. Then, and not now, would be the time for Congress to debate the question.

But again, with much noise, the ultras of both sides said *no!*

Both senators warned that if these delays continued, the Californians might not be eager to keep on knocking at a door that for so long had been stubbornly closed against them. The ultras paid no attention.

History does not tell us whether or not either of these senators, as he spoke, was looking across the Senate Chamber toward the senators from Texas. But every man in the Chamber knew that Texas had been refused admission to the Union because of this same slave-free

200

controversy, and the Texans had organized a nation of their own. The Republic of Texas had remained independent for nearly ten years, until it had at last been made a state in 1845. And now the talk was that California was astir over an idea called the Pacific Republic.

Nobody today is sure how many Californians were seriously thinking about a Pacific Republic. But the idea was there, and growing. Much of its growth was encouraged by suave, gentle hints from outside.

There had been no official proposals. But the Californians were quietly being made aware that if the country of their birth did not want them, other countries did.

For instance, France. The French people were never going to forgive Napoleon for having sold a million square miles in North America to Thomas Jefferson. But while they could not undo the Louisiana Purchase, they could, and did, let the Californians know that they yearned for another foothold on the continent. This need not be limited to California. The very name suggested for the new nation, Pacific Republic, implied that the way was open for the Oregon Territory to be part of it. This would make a nation larger than France itself, and perhaps richer. If the citizens of the Pacific Republic wanted to unite with France—well, they would be welcome.

Even more tempting than France was Great Britain. Cloth manufacture was one of the great British industries. The mills had to have cotton, and southern California could produce millions of bales a year. The British navy, which could bring vast cargoes of tea from China, could just as well bring cargoes of cotton from California.

Other nations too were assuring the Californians of their friendship. In fact, sometimes it seemed as if every country wanted California except the one country the Californians wanted: their own.

All this was recognized on the East Coast as well as on the West. The New York *Herald* for January 12, 1849, had a scorching editorial by James Gordon Bennett. He had no doubts about the real threat of the suggested Pacific Republic.

"We have every reason to believe," he wrote, "that many of the adventurers now flocking to California are full of the idea of making that region a separate and distinct republic, with the Rocky Mountains for a boundary line between it and the old states."

He went on to demand that the extremists in Congress end "their absurd, technical, and abstract debates about slavery" and give California government *now*.

No less demanding were California's early opponents, Horace Greeley and Daniel Webster.

It is true that Greeley and Webster had fought the whole idea

201

of accepting California, even as a minor appendage to the United States. Back in 1848, Greeley had been urging in his paper that California was "anything but desirable." At the same time, Webster had been urging in the Senate that the acquisition of the western lands would be "a great calamity." But it is also true that they both were wise men, and men of courage. We do not know if either of them had read the writings of that sharp-witted Irishman, Jonathan Swift. Swift had said, more than a hundred years before, "A man should never be ashamed to own he has been wrong, which is but saying in other words that he is wiser today than he was yesterday."

It takes a man of strong character to admit before a whole nation that he has been wrong, but nobody had ever called Webster or Greeley a weakling. They had been wrong about California, and now they said so. Throughout California's bitter fight for statehood, two of her best friends were Webster and Greeley. Without them, and the many others influenced by them, the fight would have been even longer and harder than it was. It might never have been won at all. Webster and Greeley were fighting not only for California but for their country.

While they fought, the extremists in Congress went on, day after day, week after week, shouting and brawling and making no progress toward anything. But in California, the dreamed-of constitutional convention was speedily changing from dream to reality.

28

Colonel Mason's letter asking to be ordered home was promptly approved. On April 12, 1849, the man who was to replace him reached Monterey.

The new military governor, Brigadier General Bennet Riley, had been a soldier in the United States Army for thirty-six years. He had spent most of this time defending outposts that ranged from the cypress swamps of Florida to the great plains of Dakota Territory. He had taken part in the Black Hawk War, when John Marsh was getting into trouble by selling illegal guns to the Sioux Indians. Later, in the Mexican War, he had commanded a brigade under Brevet Major General Persifor Smith and had received a spirited citation from General Smith for heroism at the battle of Contreras, near Mexico City.

General Riley reached Monterey on a Thursday. Friday morning he issued a proclamation stating that he was now military governor of California, and Colonel Mason was relieved of all his former duties and obligations. By Monday, the two men were deep in conference.

Mason told Riley the people had been clamoring for a constitutional convention. The two men agreed that if Congress still refused to give California a government, Riley should call this convention. They knew another session of Congress had just ended. Its adjournment date had been March 3, 1849—more than a month before Riley had reached Monterey—and this year the members had been required by law to observe the date. The reason was that a new President, Zachary Taylor, was to be inaugurated. At that time, Inauguration Day was March 4. This year, March 4 had fallen on a Sunday, so President Taylor had taken his oath of office March 5. With the new President in office, the old Congress had gone out of existence.

Mason and Riley were asking: Before adjourning on that night of Saturday, March 3, had Congress provided California with a territorial government? They did not know. Nobody had bothered to send word to the Californians.

Riley determined that he would find out right away. The place to look for this sort of information was the Mexican town of Mazatlán.

In those days, Mazatlán was the liveliest port on the west coast of North America. Besides being a center of trade, Mazatlán was the base for the Pacific squadrons of the great sea-trading nations, including the United States. Vessels from these countries were constantly moving in and out of the harbor, bringing news from outside and gathering news to be spread around. If anybody wanted to know what was going on in any country with interests in the North Pacific, Mazatlán was the place to find out.

The USS *Edith* had come into San Francisco Bay March 21. She had sailed from New York, stopping on the way at Rio and then at Valparaiso. Evidently her captain had been ordered to put his ship at the disposal of General Riley, for she stayed in the bay only long enough to replenish her supplies and get what repairs she needed after her long voyage. On April 10 she left for Monterey. She was therefore ready for service when Riley decided to get news from Mazatlán. He promptly ordered her there.

In the meantime, Colonel Mason was joyfully packing his trunk. He was about to go home.

The steamer *California*, now in San Francisco Bay, was ready to go to sea. May 1, 1849, she puffed out of the bay, bound for the Isthmus of Panama. When she stopped at Monterey, Mason went on board. Never was a man happier to see a shoreline receding.

It was Monday, May 28, when the *Edith* came back to Monterey. Nearly every American in town hurried to ask what news she had brought. Had Congress done anything at all about a government for California?

Their questions got the same old answer. No.

The *Edith* brought newspapers from the major United States cities, dated through March and the first six days of April. The exasperated Californians learned that though Congress had again refused to give them any basis for security in their daily lives, it had extended the revenue law so that they still had to pay taxes to the country that rebuffed them.

The country itself was showing signs of exasperation. The homefolk were concerned not only because of the ominous phrase "Pacific Republic" and the mounting dread lest the Californians make it a reality. They were even more concerned about the fate of the Forty-niners. Americans were leaving every day for California. They were leaving in such numbers that nearly every man, woman, and child in the States had a father, husband, brother, son, or friend on the way west. Their journey was perilous enough without their finding themselves in a land of barbaric misrule at the end. Over and over, newspaper editors were demanding that California be given an adequate civil government. They were forcefully protesting that the citizens going to California this year had as much right to the regard of their representatives as the citizens at home.

But evidently the extremists in Congress, and their supporters in the voting public, had paid no attention.

The papers carried graphic accounts of the last hours of this Congress. On the evening of Saturday, March 3, the members of the House of Representatives had passed the bill prolonging the California taxes. They had then gone back to their normal shouting and arguing about the question of territorial government. As for the senators, so far they had not even taken a vote on the revenue bill. While Senator John Adams Dix of New York was trying to get enough order for a vote, the hands of the clock in the Senate chamber were moving close to midnight. When the hands touched twelve, this Congress would come to an end as an official body, whether or not it had accomplished anything. Before this could happen, the senators stopped the clock. Word was whisked over to the House chamber, and there, too, somebody stopped the clock. The senators got quiet long enough to pass the California revenue bill. Now that both houses of Congress had agreed that the Californians must go on paying taxes, the extremists could go on wrangling about whatever they pleased. As had happened so many times before, they haggled but took no action. As day was breaking, they voted to adjourn.

The clocks in both chambers were still stopped, but the reporters' watches showed the time to be six-fifteen Sunday morning. The reporters were exhausted.

So were the members of Congress. Their tempers were on edge. While they were putting on their coats and preparing to leave, some ultra said something that some opposing ultra resented. Their argument turned into a quarrel. Other ultras took sides. The quarrel spread to both houses of Congress, and somebody's fist bumped somebody else's shoulder. The quarrels turned into fistfights, which the soberheads and the presiding officers could not control. Most of them walked out in disgust.

When the reporters wrote their accounts for the newspapers, they gave broad hints that the fights were not entirely due to fatigue or even to hot tempers. At least part of the trouble, they suggested, should be blamed on the flasks that some members had brought to ease their way through what they had foreseen was going to be a long and trying assembly.

Whatever the reason, Congress had quit and gone home, and California still had no government.

The Easterners had read this in their newspapers. Now the Westerners read it in theirs. The news of more taxation without representation appeared in the *Alta California* May 31, 1849. Two days later, Edward Gilbert published another of his blistering editorials, well expressing the anger of the readers.

At the army headquarters in Monterey, General Riley was angry too. And he had authority, which Gilbert had not. While Gilbert was protesting the deadlock in Congress, Riley was doing something about it. He issued a proclamation and sent out copies in both English and Spanish, calling for a convention to draw up a constitution for California. Delegates to the convention were to be elected August 1 and would meet in Monterey the first day of September.

There was no quibbling about the convention and no vagueness about its purpose. Now, and not in some hazy future, the Californians were to make their laws and organize their government. Then, either they would be accepted as citizens of their country or they would govern themselves.

Not every soul in California was happy to see this taking place. In any situation there are some people who are benefiting by it and do not want to see it changed. A good many such dissidents were present in California during that summer of '49. Some of them were men who had been planning to make careers for themselves in the Pacific Republic; others had left unpleasant records behind them in the States, which they did not want known in California; still others were men who sincerely believed that Riley, an army officer, had no right to order a citizens' convention.

The objectors tried in various ways to block the convention, but they found themselves a weak minority. Most of the Californians welcomed Riley's action. They were tired of living at a halfway station where they were neither wholly in the United States nor wholly outside. Except for the always paramount interest of gold, the constitutional convention became the most talked-about subject of the day.

Candidates for election in the northern districts toured the gold camps on horseback. They carried their supplies in saddlebags, or, if they had come across the plains and learned how to pack a mule, they used their skill again. Sometimes the miners were sullen, saying they had seen enough politicians back home, but more often they were hospitable, and the candidates slept alongside the miners in their tents. Or they shared the miners' meals around the campfires, breaking the monotony of beans and salt pork with onions and raisins and dried apricots they had brought with them and winning votes thereby.

Such campaigning was not luxurious. Days in the gold country were hot, but the nights were likely to be cold. A foresighted candidate would bring with him the Mexican horseback wrap called a poncho. This was a narrow blanket with a slit in the middle through which a rider could put his head. Thus he could wear the poncho as a cloak if he needed one, or he could throw it across the front of his saddle in the daytime and use it as a blanket on shivery nights.

But though these camp-stopping treks were hard, the candidates were a sturdy lot of men or they would not have survived to reach California at all. And they knew there was no other way for them to be chosen as partakers in the forming of their constitution. Most of the men in these upper districts, candidates and voters alike, had come to California in the past year or two and were strangers to all but their near neighbors. An office seeker had to make himself known by any means he could.

Candidates in southern California had a less arduous task. The southern population still included more Californios than people of any other group. The leading outsiders, such as Abel Stearns and Thomas Larkin, were men who had lived here for years and were already well known. They did not need to take so much trouble meeting their constitutents-to-be.

The elections were held August 1, with no disorder. During the last week of August, the out-of-town delegates began arriving in Monterey. Two or three, who lived in port towns, had managed to board coastwise vessels; the rest came by horseback, the usual means of travel in California. Some of them had a long way to go, and their rides took longer than they expected. The convention was supposed to begin Saturday, September 1, but on that day, not enough delegates were in town to make a quorum. By Monday, however, more of them had reached Monterey, so they assembled and began organizing. On Tuesday, September 4, they were ready to set about achieving their goal of creating a government for California.

They held their meetings in the two-story stone building now called Colton Hall. Their assembly chamber, on the upper floor, was the room that the young army officers had turned into a ballroom for their celebration of Washington's birthday, the year before. Thirty by sixty feet in size, it had been meant as a place for public gatherings and was well designed for its purpose. However, the delegates were faced with two homely but momentous problems. One problem was where they could sleep, the other was where—and what—they were going to eat.

Monterey was a town of twelve or fifteen hundred persons, most of them Californios. It had no place of public lodging for half a hundred more. These out-of-towners had to manage for themselves. With rare patience and good humor, they managed.

Most of those who had come to town on horseback had carried ponchos to use as sleeping blankets along the trails. Now they continued to use them. A few men tried to take shelter in storehouses or other such buildings, but these buildings were infested by so many million fleas that the men soon fled outside. Luckily, the winter rains had not begun, and outdoor sleeping was not too disagreeable.

Food was a greater problem. Thomas Larkin had been chosen as one of the Monterey representatives, and every day he and Rachel invited at least one delegate to their home as a guest at lunch and another at dinner. Other Monterey families were also hospitable. Between invitations, the delegates bought beef and beans and cooked outdoors. Those who had been to the mines were used to this; others learned. And somehow they all managed. But they were mighty glad when they found that they did not have to manage—at least not so strictly—for long.

Back in New York was Horace Greeley, and while he often had eccentric opinions, Greeley was a first-rate newspaper man. He realized that California was more interesting to more people than any other place in the world and had sent a keen-witted reporter, Bayard Taylor (no relation to the President), to write about it. Bayard Taylor, twenty-four years old, had crossed the isthmus and reached San Francisco August 18, 1849. Learning that the Californians were about to draw up a constitution, he set out for Monterey. As his expense account was not lavish, he walked. The distance was about a hundred miles. Carrying his poncho and accepting such rides as he could get, he reached Monterey September 9, and from that day onward he wrote a sprightly account of all he observed.

By the time Bayard Taylor reached Monterey, an ambitious Mexican had opened a restaurant—not elegant but welcome. The cook and the serving boy were Indians. The refreshments consisted of beef, corn, cucumbers, potatoes, and "execrable coffee." But unalluring as it was, this eating house did such a thriving business that soon others were opened. They improved with competition, and one or two even offered sleeping quarters. One such "hotel," run by a former soldier of the New York Volunteers, provided Taylor with "excellent board."

But though the sessions did not have a stately background, the convention itself was an impressive assemblage. There were forty-eight voting members, besides a president, a secretary with two assistants, a shorthand reporter, a language interpreter, two chaplains, and a goodly complement of clerks, page boys, and other minor personnel.

Of the forty-eight voting delegates, thirty-six had been born in the United States. By birth they represented fifteen of the thirty states then in the Union: Connecticut, Florida, Kentucky, Maine, Maryland, Massachusetts, Missouri, New Jersey, New York, Ohio, Pennsylvania, Rhode Island, Tennessee, Vermont, and Virginia. Several of them had lived for years in states other than those where they were born; thus the state representation was even wider than the list would suggest. Six delegates had been born in foreign countries: two in Spain, and one each in Germany, Ireland, France, and Scotland. Six others were native Californios.

Their average age was thirty-six, younger than that of most law-making bodies. (The average age of the Signers of the Declaration of Independence, and also of the American Constitution, was forty-four.) The oldest man in the convention, José Antonio Carrillo of Los Angeles, was fifty-three; the two youngest, James McHall Jones and John Hollingsworth, were both twenty-five and both represented the District of San Joaquin.

One of the delegates from the Sacramento District was Johann Augustus Sutter, lord of Sutter's Fort and the gold-flecked sawmill. Elam Brown, a delegate from San José, was the helpful man who had given John Bidwell the map supposedly drawn to show the way west, though the artist had left out the Rocky Mountains and put in a west-flowing river that wasn't there. But that had happened back in '41, and since then Elam Brown had learned a good deal. Five years later, in '46, Brown had left home as leader of a party that included his own family. He had brought them safely to California, and now he was a prosperous farmer.

General Mariano Vallejo, elected from the Sonoma District, was the officer who had befriended Bidwell's party when the swaggering Governor Alvarado was threatening to send them back into the snow-blocked mountains. Also from Sonoma was Joel Walker, one of the famous Walker brothers who had won renown as frontier guides and explorers.

Abel Stearns, a delegate from Los Angeles, was the man who, in 1842, had sent the United States Mint a sample of gold from the onion bed. Stearns was as influential in the southern districts as Vallejo in the north, and whatever he said in the convention would carry weight.

And who in California had not heard of Thomas Larkin? One of the first sights out-of-towners wanted to see in Monterey was the house he and Rachel lived in, with its novel blending of three styles of architecture—the California adobes, the tidy cottages of their native New England, and the verandaed plantation homes Larkin had seen when, in his twenties, he had been employed at various jobs in the Carolinas. Without planning to do anything but build a house that would fit the climate, so different from any other climate they had ever lived in, Mr. and Mrs. Larkin had devised a new type of architecture. (Now known as the "Monterey style," it is widely used in the southwestern states; the Larkin house today is a California state monument, which attracts as many visitors now as it did in the days of the constitutional convention.)

The name of Edward Gilbert, delegate from San Francisco, was familiar to all the newspaper readers. These were many, out of San Francisco as well as in. Not only was the *Alta California* sent to subscribers in the mining camps by couriers, but hardly a mule train went up to the placers, peddling food and firewater, that did not also peddle the papers. Nearly every man in the convention had read Gilbert's stinging editorials about taxation, and now wanted to meet him and shake his hand.

To serve as president they elected the towering Kentuckian, Robert Semple. A young delegate named Henry Tefft, who was engaged to be married, wrote to the father of his fiancée, "California being the tallest country in the world, 'tis perfectly proper that we should have, as we have got, the tallest President that ever served in that capacity."

They engaged as language interpreter the Englishman William E. P. Hartnell, one of the first men to scramble aboard the steamer *California* when she came into port earlier that year, the day after the Washington's birthday ball. Hartnell had lived in Monterey for twenty-seven years. Married to a native wife, father of a native family, trader and civic leader, he was almost as much a Californio as his native neighbors. More important to the convention, he was as fluent in Spanish as in his mother tongue. The Californio delegates, and those born in Spain, were shaky in their English; most of the others spoke little Spanish or none at all. Both groups were glad to have Hartnell as a link between them.

The secretary was William George Marcy. Marcy's father had been Secretary of War in the Cabinet of President Polk and now held the same post under President Taylor. The younger Marcy had come to California as a captain in the New York Volunteers.

The two chaplains, one Catholic and one Protestant, on alternate days opened the session with prayer. The Catholic chaplain was the Reverend Antonio Ramirez, pastor of the church in Monterey. His church building was already acquiring the romantic glow of a land-mark, for it had been constructed in the days when the West Coast belonged to Spain and the East Coast to Britain. In California of the Gold Rush, this seemed long, long ago.

The Protestant chaplain was the Reverend Samuel Hopkins Willey, one of the four young clergymen who had reached Monterey aboard the *California* on that well-known morning after. Mr. Willey was about to be married. His fiancée was a girl from New Jersey named Martha Jeffers, whose sister was the wife of Captain George Westcott of the U.S. Army. Martha had come to Monterey with the Westcotts aboard an army transport, which had reached Monterey shortly after Mr. Wil-ley arrived. Their wedding took place in the home of Captain and Mrs. Westcott a week after the convention adjourned.

The shorthand reporter was J. Ross Browne, a tireless rambler among the far places of the earth. Browne had come to California for the same reason he had gone to other strange places: because he wanted to see what it was like. He was no dreamer expecting to pick up bags of gold; he was a practical thinker, who had already paid his way through many lively wanderings because he knew how to write shorthand.

In those days, not many people could write shorthand. Systems of shorthand had been in use since the time of the ancient Romans, but they were so cumbersome that few writers had patience to learn them. The first really efficient system of shorthand, devised by Isaac Pittman, was still new and little known, for Pittman's first textbook had been published only eleven years before Jim Marshall found gold at the sawmill. (John Robert Gregg, inventor of the Gregg system was not yet born.) As Ross Browne's greatest joy was to be always going somewhere, he decided early that a man skilled in this rare art could find work anywhere. Then he could earn money enough

211

to go somewhere else. As a teenager, Browne had learned shorthand, and at twenty he had become a reporter for the United States Senate.

When Browne had reached San Francisco (August 3, 1849) he had not known that a constitutional convention had been called. But when he learned of it, he felt sure that if the delegates had not already found a shorthand reporter, they would be glad to have him. One of the delegates elected from San Francisco was William Gwin. A native of Tennessee, William Gwin had lived for some years in Mississippi and had been a member of Congress from that state during the time when Browne had been a Senate reporter. Browne asked him: Had the convention engaged a reporter? Of course not; Gwin had not known—nor, probably, had anyone else—that there was such a man to be found in California. In almost no time, the convention had a chronicler and Browne had a job.

His notes, under the formidable title *Reports of the Debates in the Convention of California on the Formation of the State Constitution in September and October, 1849,* were published in Washington in 1851. A Spanish translation appeared the same year.

As was to be expected, these debates were not always friendly. With their strong opinions and confident minds, the delegates had many arguments. But they never reached the stalemate of bluster and name-calling that was still paralyzing Congress. They agreed on their purposes; they disagreed only on the best way of achieving them. And unlike the ultras in Congress, they were willing to listen to each other.

They intended, of course, to ask Congress to make California the thirty-first state of the Union. But first they had to say exactly what they were asking the Union to receive. They must decide how large the state would be and draw boundaries showing what it would include and what it would not. More important, they must unite upon the terms of the constitution by which the people would live.

By the peace treaty, Mexico had ceded to the United States about half a million square miles of land. This vast domain, twice the size of Texas, with such variety of climates and resources, could hardly be accepted as a single state. There was also another fact, forgotten by nobody: As a single state, this vast domain would provide only two senators—no more than Rhode Island, with its just over twelve hundred square miles. Divided into smaller units, it would give the West six senators or maybe more.

The delegates all agreed, of course, that the western boundary would be the Pacific Ocean; the northern, the line dividing California and Oregon; the southern, the line between California and Mexico. Concerning the eastern boundary, there were many opinions, but after many speeches, this too was agreed upon. This meant that California was to be a state of almost 160,000 square miles. It was much longer than wide—as Henry Tefft had described it, a "tall country."

They found it no simple task to draw up a constitution that every man in the convention would be willing to sign. However, this proved less baffling than some of them had feared. As the Californios and some of the foreign-born members had only slight acquaintance with the United States Constitution, General Riley had commissioned two members to draw up a sample constitution. This could be used as a base to work from. One of these members was Brevet Captain Henry Wager Halleck. The other was Myron Norton, a young lawyer from Vermont.

Their only guides were the national constitution and such state constitutions as they could scrape up in this neglected hinterland. But they did their work well and won official thanks from Riley when he retired as military governor.

(The later careers of these amateur statesmen upheld their early promise. Halleck became one of the most distinguished officers in the Union Army during the Civil War, and Norton made an excellent record as Judge of the Superior Court during one of California's most turbulent stages of growing up.)

In forming their state constitution, the convention members used Halleck and Norton's model, along with the national and state constitutions, making changes to fit California. They had disputes, often noisy but not violent. What might have caused the bitterest conflict, slavery, was disposed of more smoothly than many of them had dared to hope. Most of the Californians did not want slavery and said so. Men from the slave states had seen how the system blunted the opportunities for enterprising young people there, and few of them wanted to bring it west. Nearly all the delegates who had come to California from slave states opposed slavery as much as the rest.

Nearly all, but not all. The hardest to convince were Benjamin Moore of Florida and James McHall Jones, a Kentucky native who had lived the better part of his twenty-five years in Louisiana. These two holdouts were persuaded to vote against slavery by Ross Browne's friend, former Congressman William Gwin. As Gwin owned a plantation in Mississippi, where the work was done by slaves, there was a good deal of guessing about why he opposed slavery. Some guessers said it was because he did not believe California could be admitted to the Union as a slave state but he was hoping that, once admitted, the state could be cut in half, crosswise, with slavery in the southern half. Others said it was because Gwin was ambitious: He wanted to be one of California's first senators, and wanted this so much that he would rather be a senator from a free state than no senator at all.

(And in spite of the gossip and whispering, it may be that Gwin opposed slavery in California because he genuinely did not want it there.)

Whatever his motives, Gwin brought in the last two objectors. He was a man of great charm, as well as a lot of nimble sense, and in this case he used both to advantage. When the convention met for its regular session September 11, the subject under discussion, carried over from the day before, was the Article on Rights: the right to free speech, trial by jury, and so on. A delegate from the Sacramento District, William Shannon, proposed that Section 18 of this article should read: "Neither slavery nor involuntary servitude, unless for the punishment of crimes, shall ever be tolerated in this state." The *yes* vote was unanimous.

As Shannon was a native of Ireland, it surprised nobody that he should believe in freedom. The voters who had elected him were mostly men in the mining camps, a mighty independent lot. Before the convention assembled, they had held a meeting at which they had expressed their opposition to slavery. Their delegate was glad to comply.

The convention named Tuesday, November 13, for the general vote on accepting the constitution. The plan was that on the same day, when the constitution was accepted (evidently nobody doubted that it would be accepted), the people would also elect a governor, a state legislature, and other officials. As soon as the votes were counted, the men elected would take the oath of office and California would start functioning as a state.

And so it came about that after a surprisingly short time—Tuesday, September 4, to Friday, October 12—the delegates had nothing more to do but tie up a few formal ends. This finished, they adjourned to celebrate with a grand ball that evening. It was a great occasion.

The next day (Saturday, October 13, 1849) they met to perform their last and happiest duty as a group: signing the constitution. As the ceremony began, the American flag was run up on the flagstaff outside. The guns at the fort began a cannonade to spread the news through the town, the countryside, and the ships in the bay. The listeners in the street counted, and as they heard the thirty-first bang, they

214

broke into shouts. They had taken one more step, this time a long one, toward making California the thirty-first star in the flag.

Now came another grand occasion: payday.

Not long after the convention opened, somebody had brought up the subject of remuneration for the delegates. Bayard Taylor wrote that some few of them had said proudly that being chosen for this important trust was such an honor they wanted no other reward. But the majority, being less rich, were more practical. They needed payment. Leaving their usual occupations and spending all this time in Monterey was more than they could afford. This made sense, and there was no disagreement in the convention or out. It was decided that officers and all delegates, as well as the employees, should be paid, the rates varying with the positions they held. The money was to be taken from what was called the Civil Fund. This meant the taxes on imports.

So at last, some of this tax money was going to be returned to the men who had been forced to pay it. They all resented the tax, and this was not only because of the principle of taxation without representation. Nor was it entirely a matter of the amounts they had to pay. It was an absurd sort of tangle that nobody in Congress seemed able to understand.

The tax could not be paid with uncoined gold, no matter how pure. It had to be paid with gold or silver coins, and every coin had to be brought from the United States, nearly three thousand miles overland and farther by way of the isthmus or Cape Horn. A man who had nowhere to sleep and wanted to buy a ready-made house from China could pay for the house with gold dust. But the trouble with gold dust was that he could not use it to pay the import tax. He could not get his house until he—or the seller—had paid the tax. He might have a golden fortune in his safe, but he had to wait until he could find somebody who would buy his gold dust for gold or silver coins. When at last he paid the tax, the coins were locked up in the customhouse. Neither General Riley nor any other officer could take them out except for some public expense. Behind the locked and guarded doors the coins piled up, almost useless. In the world of business outside, they were so scarce that when a desperate buyer borrowed coins to pay his tax, he had to pay the lender interest of ten percent a month. This was not greedy usury; it was the standard rate.

Since pay to public functionaries was a public expense, General Riley could order that the convention personnel be paid with coins. The coins, most of them silver dollars, were brought to the convention hall, where officers, members, and employees walked out with clinking bags of real money over their shoulders. The bags were gloriously heavy. So heavy, in fact—about thirty to sixty pounds each—that the better-paid officers could hardly lug them around. The supposedly dignified gentlemen were grotesque as they staggered down the street, their backs bent under their loads of wealth.

No matter. They had earned it.

29

The convention had named November 13, 1849, as the day when the Californians were to vote *yes* or *no* on the constitution and elect their state officers. The date was not a happy choice, but this was nobody's fault. Nobody could have foreseen that California was on its way into one of the rainiest seasons in history.

The year before, except for a few early sprinkles, there had been no winter rain until December. But this year the first downpour in Sacramento occurred October 7, and the first in San Francisco two days later. Then it rained, and rained, and rained. By the time Election Day arrived, the mud was knee deep and in some places deeper. Storekeepers sank bales of goods and even cookstoves into the mud in front of their stores, so customers would have something solid to walk on. On Election Day, showers kept falling from dawn till dark and, said the *Alta*, "the mud, which was unfathomable before, suddenly disclosed a lower deep."

This was true not only of San Francisco but of the mining camps and most of the settlements all over California. It was not surprising that the voter turnout was not large. However, among the men who did go to the polls, the *yes* vote was overwhelming. In San Francisco the votes were *yes*, 2,051; *no*, 5. The total throughout California was *yes*, 12,064; *no*, 811.

It is interesting to speculate on who these 811 *no* voters might have been. Among them were almost certainly some Californios who did not want to be Americans and took this way to say so. Others were men who had planned to make themselves important in the Pacific Republic and still hoped to bring this republic into being. Still others, like "Talbot Green" of the Bidwell-Kelsey party, had come to California because they wanted to be rid of their past lives. They did not want United States authorities to catch up with them. And some—perhaps most of them—were the sort of malcontents who are never happy anywhere, and whose reaction to every new proposal is *no!* Now in '49, California had more than the average share of such misfits.

As governor, the voters elected Peter H. Burnett. One of the U.S. Congressmen was Edward Gilbert of the *Alta California*. The other was George Washington Wright, who had come to California from Massachusetts. Wright was a picturesque figure. He had already been engaged in many occupations—newspaper work in Boston, the whale oil and candle business in Nantucket, banking, mining, and gold dust speculation in San Francisco, and varied scientific experiments on the side—just the sort of man the adventurous voters of California wanted at this juncture to speak for them. When he reached Washington, the reporter for the New York *Herald* described him as "a fine, intelligent-looking man."

The California State Legislature met in San José Monday, December 17, 1849. On the morning of Thursday, December 20, in a joint session of both houses, Governor Burnett and Lieutenant Governor John McDougal were formally installed. In his acceptance speech, Burnett said California should "assume all the functions of sovereignty now." He added that if California were refused admission to the Union, she would still be a sovereign state. It was a clear warning. *Remember Texas. Remember the Pacific Republic.*

That afternoon the legislature turned to the duty of electing the senators from California. (At that time, U.S. senators were still being chosen by the state legislatures instead of by direct vote of the people.) Several ballots were necessary. But before they adjourned that evening, the members of the legislature had agreed upon John Charles Frémont and William Gwin.

Some outsiders suggested that the legislators had chosen strong personality and charming ways instead of more solid qualities. This may have been true. But in this case, Frémont and Gwin were better than men less flamboyant would have been. The legislators were well aware of the barricade the senators-elect would have to face in Washington. They were going to need all the friends, admirers, and advocates they could get. A romantic reputation like Frémont's and an engaging manner like Gwin's were assets not to be ignored.

The four delegates to Congress left San Francisco New Year's Day, 1850, aboard the steamer *Oregon,* bound for Panama. With them was

218

an unofficial diplomat. This was Mrs. Frémont, the former Jessie Benton, daughter of Senator Thomas Hart Benton of Missouri. One of the most brilliant and beguiling women of her day, Jessie was to be a great winner of allies for California.

Their plan had been that the whole party would go together across the isthmus with the troops that escorted the mail. Gilbert, Wright, and Gwin did cross with the troops. But the Frémonts were delayed because they both fell victims to one of the tropical infections lumped under the general name "Chagres fever." However, they both recovered and finished their journey, though they were several weeks behind the others.

These others reached Washington early in February. At once they set about meeting important people, making friends, and smoothing California's way toward statehood. Said the Washington correspondent of the New York *Herald* February 14: "The arrival of Messrs. Gwin, Wright, and Gilbert, from the new state of California, has created considerable sensation here in Washington." He went on to tell how they were being received by such outstanding men as senators Henry Clay and Thomas Hart Benton, Speaker of the House Howell Cobb, and Vice-President Millard Fillmore; how often they had been invited to the White House to discuss affairs in California with President Taylor and members of his Cabinet; and how they were being welcomed by the social leaders of the capital.

Plainly, the men from California were gaining respect for their political acumen as well as popularity for their genial spirits. When the Frémonts arrived, they too were met with enthusiasm. Frémont had faults but dullness was not among them, and Jessie was a delight in any gathering. Their schedule was bright and crowded.

A copy of the California state constitution had been sent to the President by a special messenger, John M. Hollingsworth, who had been a lieutenant in the New York Volunteers and a member of the constitutional convention. It was reprinted all over the country. Governor Burnett's speech to the legislature had also been sent east, and newspapers from New England to the Gulf of Mexico published it in full. Many papers also published the complete results of the California elections, with names of all the candidates and the number of votes given each. Edward Gilbert was guest of honor at a banquet in Albany, New York, where he had once worked as a newspaper reporter. Now the citizens welcomed him as a hero. His speech was interrupted over and over by cheers and applause.

The first newspapers with these glowing accounts reached San

Francisco March 20, 1850. The Californians were happy to see that so many Easterners were taking it for granted that California statehood was assured. Many writers, in fact, were writing as if California were a state already. The reporter who announced the arrival of Gwin, Gilbert, and Wright said they had come from "the new state of California." An article in the New Orleans *Picayune* began, "One of the senators from the new state will be in Washington probably in the course of this week." The New York *Tribune*, summarizing the bills passed by the California Legislature, said nearly all had been "directly necessary to the thorough organization of the state government." The *Herald*, listing the names of the officeholders, headed the column "The Officers of the New State."

But Congress was taking no steps toward making California a state.

On both the East and West coasts, people in general had assumed that the Californians would accept their new constitution and elect officers. Then they would not merely ask for admission to the Union, they would claim it as their right.

The majority of the men in Congress wanted to say yes. But it was well known, in Congress and out of it, that the ultras (and the voters who had elected them) wanted California admitted only on their own terms. If they could not have their way, they would do all they could to keep California out.

The pro-slavery extremists wanted California to be cut crosswise to make two states, with slavery to be legal in one of them. Up to now, the slave and free states had been evenly balanced in number, thus assuring an equal number of senators for each point of view. (Slavery was allowed also in the District of Columbia, but in those days, residents of the District could not vote and were governed directly by Congress.) If California should be admitted as a single state, with a no-slavery constitution, this would slant the balance in favor of the free states.

The Southerners justified the split by the Missouri Compromise. This compromise had been agreed upon thirty years before, in 1820. Missouri had asked for admission as a state with slavery, Maine as a state without it. In both Houses of Congress, men from free states had objected to Missouri's being admitted as a slave state. They feared that this would open the northern part of the Louisiana Purchase to slavery. By the terms of the compromise, both Missouri and Maine would be admitted as they were; but thereafter, no state formed from any part of the Louisiana Purchase north of the southern boundary of Missouri was to be admitted as a slave state. This boundary, usually called the "compromise line," was 36 degrees 30 minutes north latitude. At that time, the American people had expected that this line would forever divide the free and slave states. But back in 1820, few if any of the American people had been bold enough to dream that their country would one day reach the Pacific Ocean.

The proposed "tall state" of California lay both north and south of the compromise line. But California was not part of the Louisiana Purchase. California was part of the land ceded to the United States by the treaty that had ended the Mexican War. The southern extremists wanted the compromise line to extend to the Pacific Coast and cut California into two states. The line would cross California a short distance south of Monterey, placing San Francisco and Sacramento in the northern state, Los Angeles and San Diego in the southern. Unless this was done, said the southern extremists, they would not vote to admit California at all.

The northern extremists insisted that if California were admitted, it would be as one state, with no slavery. But they wanted more than this, if they were going to vote yes on the admission bill. Not only must California be a free state, but Congress must prohibit slavery in all the western country not yet organized into territories. And they wanted Congress to abolish slavery right now in the District of Columbia.

The western country not yet organized was an area of more than a million square miles. Most of it was thinly populated, but few people thought this would last much longer. Several states would be made of it. Already Congress had been asked to give territorial governments to the areas that are now the states of Utah and New Mexico.

The moderates might warn again and again that they were sure the United States Constitution did not give Congress the right to control slavery until the would-be state asked for admission to the Union. The northern extremists would not listen. One senator, William H. Seward of New York, exclaimed in a speech on the floor of the Senate that there was "a higher law than the Constitution."

This was probably an impulsive line shouted in the heat of debate. Seward, a former governor of New York State, was not accustomed to making drastic threats. But hundreds of Americans who had heard his speech, or read it in the papers, said his words were close to treason. James Gordon Bennett, in the New York *Herald,* said Seward had "proclaimed his intention of over-riding the Constitution and trampling that sacred instrument under foot." It was useless for Seward to protest that he had meant to imply nothing of the sort. Too many readers agreed with Bennett.

The debates were loud and violent. So far, most of the violence was in the Senate, as the Senate was first to vote on an admission bill, but signs of wrath were appearing in the House as well. In both bodies, the extreme factions were minority groups. But if these groups, so furiously opposed to each other, should unite in voting no, they could keep California out of the Union.

It was an explosive situation. If all the ultras should vote no, the result would be a blow from which the country might never recover. Denied statehood, California would be likely to organize as an independent nation, as Texas had done. After nearly ten years of independence, Texas had at last been made a state. But after nearly ten years, the Texans had still wanted to be a state; California, angry and defiant, might prefer to stay independent. And nobody could foretell how much of the western country would want to stay with her. As Peter Burnett had reminded them, the Pacific Republic was still possible.

Was there no way to stop such a tragedy?

This crisis roused Henry Clay to one of the most notable achievements of his life. Born in Virginia and elected from Kentucky, Clay was a Southerner and a slaveholder. He was also a patriot and a peacemaker. He wanted to save the Union. He believed that in a contest neither side could or should expect to win everything. Give something here, hold something there—this was the only way to keep the two factions from destroying California's admission to the Union and perhaps the Union itself. In a word, *compromise.*

Clay was now past seventy and his health was poor. Probably the disease that was to kill him, tuberculosis, had already begun its attack. But in one of the noblest speeches he ever made, he presented what came to be known as the Compromise of 1850.

His proposals were simple and well balanced: Admit California as a state, with her anti-slavery constitution; organize the western country into territories without allusion to slavery and let the people make up their own minds; allow the slaveholders in the District of Columbia to keep the slaves they already had but forbid the slave trade in and out of the District; and deny the right of any state to obstruct the slave trade between other states where the trade was legal. Another section provided for settling the boundary between Texas and New Mexico, which had never been fixed to the satisfaction of both.

His plan, his lucid presentation of it, and above all his plea for the Union made most of Clay's hearers think about the subject more earnestly than they had ever thought of it before. But among the real ultras, Clay pleased neither side. Quarreling broke out again. The New York *Tribune* published a daily column headed "Yesterday in Congress" in which Horace Greeley well described the long, long argument over the Compromise Bill: "First, a Northern Free-soiler will rise and denounce the measure as one which surrenders everything to the South; next, a Southern propagandist will assail it with equal vehemence as giving the North all the territories with half of Texas [too]."

A few days later he tersely reported, "Butler and Hale, Chase and Clemens, Baldwin and Soulé, united in denouncing the measure upon grounds as inconsistent as possible." (He was referring to senators Andrew P. Butler of South Carolina, John P. Hale of New Hampshire, Salmon P. Chase of Ohio, Jeremiah Clemens of Alabama, Roger S. Baldwin of Connecticut, and Pierre Soulé of Louisiana.)

And the *Alta California* acidly observed, "Members appear merely desirous of talking and seeing their names in print."

In the midst of this dreary tumult, Daniel Webster took the floor of the Senate. The day was March 7, 1850.

Webster was also in his seventies and his health too was failing fast. He was no longer the stirring orator he had been. His once many-toned voice was reduced almost to flatness. But his speech was one of the finest of his long career.

Born in New Hampshire and elected from Massachusetts, Webster was a Northerner and he hated the slave system. But like Henry Clay, he believed the country's most important goal now was to save itself from falling to pieces. Both he and Clay wanted the United States to be a mighty nation that reached from sea to sea. They did not want it to break into a lot of squabbling little principalities, no one of which was strong enough to be of much importance in the world.

He began, "I wish to speak today, not as a Massachusetts man, nor as a Northern man, but as an American. I speak today for the preservation of the Union."

His words came slowly. Sometimes he made long pauses between his sentences, as if to gather strength to go on. Sometimes his listeners had to lean forward, almost holding their breath, to hear what he said. But they heard it, and it was not a speech they were likely to forget.

When he finished, the battle for California was not yet won. Months of more quarreling, more acrimony, more uncertainty lay ahead. But these two tired, sick, and aging men had opened the way for California to come in.

And California, though not a state, with golden bravado was acting like one.

The ultras in Congress did not shout and argue all the time. They had interludes of quiet. (Or maybe it was just hoarseness.) Anyway, in such interludes, the two houses had each approved a bill asking each state to send a block of its native stone to be used in the building of the Washington Monument. On June 1, 1850, when the *Oregon* steamed out of San Francisco Bay on her regular voyage to the isthmus, she carried a block of gold-spangled quartz as California's contribution.

The quartz block had been hewn from a mountainside of the Sierra Nevada, at the Mariposa mines. Governor Burnett had entrusted it to the care of two leading citizens. One of them was John Bidwell. By this time, Bidwell had been living in California nearly seven years and was the owner of 22,000 acres. (The modern town of Chico, eighty miles north of Sacramento, stands on part of what used to be his ranch.) The other custodian was Henry Schoolcraft, one of the New York Volunteers, now alcalde of Sacramento.

On the Fourth of July the quartz block and other stones were accepted in a ceremony at the site where the monument was to stand. President Taylor and many distinguished men took part.

Then came a blow that shocked the nation. Five days after the ceremony, President Taylor died.

His biographers have not agreed on the cause of his death. While greeting friends and visitors at the monument site, the President had seemed in his usual health. He had grumbled about the weather, but so had everybody else; midsummer days in Washington are often hot and humid, and this day was even muggier than most. When he was back at the White House, he had taken a glass of his favorite summer refresher, described as "iced milk with cherries." Later in the day, he had shown the beginning of his fatal illness.

Storage methods of that time were not as dependable as they are today. Some writers have suggested that the milk, and perhaps the cherries too, had become tainted and unfit for use. Others have said that although he had seemed to recover from an attack of cholera in his army days, the infection had stayed with him and had recurred several times, and this time he could not resist it. Still others, citing the various doses and treatments his doctors gave him, say he would have had a better chance to get well if they had let him alone. Whatever the cause, President Taylor died July 9, 1850. Vice-President Millard Fillmore took his place.

It is always unsettling to the country when a new President is called into office partway through a term. In 1850, the people wondered about Millard Fillmore.

Before long, they began to feel encouraged. They recalled that while presiding over the Senate during the violent clashes of the weeks past, he had been carefully impartial to both sides. Looking back further, they could see by his record that while he was not a brilliant man, he was a man of solid character.

Born in a log cabin near Lake Cayuga—which in 1800, the year of his birth, was away in the backwoods of New York State—Fillmore had worked hard to get the education he knew he must have if he did not want to spend his life in the backwoods. He made up his mind to study law. He worked at various jobs, taking care that each one be near some kind of school so he could be always learning something in his free time. At a class one day, he met a girl named Abigail Powers, and this was one of the luckiest days of his life.

Daughter of cultured parents who were also democratic in the best sense of the word, Abigail had no snobbery about her. She liked her eager fellow student and admired his ambition. She helped him with his studies and gently smoothed his rustic manners. Fillmore was admitted to the bar, and in 1826 he and Abigail were married.

In 1828 he was elected to the New York State Assembly. Three years later he was elected to Congress. His most important achievement in Congress came about when he was chairman of the Ways and Means Committee. Samuel F. B. Morse, inventor of the telegraph, had asked Congress to give him funds to put up a wire from Washington to Baltimore, so he could prove that his machine could send a message between two cities forty miles apart. The resistance was almost overwhelming. One objector is said to have exclaimed that if they started handing out public money for this kind of foolery, next year some dreamer would be wanting funds for some kind of contrivance that would take him to the moon. (As we know now, the objector was not wrong, merely premature.)

Fillmore and his supporters fought back. At last, after midnight of the last day of the session of spring, 1843, the grant was made. By the time Fillmore became President, wires linked all the major cities from the Atlantic Coast to the Mississippi River.

He took the oath of office Wednesday, July 10, 1850. Congress spent the rest of the week in speeches eulogizing the late President.

There were six speeches by senators and eight by representatives. On Monday, July 15, Fillmore named Senator William R. King of Alabama as presiding officer of the Senate in his place. This done, both houses began wrangling again.

If it were possible, the arguments seemed even more furious than before. In the Senate, men who hated each other shouted "personal remarks" across the floor with such vehemence that Presiding Officer King, perhaps not as patient as Fillmore had been, called them to order by name.

In the *Tribune's* column headed "In Congress Yesterday," one day's report is typical. "The Senate effected nothing, but talked garrulously. In the House, rather less than nothing was accomplished. *When shall there be an end of it?*"

Nobody could answer. The members of Congress were arguing now about Henry Clay's compromise bill. They tore the bill to pieces, made amendments, voted on it, piece by piece. The extremists seemed to be fighting to keep the California admission bill from coming to a vote. Congress could not stay in session forever, and this session appeared about to end as others had ended, leaving California in a haze of uncertainty: not a state, not a territory, nothing but a payer of taxes. At length, on August 1, the moderate senators—helped by some northern extremists who were gradually being won over to a more flexible frame of mind—managed to get the admission bill named the next in order for consideration. But they had no power to put an end to the speechmaking.

So it had been going, and so it seemed to be going still. Every day the summer heat and dampness seemed harder to bear. Henry Clay had nearly collapsed before it and had been ordered by his doctor to leave town and take a rest at a seaside resort.

President Fillmore had been calm, as calm as he had been when he was presiding over the quarrels in the Senate. But when he delivered his Message to the Senate August 6, 1850, Fillmore was patient no longer. He urged—he almost ordered—the senators to stop talking and vote on the admission of California. He did not tell them they should vote yes or no, he simply told them to *vote.* This, he reminded them, was what they were here for.

And now at last came a day when even the stubbornest men in the Senate found themselves powerless to "postpone" any longer the vote on statehood for California. This day was Tuesday, August 13, 1850.

Of the thirty states in the Union, fifteen were slave and fifteen free. Each state was represented by two senators. When the roll was called, of the sixty senators, 34 voted *yes,* 18 voted *no,* and 8 did not vote at all.

The former northern extremists made no attempts to block the admission of California. Henry Clay's clearest, most valid statement about his compromise bill, repeated many times since by other senators in their speeches and in private conversations, had persuaded these men, or most of them, that they no longer had any reason to insist on having their own way all at once. Clay had said to them, plainly and forcefully, "You have Nature on your side."

California had already voted against slavery, he reminded them, and they need not try to forbid slavery in other parts of the Southwest. It was already forbidden by Nature itself. The Southern plantation economy, which was the base and backbone of the slavery system, simply could not flourish there. The areas that are now the states of Nevada, Utah, New Mexico, and others in that part of the Union, were not suited for vast expanses of sugar cane and cotton and rice. As for the District of Columbia, not many slaves were held there, and the slave trade was to be no longer allowed in and out of the District. Convinced that they were getting what they wanted anyway, the former northern extremists voted *yes* on the California admission bill.

The senators from two states voted against each other. Sam Houston of Texas voted *yes;* his colleague, Thomas J. Rusk, voted *no.* Thomas Hart Benton of Missouri voted *yes;* his fellow Missourian, David R. Atchison, voted *no.* These differences are understandable. But still baffling are the men who chose not to vote on either side.

One of the eight nonvoters, Henry Clay, could not vote because he was too ill to be present that day. (He returned to the Senate shortly afterward, when his health had improved.) As for the other seven nonvoters, who represented both the northern and southern sides, historians have speculated but never agreed as to what their motives might have been. These seven men included both senators from North Carolina, George E. Badger and W. P. Magnum; James A. Pearce of Maryland, William L. Dayton of New Jersey, S. W. Downs of Louisiana, Solon Borland of Arkansas, and John H. Clarke of Rhode Island.

However, the nonvoters had no effect on the result. The needed majority had voted *yes.* The first battle for California was won. But the fight was not over.

On Monday, October 7, 1850, the steamer *Carolina* reached San Francisco from the isthmus. She brought enough United States coins to ransom eight hundred ounces of gold, and she also brought a bundle of American newspapers. The latest of them was dated August 28.

These papers told the news that the Senate had passed the California admission bill. "So it seems certain," hopefully said the *Alta California* the next day, "that we will soon be a state."

The young editor, Edward Kemble, was trying to keep everybody bright and confident. But basically he was trying to keep himself bright and confident, and his readers knew it. The Senate had passed the bill August 13. Word of this had reached San Francisco October 7. Fifty-four days. In those fifty-four days, what might have happened?

For California to become a state, the Admission Bill must be passed by *both* houses of Congress. It must then be signed by the President. The bill had gone from the Senate to the House of Representatives, and the papers made it clear that the ultras in the House had started at once to do all they could to block it. If they did block it, the fight would have to be held over until the next session of Congress, and maybe the next and the next. And the advocates of that bleak substitute, the Pacific Republic, would be growing stronger all the time.

The papers had brought good news, yes. But not the great, final, welcome-home news the Californians were yearning for. They had been waiting so long and thwarted so often that they could not feel confident now.

They were homesick. They were Americans and they wanted to stay Americans. They did not want their country to reject them again and push them into a new political creation. They wanted to come home, and they wanted to bring California with them.

30

The extremists in the Senate had managed to drag out the debates on the California Admission Bill from February to August. No doubt there were some in the House who would have liked to equal this performance. But the fact was that citizens all over the country were getting tired. True, some of the voters who had sent these extremists to Congress were themselves violent fanatics. But not all. Many of the voters were out of patience with their deputies, and they were not timid about saying so.

So it came about that the Admission Bill, which in the Senate went un-voted on for six months, had to wait less than a month in the House.

Of course, some members were still inflexible. Over their objections, after the Senate had approved the Admission Bill, one of the first acts of the House was to approve another bill already passed by the Senate. This bill made Utah a territory. It left the question of slavery to be decided by the people of Utah when they should ask for admission to the Union. After a few more arguments, on Saturday, September 7, the moderates in the House succeeded in getting a vote on the California Admission Bill. The result was 150 votes yes, 56 no. The bill was then sent to the Executive Office to wait for the signature of President Fillmore.

Nobody seemed to doubt that he would sign it. Before he had even had a chance to do so, a hundred cannon in Washington, firing with a one-minute pause between shots, were booming a welcome to the new state. Flags appeared on hotels and public buildings around the Capitol. That evening the city of Washington celebrated with a fireworks display. The President attended to no business on Sunday, but on Monday, September 9, he signed the Admission Bill.

When Congress was officially notified that the President had signed the bill, both houses voted with enthusiasm to adjourn September 30. This gave them three weeks to catch up on unfinished business, and the weary men in Congress felt that this was all the country had a right to expect of them. The next morning, in the *Tribune*, Horace Greeley announced the event in his own particular style: "Congress has agreed to adjourn on the 30th inst. We believe *this* vote will be hailed with universal approbation."

About the admission of California, Greeley was exultant. Congress had already made Utah a territory; the day Fillmore signed the Admission Bill Congress gave territorial status to New Mexico, again with no requirement about slavery. Referring to the territories as "organized members" of the United States, Greeley proclaimed that the nation now reached across the continent "in one unbroken arch, whose base is washed by the world's two great oceans." He added, "May it stand through the coming centuries!"

Less dramatic, but just as glad, James Gordon Bennett reported the good news in the *Herald*. In a thoughtful editorial, he urged:

The statesmen who stood together shoulder to shoulder, in restoring harmony in our public councils as well as throughout the country, must not be overlooked. To the efforts of Messrs. Clay, Webster, Cass, Foote, and Dickinson, supported by Mr. Hilliard and others in the House, is the country indebted for the adjustment of a question which at one time wore a dreadful and ominous aspect.

Besides Clay and Webster, the senators Bennett was praising here were Lewis Cass of Michigan, Henry Stuart Foote of Mississippi, and Daniel S. Dickinson of New York. The congressman was Henry Hilliard of Georgia.

The day after the President signed the bill, the senators from California, William Gwin and John Charles Frémont, formally took their seats in the Senate. It was a ceremony well planned. The theme was, "Let's all act as if we liked it. Let's put on a good show." As arranged beforehand, the proceedings were to be brief, terse, and right to the point.

Senator Stephen A. Douglas of Illinois presented Gwin's credentials. Senator Robert A. Barnwell of South Carolina presented those of Frémont. As Senator Douglas was well known as an advocate of statehood for California, his presenting Gwin's credentials surprised nobody. But Senator Barnwell, though never one of the violent extremists, had voted against California's admission to the Union. To make clear his position, when he presented Frémont's credentials Barnwell made a short statement of his own. He said he had doubted the wisdom of making California a state. But this was now an accomplished fact. And as he felt no personal objection to Mr. Frémont, he had accepted when he was asked to present the senator-elect to the Senate.

Not everybody was so cooperative. Senator Jefferson Davis of Mississippi (later President of the Confederate States) stood up to say it was his duty to challenge the seating of both gentlemen from California. The California Legislature had elected them before California had become a state, and therefore their election had not been valid. He moved that their credentials be submitted to the judiciary committee for further consideration.

This meant further shouting matches, and the senators had had enough. By a more than two-thirds majority they voted down the motion. Gwin and Frémont were officially welcomed and escorted to their seats.

In the House of Representatives it took a little longer. First in their order of business that day, September 11, was a bill concerning mail between the United States and Great Britain. When they had disposed of this, which took only a short time, Representative Linn Boyd of Kentucky, chairman of the Committee on Territories, stood up and was recognized. He said the congressmen from California, Messrs. Wright and Gilbert, were present in the hall outside the chamber, ready to be sworn in.

Several members objected at once. Their leading spokesman, Abraham Venable of North Carolina, said Wright and Gilbert had not been legally elected. This time the reason given was that they had been chosen at the same election at which the Californians had voted on whether or not they would adopt their state constitution. At the time Gilbert and Wright were elected, he said, California had had no constitution. Therefore the people had had no right to elect anybody to Congress.

The arguments began again. The speeches went on until most of the members were worn out and ready to quit for the day. They voted to adjourn and went home without having accomplished anything.

However, the next day the Speaker of the House, Howell Cobb of Georgia, managed to bring the matter to a vote. The representatives accepted the Californians by a vote of 150 yes, 50 no.

A page boy opened the door. Linn Boyd went to tell the new congressmen that they were to enter. A moment later a dozen voices exclaimed, "Here they come—there they are!" There was a shuffling sound as nearly every man in the chamber turned in his chair to see the newcomers. Down the aisle came Boyd, followed by Wright and Gilbert. Boyd conducted them to the foot of the steps that led to the platform on which stood the Speaker's chair. Speaker Cobb came down to meet them, administered the oath of office, and made a low bow. Then, as one newspaper reporter put it, "he resumed his dignity and station."

The others were less dignified. Once the solemnity of the oath was done, all over the chamber men sprang to their feet. They crowded toward the front, as if every one of them wanted to be first to shake hands with his new colleagues and say, "Glad to have you!" Apparently nobody paid any attention to those of the ultras who were still sulking. After a good deal of gavel-pounding and calls to order, the Speaker finally got the celebrants to sit down. He told them they must now turn their minds to another piece of unfinished business. The task was necessary, but Cobb could not pretend that today it would be interesting. This piece of business concerned a contested election in Pennsylvania. Cobb must have felt like a schoolmaster calling little boys from their games to their lessons, but it had to be done.

And so, on September 9, 1850, two years, seven months, and sixteen days after Jim Marshall picked up those shiny bits in the tailrace of the sawmill, California became a state of the Union.

But the Californians did not know it.

They could not know it until some vessel took the news to Chagres, some mule or donkey carried it across the isthmus, and a second vessel brought it up the coast to California. They had waited and waited for this, and they were still waiting.

But rumors do whisk around. They move by means nobody can measure nor understand. In Mazatlán, gathering place of international gossip, a man from one ship said to a man from another ship, "Is it true what I've heard? That California's in the Union at last?" Nobody was sure.

Soon the rumor was seeping into California. The Californians wanted to believe it. But they had been disappointed so often that they were no longer in a mood to believe something just because they wanted to believe it. They wanted to *know*.

Their last definite news about statehood had reached them October 7, when the *Carolina* had brought word that the Senate had passed the Admission Bill. Since then, many other vessels had come into port, but none had brought any later information on the subject. However, whether good or bad, the news must reach them sometime, and they knew what ship was likely to bring it. This was the *Oregon,* one of the three sidewheel steamers of the Pacific Mail Line, licensed by the government to carry officials and official dispatches.

Two of these steamers, the *Oregon* and the *California,* were now away on their regular trips to Panama. As the *Oregon* had been the first to leave San Francisco, she would no doubt be the first to return. She should be back before long.

But how long? wondered the waiting Californians. When *would* they learn the fate of the Admission Bill in the House? Who was it that said "Time flies"? What a wronghead! Time was just loafing along.

Telegraph Hill, overlooking the sea, was nearly three hundred feet high. All day, every day for some months now, the city had kept watchmen posted on the hill so they could see incoming vessels a long way off and send signals to the people in town. At the top of the hill was a semaphore. By different positions of its mechanical arms, and pennants of assorted colors, the semaphore could announce that a vessel was in sight, what sort of vessel she was, and various details about her.

The steamer voyage between Panama and San Francisco took about twenty days each way. The steamer would stay two weeks (sometimes more) at Panama to take on mail, cargo, and passengers. If all went well, total time for the round trip would be seven or eight weeks.

The *Oregon* had left San Francisco September 1. If she made the round trip with no delays she should be back about October 20. Seven weeks. Of course, she might run into a storm. Or she might have been given orders to wait for somebody important. The San Franciscans tried not to worry about this. They tried to keep their minds fixed on October 20 as the day when they could expect the semaphore on Telegraph Hill to give the signal that would tell them the watchman on duty had sighted a sidewheel steamer.

But she might, she just *might,* be earlier. The semaphore was announcing arrivals at an average of eleven or twelve a day. As October 20 drew near, eleven or twelve times a day the San Franciscans interrupted whatever they were doing to watch the semaphore and see what sort of vessel was coming in now. Eleven or twelve times a day they were disappointed. A Cape Horner from Boston, a trader from Hong Kong, a transport from Honolulu—but no sidewheel steamer from the isthmus.

They waited.

It was not a do-nothing sort of wait. In this tense October, San Francisco was one of the busiest cities in the world. The *Alta California* told what it was like:

Streets are crowded all the time. Even the idle cannot seem idle. They are obliged in self-defense to move on, and move quickly, or they will be run over. All is activity—cracking of whips, rumbling of wheels; tumbling of boxes, barrels and bales; crowding and crushing of carts, locking of axles; noise, din, and dust.

This was published Tuesday, October 15. Three days later, Friday, October 18, the *Alta* appeared as it did every morning—mirror of this blustery town pushing in all directions at once. New placers found in the hills. Another of those murders. Names of the vessels that had come in yesterday, their captains and their home ports. Lists of vessels about to sail for Panama and Mazatlán; riverboats to Sacramento, Stockton, San José. Offers from local branches of New York banks to take gold dust across the isthmus "safely and speedily" and bring back its worth in coins. Programs of Rowe's Olympic Circus, featuring tightrope dancers and "equestrian performances," and Foley's Amphitheater, presenting stage plays every evening but Sunday. Stores advertising silks from China, cigars from Cuba, oatmeal from Scotland, wines and toilet soaps and women's bonnets from France. Another boisterous, clattery day, and people rushing about their business as usual.

They rushed about until all of sudden, not long before noon, they heard a thunder of cannon from the sea. One roar—another roar— and a mighty shout in the street. It sounded as if every man, woman, and child had shouted at once. On Telegraph Hill the semaphore was signaling *sidewheel steamer!*

A pennant assured them that the steamer firing the guns was, as they had thought, the *Oregon.* Another pennant said she was still outside the Golden Gate, but near it; she would soon round the headland and come into the bay. She was coming in with flying colors; this meant she brought good news.

And she was cannonading a glorious "Good morning!" Only one item of news in the world could be so grand as to merit all this.

Nearly every soul not already outdoors dashed out now. The only people who stayed in were those whose dwellings or places of business were on hills high enough for them to see the bay from their windows. And at last—it was not a long time but it seemed long—at last they saw the steamer.

Never was a vessel more gorgeously arrayed. She was flying American flags everywhere she had room for them. She was draped with bunting, hundreds of yards, red-white-and-blue and whatever other bright colors the passengers had been able to find in the city of Panama.

From mast to mast hung an enormous sheet of canvas on which was painted, in enormous letters, CALIFORNIA ADMITTED! Facing the other side was another vast sheet bearing the words CALIFORNIA IS A STATE! The first sign had been prepared by friends of California in New York. They had sent it to Panama to be given to the captain of whatever vessel was to bring the great news to San Francisco. The second had been made on board the *Oregon* by her excited passengers.

The *Oregon* was bringing 165 passengers. Two of them were John Bidwell and Henry Schoolcraft, on their way home after taking the gold-spangled block of quartz to Washington. Also on board were a few other returning Californians, but most of the passengers were men and women about to see California for the first time. If at the start of the voyage these newcomers had not realized the magnitude of the news they were bringing, they certainly knew it now. The ship-master, C. P. Patterson, had a special reason for being a proud man. Aided by good weather and a happy crew, he had brought his ship to port in sixteen days. It was the quickest passage any of the mail steamers had ever completed between Panama and San Francisco.

Aboard the *Oregon*, in addition to the cannonade, some fellow was lustily ringing the ship's bell. Everybody who had a musical instrument was playing some sort of tune on it. The rest of them were singing, shouting, and otherwise contributing to the janglefest. As the steamer threaded her way among the other vessels in the bay, their captains hailed her with more firing of guns. The first welcoming shot was fired by a British bark from Liverpool. It seems that her captain, a patriotic man named Harrison, had made up his mind that among these ships from half the world his Britisher would be the first to congratulate the Americans. In a second or two, other guns were booming from other vessels, and cheers were sounding from every craft that still had a crew on board.

The *Oregon* did not pause. Rowboats went out to meet her, and her crewmen threw off bundles of newspapers for the boats to pick up. The *Oregon* puffed on to Sausalito, three miles away, to give the gladdening news to the garrison there. In the meantime, the garrison at the Presidio in San Francisco fired a salute of thirty-one guns.

The town was hilarious. Everybody hugged everybody else, regardless of age, sex, and place of origin. Some people laughed and hurrahed; some people tried to say how happy they were, and burst into tears, and made no apology for it. The *Alta California* brought

235

out an extra dated "Friday at 2 o'clock." On the front page was the picture of a rippling Stars and Stripes, and across the flag was printed CALIFORNIA ADMITTED! Every storekeeper who had fireworks for sale soon found his shelves empty, and many a bartender felt his pockets grow heavy with gold dust. As the early darkness of October drew in, lights blazed from windows up and down the streets, a general illumination to express the general delight.

On the plaza, now called Portsmouth Square, stood a flagpole 111 feet tall. It had been presented on the Fourth of July by the people of Portland, Oregon, to the people of San Francisco. A city employee, doing the work he was being paid to do, had lowered the flag at sunset. But who wanted the flag down now, when the people of California had just been made American citizens and could vote for the next President? An exuberant young man scrambled up the pole to the top and set Old Glory waving in the wind again. When he came back to earth he found that the applauding onlookers had taken up a collection of nearly $300 to reward him.

The people celebrated all night. They feasted, danced, gathered at every sort of impromptu merrymaking. When dawn appeared they were still shooting off firecrackers in the street. The look and racket of the town suggested that nobody had been to sleep, and champagne was still splashing at the bars.

The young editor of the *Alta California* somehow managed to bring out his paper that morning. His columns told about the glittering yesterday. Then he added some comments. He said:

We only wish that those who have so long prevented this act of justice to the wishes of California could have witnessed this scene. We are now in the Union, thank God! We are in the United States of America once more. We are admitted!

While he was writing this, already couriers were riding toward the mining camps and inland settlements, every man of them no doubt hoping he would be the first to tell the news at his stopping place. At last, the people of California had won the rare joy of a dream turned to fact.

They had come home, and they had brought California with them.

Additional Reading

These books are not ones that I drew on heavily, but they should be interesting to readers who want to know more about some of the more picturesque characters referred to in *Golden Dreams*.

Belden, Josiah. *Overland Pioneer, the Memoirs of Josiah Belden.* Edited by Doyce Nunis, Jr. Georgetown, Cal.: Talisman Press, 1962.

Brown, John Henry. *Reminiscences and Incidents of Early Days in San Francisco.* With introduction and reader's guide by Douglas Sloane Watson. San Francisco: The Grabhorn Press, 1938.

Browne, John Ross. *J. Ross Browne; His Letters, Journals, and Commentary by Lina Fergusson Browne.* Albuquerque: University of New Mexico Press, 1969.

Clappe, Louisa Amelia Smith. *The Shirley Letters from the California Mines, 1851–52.* With introduction and notes by Carl I. Wheat. New York: Alfred A. Knopf, 1945.

Colton, (Rev.) Walter. *Glances into California.* Los Angeles: Glen Dawson, 1955.

Giffen, Helen S. *Trail-blazing Pioneer: Colonel Joseph Ballinger Chiles.* San Francisco: John Howell Books, 1968.

Gudde, Erwin C. *Bigler's Chronicle of the West: The Conquest of California, Discovery of Gold, and Mormon Settlement, as Reflected in Henry William Bigler's Diaries.* Berkeley: University of California Press, 1962.

Hafen, LeRoy R., and W. J. Ghent. *Broken Hand: The Life Story of Thomas FitzPatrick, Chief of the Mountain Men.* Denver: The Old West Publishing Company, 1931.

Johnston, William G. *Overland to California, by a member of the wagon train first to enter California in the Memorable Year of 1849.* Foreword by Joseph A. Sullivan. Oakland, Cal.: Biobooks, 1948.

Lienhard, Heinrich. *A Pioneer at Sutter's Fort, 1846–1850.* Translated from the German, edited and annotated by Marguerite Eyer Wilbur. Los Angeles: The Calafia Society, 1931.

Lyman, George D. *John Marsh, Pioneer: The Life Story of a Trail-Blazer on Six Frontiers.* New York: Charles Scribner's Sons, 1930.

Megquier, Mary Jane. *Apron Full of Gold. Letters of Mary Jane Megquier from San Francisco, 1849–1856.* Edited by Robert Glass Cleland. San Marino, Cal.: Huntington Library, 1949.

Royce, Sarah Bayliss. *A Frontier Lady.* New Haven: Yale University Press; London: H. Milford, Oxford University Press, 1932.